Moving

the Image:

INDEPENDENT

ASIAN PACIFIC

American

Media Arts

Edited and Introduced by **Russell Leong** UCLA Asian American Studies Center

With a Preface by **Linda Mabalot** Executive Director of Visual Communications

A collaborative project of

UCLA Asian American Studies Center *and*

Visual Communications, Southern California Asian American Studies Central, Inc.

Joint Copyright© 1991
by the UCLA Asian American Studies Center, 3232 Campbell Hall, University of California, Los Angeles, California 90024, and Visual Communications, Southern California Asian American Studies Central, Inc., 263 S. Los Angeles Street, Suite 307, Los Angeles, California 90012

Printed in the United States of America.

Library of Congress Catalog Card Number: 90-71789

ISBN 0-934052-15-8
ISBN 0-934052-13-1 (pbk)

Editor Russell Leong

Assistant Editor Joyce Nako

Publisher Linda Mabalot

Art Direction and Design Qris Yamashita

Writing Assistant Chris Komai

Computer Operators Esther Belin, Cindy Tomita, William Vu Tam Anh

Editorial Assistance Janice Tanaka, Allison Tom, Jean Pang Yip

Production Co-ordinator Charlene Narita

Production Assistants Vicki Kato, Russell Oshita, Terry Song, Susanne Takemoto

Indexer Sachi Yagyu

Typography Andresen Typographics, Tucson, Arizona

Funds provided in part by the Los Angeles Cultural Affairs Department, J. Paul Getty Trust Fund for the Visual Arts, John D. and Catherine T. MacArthur Foundation, Manabi Farms Incorporated, and community donations.

Special thanks to the Morimoto Family for donation of word processing hardware and software used in the production of *Moving the Image*, *Rafu Shimpo* for conversion of IBM software to Apple Macintosh software, and use of Japanese American Cultural and Community Center and Douglas Aihara's Macintosh computers.

Cover photograph provided by Curtis Choy.

After twenty years of productive effort, we, the makers of independent alternative media, still confront basic obstacles daily: a lack of understanding, a lack of money, a lack of access, a lack of space, a lack of honesty and truth, a lack of respect, a lack of power—and a lack of even momentary relief from these burdens. Borne of this frustration and anger, *Moving the Image* emerged initially as an emotional response to the uninformed, uncaring, and repressive environment that this country has become for artists in the past decade.

During our research, reflection, and analysis in the making of the book however, we discovered an optimism and unearthed a spirit of celebration and accomplishment among ourselves. For *Moving the Image* is a tribute to those individuals and institutions committed to Asian Pacific Media Arts in the past, as in the present.

Nineteen ninety marked the shared twentieth anniversaries of UCLA's Asian American Studies Center and of Visual Communications, two institutions linked to the inception of the Asian American Movement in Los Angeles and in the nation. This publishing collaboration, an open dialogue among those involved in the media arts and in Asian American Studies, reaffirms our commitment to, and active participation in, the growth of Asian Pacific American communities.

Moving the Image is by no means the definitive publication on independent Asian Pacific American media arts. Our intent, in publishing the book, was fourfold:

1. To provide a sense of the "faces" and "voices" of Asian Pacific media artists;
2. To question traditional assumptions and approaches toward looking at Asian Pacific American culture;
3. To begin to develop new languages—both critical and cinematic, for assessing our work—a new "cultural literacy" which places cultures of color at the core;
4. To establish a basis for discussing, debating, and resolving issues around media, funding, and education which affect all alternative media.

Therefore, *Moving the Image* is dedicated to all who are concerned with broadening and defining the audiovisual images of women and men of color. We hope that this book will speak to international communities of media artists, cultural workers, programmers, critics and historians, media arts and ethnic studies centers, students, teachers, and funders.

The growth of alternative media, as in the previous twenty years, will not occur without pain. The hard issues of monetary and artistic survival remain with us: the institutional censorship of works produced by people of color— because of the token and minimal funding given to us; the Eurocentric exclusionary attitudes and practices of programmers and funders in defining what is American Arts and what is quality; the lack of knowledge by programmers on how to effectively exhibit and contextualize our productions; and the denial of recognition by, and access to, major arts institutions and public broadcasting systems.

Our goal in producing *Moving the Image* was to provide a greater understanding of the full implications and possibilities of alternative media, one which integrates communities and cultures in relation to issues of form and function, and to content and control. We are indebted to the media artists and writers who invested thought, time, and care in their individual pieces; without their sharing this open dialogue would not have come into being.

In publishing this book, our funders were key, and we are grateful to them: The City of Los Angeles Cultural Affairs Department, National State County Partnership Program; the J. Paul Getty Trust Fund for the Visual Arts (a program of the California Community Foundation), the John D. and Catherine T. MacArthur Foundation, "American Generations: The Asian Pacific Program" (Rockefeller Foundation/Humanities Division), and Manabi Farms Incorporated. Countless individual donors also deserve our thanks for their generous support—both of this publication and of the continuing endeavors of media artists and organizations. Their help has been a source of hope, and a source of optimism for the future.

Read. Enjoy. Re-Act. Continue to move the image. May the next twenty years move us even further than the last, and bring America closer to the heart.

Linda Mabalot
Executive Director
Visual Communications
November 1990

We must not turn our back from
the community, from our tribal
family, our ancestral link...
We must remember that the
uranium was stolen from the
Sacred Land of the Hopis and
Navajos to kill and destroy an
Asian country of mothers,
fathers, and children.
How ironic! Our tribal family is
more than just across the way;
they are brothers and sisters
under the same skin; they cross
their blood with ours — the
plight and struggle. They are
not a mere historical picture in
some phoney two-bit Hollywood
movie."

AL ROBLES

"Hanging on to the Carabao's Tail"

Amerasia Journal, 1989

TO OPEN THE FUTURE
RUSSELL LEONG

Moving the Image is the first effort to define independent Asian Pacific American media arts and to describe its development from 1970 to 1990. In conceiving the book, we sought to carry into the future the momentum, the movement, and the energies unleashed at the birth of independent Asian American media.

The words, essays, and statements by the fifty media and cultural workers in this book challenge, celebrate, and contradict each other. Read together, these writings convey a sense of how Asian and Pacific Americans have viewed themselves during the past twenty years, and have created film, video, and radio alternatives to Hollywood portrayals and mass media images.

In selecting veteran and younger media artists from both immigrant and American-born backgrounds, we have committed ourselves to a wider dialogue, on emerging, rather than fixed, positions on generation, and gender, ethnicity and nationality. These writings thus can serve as a basis to further examine and question the premises and perspectives contained within Asian and Pacific American media culture.

Imagery for Action
The world had to be shown what its eyes were turned away from.
Leo Hurwitz, New York Workers Film and Photo League[1]

Independent Asian Pacific American media arts in the United States emerged with the Civil Rights and ethnic studies movements of the late 1960s.[2] Most of the writers in this book who were born before 1960 allude to this period as instrumental in their development as Asian and Pacific Americans and as artists/cultural workers. Theory and action were grounded in the Black Power movement in the Americas and internationally in the post-World War II liberation and anti-colonial struggles of Cuba, China, Vietnam, Kampuchea (Cambodia), Algeria, and other Third World countries. These liberation movements not only attempted to reclaim national integrity and restore cultural identity, but also to move, mobilize, and reposition images of their peoples in relation to their colonized past, toward future effect. An independent alternative, or Third cinema, was vital to a culture of the future.

By creating imagery for action—whether by painting murals on public buildings, postering "Post No Bills" walls, organizing basement poetry readings or jam sessions, or protesting U.S. military interventions in Southeast Asia with felt tip pen and cardboard caricatures—we sought to mark the day and project our image of a new dawn. An important part of this movement of imagination, critical to the production of our works, was the unity between maker and audience. As muralists, filmmakers, photographers, dancers, or poets living in Asian or Third World communities—we did not separate ourselves or our "imaging" from everyday activities of eating, drinking, working, or making love, in our neighborhoods. We did not see ourselves as "making art" for others to consume. Rather, community collaboration was integral to planning, producing, and presenting our works. We shared a common experience, lived a common agenda, took part in a common scenario. This give and take between artists and community characterized the works of, for instance, Asian, Chicano, Native American, and Afro-American filmmakers who founded and graduated from UCLA's Ethno-Communications program in the 1970s.[3]

Selective Traditions

In a society as a whole, and in all its particular activities, the cultural tradition can be seen as a continual selection and re-selection of ancestors.

Raymond Williams

Williams, in *The Long Revolution*, discusses the nature of "selective tradition," how, "from a whole body of activities, certain things are selected for value and emphasis." Such a selection process goes beyond the mere documentary recording or preserving of a tradition. "For it is not an absolute body of work but a continual selection and interpretation," subject to "reversals, and re-discoveries," as determined by class interests and contemporary values, according to Williams.[4] Closer to home, writer Frank Chin, in his defining of a literate Asian American culture, demarcates what is "real" and what is "fake": forging languages and creating images as a strategy against assimilation.[5]

From experience, new media strategies emerged, and revealed new areas of production and interpretation. *Moving the Image* thus serves as a beginning handbook to reclaiming memory and the future. It is akin in spirit to Sun Tzu's *The Art of War*, a manual of theory and strategy written between 400 and 320 B.C. Epigrammatic and episodic in form, this ancient manual analyzes terrain—mountain and valley, water, fire, wind, weather—and the forging of winning strategies through the correct analysis of human and natural forces. Such strategies, then as now, require a keen eye, fast hand, and strong heart—as basic to warfare, sports, or dance, as to media arts. As one passage in Sun Tzu's work goes:

Sometimes we make artificial animals' feet to put on our feet; at others we put artificial undergrowth. After this, we listen carefully for distant sounds and screw up our eyes to see clearly. We concentrate our wits so that we may snatch an opportunity. We observe the indications of the atmosphere; look for traces in the water to know if the enemy has waded a stream, and watch for movement of the trees which indicates this approach.[6]

Like Sun Tzu's treatise, *Moving the Image* synthesizes the thoughts and strategies of many individuals. The experiences of Asian and Pacific Americans gathered here form a whole, but not homogeneous, work greater than its parts. Some, in their short "on-line" statements which are personal or anecdotal, share the ways they "see": images they capture or liberate, voices they contain or release. Others, in longer essays, analyze the field, twists and turns of the road, as well as chances for victory, compromise, and defeat as independent artists. In their visual work they deploy the elements of light, shadow, speed, and sound; create artifice and rearrange nature, develop short-and long-term strategies, and "concentrate wit and snatch opportunities." Together, their accounts raise questions and reveal strategies for the future, be it shooting film "from between the legs" (Christine Choy); inscribing immigrant images (Supachai Surongsain, Cindy Hing-Yuk Wong); uncovering the real faces of a community (Loni Ding, Van Troi Pang, John Esaki, Karen Ishizuka, Robert Nakamura); creating new visual emblems which cross traditional ethnic, gender, and genre lines (Trinh T. Minh-ha, Roddy Bogawa, Cheng-Sim Lim, Janice Tanaka, Wayne Wang, Nicky Tamrong, Fu-Ding Cheng); including lesbians and gays within Third World and Asian American visions (Gregg Araki, Richard Fung); and, linking Asian American communities and immigrant homelands via video, radio, and film (Hye Jung Park, Maricel Pagulayan, Kyung-Ja Lee). Whether born in the Americas, in Asia, or the Pacific, the filmmakers gathered here directly organize and transform memories: personal lore and public living into materials which attempt to transform our perceptions into a level "more intense, more concentrated, more typical, nearer the ideal, and therefore more universal than actual everyday life."[7]

Moving the Image is not fixed by formula, plotted to Hollywood timeframes, or arranged according to academic or Asian American Studies schemas. Instead, we developed the book as an "open work," which "assumes different shapes depending on the angle from which it is viewed."[8] Each chapter begins with quotations, epigrams, poetry, or prose fragments by Asian and Pacific writers and visionaries.[9] These form active responses to life as it has been seen, lived, and questioned: anonymous wall graffiti written on Angel Island in the early twentieth century; a cry today for Samoan unity; the journey of water and blood of Vietnamese refugees; smoldering memories of a Japanese American writer who worked for an Afro-American newspaper in Los Angeles; a Filipino novelist who found "America is in the Heart"; a poet unraveling the myth that the Pacific and the Philippines were "discovered"; a Korean writer urging us to see farther than we wish. These fragments hint at richer and complex origins, yet, freshly juxtaposed they form a "freefloating montage" of memory. Hannah Arendt, in discussing the work of Berlin critic Walter Benjamin (1892-1940), for example, states that his selection of quotations led to "a forcing of insights" otherwise unattainable.[10]

To select, question, and conserve collective memory in life, as in film, serves to mark identity, to move the present, and to motivate the future.[11] Korean American journalist K.W. Lee, speaking before an Asian American journalism class at UCLA, stated: "You are an Asian American only if you are in touch with your collective memory, if you hear the voices of your ancestors within you." One becomes Asian and Pacific American no longer by birth, but by choice.

Visual anthropologist Cindy Wong, de-exoticizing "ritual" in her documentary on Chinese Vietnamese Buddhists in Los Angeles, depicts community folk elements—but not in the way to cater to Eurocentric biases and fascination with the "East." Wong, in her essay, "Rituals Revisited," states:

Had I concentrated on the ceremonial aspects of their lives, the audience would think that the monk's and nun's lives are totally ritualized. They would fulfil stereotypes of exotic Asians who live their lives by these wonderfully elaborate and bizarre ceremonies, thus perpetuating orientalist attitudes to the viewer. If I had chosen to emphasize ritual, I would not be lying, but retelling actual happenings in real life. But what truth am I telling?

Moving the Image is divided into nine chapters which can be read as strategic maneuvers, subject to changing climate, rather than as ironclad positions. "Moving the Image" and "Through Ourselves" (chapters one and two), interpret the body of visual images created by Asian Americans who have seen themselves as situated historically within the community. As these filmmakers have been moved, by a memory, an event, an observation, by someone's story, they intervene with camera, pen, or sound recorder. Their interventions are a *conscious strategy to move what is lived and felt into image and word for continuing life.*

This does not mean that a perspective cannot be criticized; Gregg Araki points to the status quos which he sees developing within Third World, women, and gay filmmaking. Canadian filmmaker Richard Fung observes in his article that "both Asians and gay people are used primarily as signs," to conjure mystery, humour, or danger, and that both groups are relegated similarly to the margins of popular media fare.

The act of "moving" means a constant revision of where we stand, where we are, in relation not only to yesterday, but through tomorrow.

Framing the Questions

While the origins and perspectives of earlier independent Asian Pacific American media arts are clear, what is less evident is how this past movement of imagery for action and artistic consciousness can be carried forth today, twenty years later. If we do not have all the answers, at least we can frame the questions. These include, but are not limited to, the following interrelated issues and concerns:

Given the foundations we have built for Asian Pacific American media arts and culture, how do current ideas around Asian Pacific, the Pacific Rim, and the Pacific Century challenge our perspectives and premises?
What are the implications of the critical academic terms and cultural/ political definitions used to view and interpret our media works? Do terms such as postcolonial and postmodern, for instance, apply to Asian Pacific American media arts?
In turn, how do we develop our own interpretive critical language, and create our own metaphors for experience?
How can our media arts productions serve as a tool to educate for action?

In fact, Asian and Pacific Americans do not come from common communities or nations linked by their politics, culture, language, land, or seas. Moreover, not all peoples of Asian and Pacific descent are immigrants. Native Hawai'ian Haunani-Kay Trask, in a recent *Amerasia Journal* article, reminds us that the "typically American line to reiterate, 'we are all immigrants,'" is false: as native Hawai'ians and other native Pacific Islanders are not immigrants. Native Hawai'ians, for example, "are Native to Hawai'i and therefore not American; on an ideological level (neither Western nor Eastern but Native Pacific Islanders); and on a cultural level (we are not transplants who are 'new' to Hawai'i but an ancient people who have learned to live in and with our place and whose culture is the least destructive and the most beneficial to the land").[12] Therefore, most statements and views on Asian American filmmaking in this book probably do not apply to Pacific Islanders. Like their Asian American counterparts, however, "Pacific filmmakers are beginning to respond to stereotyping with their own work," according to Diane Mei Lin Mark, in her article, "The Reel Hawaii." She urges Pacific Island peoples from Hawaii, Guam, Truk, Ponape, Bikini, Samoa, Tahiti, New Zealand, Australia, and the Philippines, to go forward, "imua," in preserving "the soul of tradition and history," of their peoples.

In further analyzing Asian American cinema in this book, Renee Tajima offers an operational definition, describing it as one which is: "socially committed, created by a people bound by race, interlocking cultural and historical relations, and a common experience of western domination." At the same time, it is characterized by "diversity shaped through national origin, and the constant flux of new immigration flowing from a westernizing East into an easternizing West." The definition is plausible and provocative, yet it raises questions about where Asian American practitioners, critics, and interpreters are locating media culture.

Should Asian Pacific Americans, or even the term itself, be viewed as a composite which reflects interlocking racial, cultural, and historical relations threaded by the common experience of western domination? This melding of relations, while convenient for discussion, places the analysis of our culture, be it cinematic, literary, or other, into the current "postmodern" or "postcolonial" discourse. Though some Asians in this book hail from formerly colonized nations such as Vietnam, India, or the Philippines, part of what has been considered the "other" by the West in orientalist terms—what is more crucial is that, once here, these film and media makers confront new realities of race, class, and economics. These confrontations cannot be compared to those in the emigrant country. They constitute, uniquely, what Trinh T. Minh-ha calls a "Third World in every First World, and vice versa."[13] Thus, Asian Pacific American artists live in at least two or or more worlds of being which affect the form and sense of their work.

The linear way in which we are taught to accept Eurocentric historical definitions and processes also appears in the linking of our culture and history primarily to the experience of western domination, rather than to any other measure, criterion, or non-western historical framework. In so doing, we adopt a particular view of history, and our affinities are linked and limited to the debris that can be salvaged from colonization and domination.[14]

To broaden this argument to other peoples of color, Cornel West, in an essay, "Black Culture and Postmodernism," states that the debate over African American culture seen in terms of postmodernism is based on "historical coordinates" roughly corresponding to European colonization of the globe (1492-1945), the rising of the U.S. (1945-1972) as the global world power, and the current "second decolonization" of Third World peoples in their opposition to the First World (Iraq, for example). Further, "every conception of postmodernism presupposes some idea of the modern—when it began, when it peaked, when it declined, when it ended."[15] West concludes that the term itself, as it is used by First World critics, does not adequately address the complexities of Third World histories and cultures.

Nor does the periodization of what is seen as the rise and decline of the "modern world," whether of history or of culture, summarize the Asian and the Asian American experiences. For example, Wen Guangyi, of the People's Republic of China, observes that the history of the Chinese who left China and now live abroad may be cast in more than one way: whether according to local historical periods, to Chinese historical time frames, to the chronology of emigrant history, or of regional developments in the places of settlement, i.e., the United States or Southeast Asia.[16] In looking at the histories of other immigrant and refugee groups in the U.S.—the Vietnamese, Koreans, Asian Indians, and Filipinos for example—can we merely analyze their histories and demarcate their cultures according to "postmodern" or "postcolonial" as defined by the West? N.V.M. Gonzalez, the noted Filipino writer states:

I think this differentiation is hardly adequate. Any art, literature, or film which comes from these new immigrant populations must be understood on their own terms. Asian and Asian Pacific American cultures must be seen vertically in the complex strands of the past and present entwined.[17]

While Asian, Asian American, and Pacific Islander cultures certainly are "diverse," such diversity should be seen in terms beyond migration—whether of filmmakers, professionals, or workers—from Asia and the Pacific into the West. Connected to this Asian Pacific diversity, I believe, are notions of the Pacific Rim, or the Pacific Century—of a "westernizing East into an easternizing West," as Renee Tajima puts it. Ideas around "Pacific Rim" usually emphasize investment, trade, and professional migration, to the exclusion of nationalistic, ethnic, and cultural movements for self-determination of Asian and Pacific peoples in Asia, the Pacific, and the Americas. As applied to Asian Pacific American film culture, "East/West" or "Pacific Rim" concepts invariably promote or enhance certain elements beneficial to the West, while excluding others that do not fit.[18]

As Asian and Pacific peoples, we need to scrutinize the terms which are being applied to us, whether it is in the form of film discussion or even the well-intentioned 1990 L.A. Festival of the Arts, with a focus on "bringing Pacific Rim cultures" to the City of Angels. Peter Sellars, the director of the L.A. Festival, states in his introductory essay to the official program that "We might as well plunge ahead. Straight into the 'Pacific Century.'" He continues:

We live in a culture of exile. . . . Just as America was beginning to notice the 'third world,' the 'fourth world' has become the immediate reality, a reality which is inevitably linked in our minds to an acute awareness of a range of internal exiles in our own country, people who, for one reason or another, remain unseen and unacknowledged by most of us, people whose very existence serves as a persistent reminder of an unnamed internal exile from our own selves: loneliness, otherness, doubt, and denial. It is no wonder that our reactions to issues of homelessness, AIDS, immigration, and integration tend to be so irrational.[19]

These ideas, though not uncommon in the mass media, suggest that Asian and Pacific Americans, and other peoples of color are not Americans, and that we are still part of the "other"—foreigners, internal exiles, exotic, diverse, colorful multiples of multiculturalism, for festive exhibition, cultural profiteering, and liberal largess. As questionable is the interlinking, implicitly, of issues of poverty, disease, immigration, and integration to Third World origins and influences, whether from groups within or without the country.

Whose eyes, ultimately, are seeing? What do they see, and what do they do with what they have seen?

Interpreting the Image

In contrast to merely adopting wholesale the concepts and languages above, we must look to our own experiences once again. I believe that a vital interpretive language—visual, visceral, and vocal—grounded in the metaphors of our communities will emerge, driven by the contradictions we face in our daily lives.

Animator Arnie Wong, for instance, feels that artists and women are treated as second-class citizens within Asian and Asian American patriarchal traditions. He imagines his strict parents looking critically over his shoulder: "Whenever I felt a passionate vision come into being, I would find myself face down in the bitter soup."

Some question the Hollywood system which accepts only one kind of cinematic language, but not others. Malaysian-born Cheng-Sim Lim states:

These days I am trying to unlearn the language of Hollywood. I am doing it because I know it is not my language. I am trying to remake my image in myself.

She proceeds to talk about her grandmother's gastronomic metaphors: "*rojak*," referring to her grandchildren, and also, to a salad made from pineapple, mango, guava, jicama, tofu, squid, hoisin sauce, chili peppers, ground peanuts, and shrimp paste. It is unlikely, she feels, that such images will appear on the big screen soon. Lim's essay, and writings by Supachai Surongsain, Cindy Hing-Yuk Wong, Janice Tanaka, Roddy Bogawa, and Mar Elepano are found in chapter seven, "Directing Memory."

Extending our "frame of vision" in chapter eight are commentaries on video and television by Anthony B. Chan, Art Nomura, Fu-Ding Cheng, and Valerie Soe, on the context of American experimental filmmaking by Daryl Chin, on community radio by Theo-dric Feng, and on a young filmmaker's frustration by Jon Moritsugu.

As stated earlier, the main intent of this book was not to respond to Hollywood stereotyping and racial and gender role subordination; Eugene Franklin Wong in his book, *On Visual Media Racism: Asians in the American Motion Pictures,* has done a thorough study of the subject.[20] Despite exclusion from the Hollywood industry however, Asian Americans have been involved from the silent screen period onward. Asians, Native Americans, Afro-Americans, and Chicanos and Latinos have always worked behind and appeared on the big screen, as pioneer Afro-American filmmaker Carlton Moss notes in his essay for this book.[21] Other articles, by Charles L. Leong, Yoshio Kishi, John Kuo Wei Tchen, and an interview of James Wong Howe by Frank Chin, view Hollywood from the perspective of its participants and observers.[22] These essays form an active, if incomplete, response to the industry in the context of the pre-1960s period and well before Asian Pacific American independent filmmaking. Asian Americans who currently work in the industry also share their views: on film editing, Irvin Paik; costume design, Terence Tam Soon; boom, George Leong; sound, Curtis Choy; and camera, Geraldine Kudaka, Michael Chin.

In this volume, many independents who now work in camera, sound, and radio began their work as poets and writers. Not surprising, for filmmakers and poets share a common visualizing capacity, know how to maneuver and condense time, and seek the metaphor of the day—be it in their film, writing, or life. Poetry, in frame. Navajo filmmaker Esther Belin, a 1990 summer intern at Visual Communications, wrote a poem, "Surviving in This Place Called the United States," in response to reading the articles in this book. During her writing, she wondered what images African slaves, and early Asian immigrants first saw in "the new world,"—albeit an "old world," for Native Americans.

Whether old world or new, we peoples of color in Asia, Africa, or the Americas, survive because of our different histories which link our responses across histories, seas, and continents. Thus, N.V.M. Gonzalez, comparing the origins of culture—from a Philippine barrio in his native land, to a village in India—can say: "We share a transgeographical and transcultural community—a community of peoples asking of History and of the future fairly similar questions."[23]

Asian and Pacific Americans can play a unique role in reframing the logic of historical thinking. The 1990 Los Angeles screening of Linda Mabalot's and Antonio DeCastro's *You Still Can Hear Me Singing,* a documentary on hunger among children in the Philippines, and Kaz Takeuchi's *Shimon,* on the fingerprinting of Koreans in Japan, are examples of this role. Both films about political issues in Asia were made by Asian Pacific Americans raised here. These filmmakers did not cross a "bridge of cultural understanding to Asia," or "translate" the rich texts of the Pacific Rim for corporations. Rather, their role was that of Third World media artists who utilized film in order to educate. As persons of color, and as part of Third World communities in the First World, their sensibility was informed by both systems. Their consciousness went beyond simple racial oppression or ethnic identification, but took on more complex colorings on class, politics, and race within an international context. Their stance helps to unite, rather than to divide, immigrant and native-born Asian and Pacific American communities.

The lessons of the 1960s and 1970s are thus being carried forward by media artists and cultural workers into the 90s.

The act of filmmaking is essentially an act of education for action. However, such acts can take multiple creative forms: didactic, descriptive, propagandic, poetic. New York-based documentary filmmaker Hye Jung Park returned home to Korea this year and observed and videotaped students with VHS video cameras risking their lives to film farmers, workers and students demonstrating. In her essay, she asks:

Those tapes on my shelves are not video tapes. They are the voice and life of our oppressed people who are struggling to build a better world. What shall I do with these videos? How can I make them useful for my country and other oppressed countries?

Alternative media can imprint images and carry voices in the form of the "film letter, film poem, film essay, film pamphlet, film report."[24] Finally, the hue and cry of community media arts is tempered by our political commitment, as Peter Kiang reminds us in his address, "A Talk Story Poem for Open Dialogue II," published here.

Hue and Cry

The struggle to define and redefine Asian Pacific American media arts and the role of its institutions can never end. Stephen Gong, in his history of Asian Pacific media arts organizations in this book, terms it: "a history in progress." As we struggle to define our media, we struggle also to produce, exhibit, and broadcast our works. In relation to public broadcasting, James Yee and Norman Jayo in their articles advocate more than a liberal change of heart. They demand that peoples of color have access to the fiscal resources and decision-making structures to carry out more programming on public television and radio.

At the same time, much needs to be done in the research arena: historical studies of independent filmmakers from earlier eras as well as those in Hollywood, biographical monographs of pathbreakers such as Joseph Sunn Jue, a Chinese American who made films in the 1930s and 40s in San Francisco's Chinatown, and research into early Filipino student filmmakers at the University of Southern California in the 1920s.[25] In-depth analyses of specific genres, and studies of Asian Pacific film, video, and radio in immigrant and non-English tongues are lacking. The relationship between media arts and the mass media require discussion. The representation of Asian Pacific popular culture on commercial and non-commercial television would yield insight into the newest immigrant communities. Student-and smaller-format productions need attention. To chronicle the lives and stories of Asian American actors and performers will require biographies and oral histories. Comparisons of specific films, and video and radio programs across generations and eras, and the placing of Asian Pacific media arts within larger national and international contexts demand curiosity, innovation, and stamina.[26]

As Asian and Pacific Americans involved in the media arts, we continue to question History. To the next generation, we hand over film, reels, tapes, microphones, cameras, lightbulbs, filters, notebooks, nagras, scripts, music— the material sum of our experience. We tailgate the century ahead: drive the hard questions, hurtle through space and time.

In moving the image, we open the future.

NOTES I would like to acknowledge and thank the following individuals who read earlier drafts of the manuscript and/or shared their uncommon insights, imagination, and information: N.V.M. Gonzalez, Glenn Omatsu, Teshome H. Gabriel, Linda Mabalot, Yoshio Kishi, Carlton Moss, Alexander Saxton, Yuji Ichioka, Eugene Ahn, John Esaki, Abe Ferrer, Joyce Nako, Jean Pang Yip, Him Mark Lai, Terence Tam Soon, Yen Le Espiritu, Renee Tajima, Marjorie Lee, Agnes Villero, Don Nakanishi, Enrique de la Cruz, Michael Soo-Hoo, Robert Ku, Janice Tanaka.

1. Leo Hurwitz, "One Man's Voyage: Ideas and Films in the 1930's," *Cinema Journal* (1975), 9, as quoted in William Alexander, *Film on the Left: American Documentary Film from 1931 to 1942* (Princeton: Princeton University Press, 1981), 17.

2. "Salute to the 60s and 70s, Legacy of the San Francisco State Strike," commemorative issue of *Amerasia Journal* 15:1 (1989), see Glenn Omatsu, "The 'Four Prisons' and the Movements for Liberation," xv-xxx; Karen Umemoto, "'On Strike!' San Francisco State College Strike, 1968-69: The Role of Asian American Students," 3-41; Russell Leong, "Poetry within Earshot: Notes on an Asian American Generation 1968-1978," 165-193.

3. Renee Tajima, "Ethno-Communications: The Film School Program That Changed the Color of Independent Filmmaking," *The Anthology of Asian Pacific Film and Video* (New York, Third World Newsreel, n.d.), 38-42. For influences of other Third World cinematic movements on Asian Americans, see: Jorge Sanjines and the Ukamau Group, *Theory & Practice of a Cinema with the People*, translated by Richard Schaaf (New York: Curbstone Press, 1989), and Michael Chanan, editor, *Twenty-Five Years of the New Latin American Cinema* (London: British Film Institute, 1983) with articles by Glauber Rocha, "The Aesthetics of Hunger," Fernando Solanas and Octavio Getino, "Towards a Third Cinema," and Julio Garcia Espinosa, "For an Imperfect Cinema."

4. Raymond Williams, *The Long Revolution: An Analysis of the Democratic, Industrial, and Cultural Changes Transforming Our Society* (New York: Columbia University Press, 1961), 52, and chapter two, "The Analysis of Culture," 41-71; and Williams, "Culture is Ordinary," in *Resources of Hope: Culture, Democracy, Socialism* (London: Verso, 1989), 3-17.

5. See Frank Chin, "From the Chinaman 'Year of the Dragon' to the Fake 'Year of the Dragon,'" *Quilt* 5 (1986), 58-71; "The Most Popular Book in China," *Quilt* 4 (1984), 6-12; "This Is Not An Autobiography," *Genre* 18:2 (1985), 109-131; Russell Leong, "Frank Chin: An Authentic One," in *Amerasia Journal* 14:2 (1988), 162-164; and Robert Murray Davis, "Frank Chin: An Interview with Robert Murray Davis, *ibid.*, 81-95.

6. Sun Tzu, *The Art of War*, translated with an introduction by Samuel B. Griffith (London: Oxford University Press), 105.

7. Mao Tse-Tung, *Talks at The Yenan Forum on Literature and Art* (Peking: Foreign Languages Press, 1967).

8. Umberto Eco, *The Open Work* (Cambridge: Harvard University Press, 1989), especially chapters three and four, "Openness, Information, Communication," and "The Open Work in the Visual Arts," 44-104; and, Renato Rosaldo, *Culture & Truth: The Remaking of Social Analysis* (Boston: Beacon Press, 1989), on the dynamic, changing nature of social reality.

9. Sources for chapter quotes: introductory essay: Al Robles, "Hanging on to the Carabao's Tail," *Amerasia Journal* 15:1 (1989), 195-218; chapter one: line from poem 58, in Him Mark Lai, Genny Lim, and Judy Yung, translators and editors, Island: *Poetry and History of Chinese Immigrants on Angel Island 1910-1940* (San Francisco: Hoc Doi Project), 122; chapter two: spoken line from *Omai Fa'atasi*, a film produced by Visual Communications, 1979; chapter three: lines from Quach Quynh Hoa, "Spring Night on the Island," in *Vat Nang* (Boulder: Vietnamese Students at Boulder, 1990), 33-35; chapter four: Emilya Cachapero, lines from "miss philippines at the miss universe contest," in *Liwanag* (San Francisco: 1975), 33; chapter five: anonymous, line from poem 13, in Marlon K. Hom, *Songs of Gold Mountain: Cantonese Rhymes from San Francisco Chinatown, 1911-1915* (Berkeley: University of California Press, 1987), 86; chapter six: Curtis Choy, "'Suckcess' above the Line: from Here to Obscurity," in *Moving the Image: Independent Asian Pacific American Media Arts 1970-1990* (Los Angeles: Visual Communications and the UCLA Asian American Studies Center, 1990); chapter seven: paragraph from Hisaye Yamamoto DeSoto, "A Fire in Fontana," *Rafu Shimpo*, December 23, 1985; chapter eight: lines from Theresa Hak Kyung Cha, *Dictee*, (New York: Tanam Press, 1982), 47; chapter nine, Carlos Bulosan, *Sound of Falling Light, Letters in Exile*, edited by Dolores S. Feria (Philippines, 1960), reprinted in "Selected Letters of Carlos Bulosan 1937-1955," selected by E. San Juan Jr., *Amerasia Journal* 6:1 (1979), 153-154.

10. Walter Benjamin, *Illuminations*, edited with an introduction by Hannah Arendt (New York: Schoken Books, 1978), 1-53, and, Roger S. Jones, *Physics as Metaphor* (Minneapolis: University of Minnesota Press, 1982) on the role of consciousness in reality and its relation to the physical world and science, an approach which may be useful to looking at film.

11. See Teshome H. Gabriel, "Towards a Critical Theory of Third World Films," in *Questions of Third Cinema*, edited by Jim Pines and Paul Willemen (London: British Film Institute, 1989), 30-52, and "Third Cinema as Guardian of Popular Memory: Towards a Third Aesthetics," *ibid.*, 53-64.

12. Haunani-Kay Trask, "Politics in the Pacific Islands: Imperialism and Native Self-Determination," *Amerasia Journal* 16:1 (1990), 1-19.

13. Trinh T. Minh-ha, ed., "Difference: A Special Third World Women Issue," *Discourse* 8: (1986) 11:32, and "(Un)Naming Cultures," *Discourse* 11:2 (1989), 5-17. On multiple kinetic worlds, see the dance works of Long Nguyen, born in Saigon and currently in Seattle.

14. See Martin Bernal, *Black Athena, The Afroasiatic Roots of Classical Civilization* (New Brunswick: Rutgers University Press, 1987), and Samir Amin, *Eurocentrism* (New York: Monthly Review Press, 1989).

15. Cornel West, "Black Culture and Postmodernism," in Barbara Kruger and Phil Mariani, eds., *Remaking History*, Dia Art Foundation, Discussions in Contemporary Culture (Seattle: Bay Press, 1989), 87-96; also, Raymond Williams, *The Politics of Modernism: Against the New Conformists*, edited and introduced by Tony Pinkney (London: Verso, 1989), 31-48.

16. Russell Leong, "Chinese Americans: Who Defines Us?"*Amerasia Journal* 14:2 (1988), vii-ix.

17. Gonzalez to Leong, phone conversation, September 1990.

18. See a typical mass media analysis of Third World and Southeast Asia: Michael Elliot, "Inside the Monolith: Third World Diversity," *Los Angeles Times*, September 30, 1990.

19. Peter Sellars, introduction to Los Angeles Festival 1990, program book (Los Angeles: 1990), 15. For a perspective on how western texts program politics and culture, see: Paula A. Treichler, "Aids and HIV Infection in the Third World: A First World Chronicle," in Barbara Kruger and Phil Mariani, eds., *Remaking History*, Dia Art Foundation Discourses in Contemporary Culture (Seattle: Bay Press, 1989), 32-86.

20. Eugene Franklin Wong, *On Visual Media Racism: Asians in the American Motion Pictures* (New York, Arno Press, 1978).

21. Thomas Cripps, *Black Film as Genre* (Bloomington: Indiana University Press, 1978), 100-114.

22. See also Todd Rainsberger, *James Wong Howe: Cinematographer* (New York and San Diego: A.S. Barnes and Company, 1981).

23. N.V.M. Gonzalez, *Kalutang: A Filipino in the World* (Manila: Kalikasan Press, 1990). On migration and cultural transformation, also see, Jatinder Verma, "Transformations in Culture: the Asian in Britain," *RSA Journal* vol. CXXXVII, no. 5400 (1989), 767-778.

24. Solanas and Getino, "Towards a Third Cinema," and Roy Armes, *Third World Film Making and the West* (Berkeley: University of California Press, 1987). An excellent introduction to video as a communication medium in its own right is Roy Armes, *On Video* (New York: Routledge, 1988).

25. Richard Springer, "Saga of a Little-Known Chinese American Film Pioneer: Joseph Sunn Jue," *East/West* News, June 11, 1987.

26. For example, see Alexander Saxton, "The Racial Trajectory of the Western Hero," *Amerasia Journal* 11:2 (1984), 67-79.

To cross the green waters
is the most difficult of
difficulties.

ANONYMOUS WALL GRAFFITI

Angel Island Immigration Station

circa 1910-1940 San Francisco

A HISTORY IN PROGRESS:
ASIAN AMERICAN
MEDIA ARTS CENTERS
1970-1990
STEPHEN GONG

Asian American media arts organizations are at a critical juncture: arguably the best organized of any alternative media arts by people of color in the United States, yet, they are too fragmented to constitute an effective national network. Asian American media arts organizations consist of three major centers: Visual Communications (Los Angeles), Asian CineVision (New York), and the National Asian American Telecommunications Association (San Francisco). These are complemented by three smaller organizations: King Street Media (Seattle), Asian American Resource Workshop (Boston) and Asian American Arts and Media (Washington, D.C.). Several other groups also serve Asian American filmmakers and media artists, like Third World Newsreel, Women Make Movies, and the Downtown Community Television Center (all located in New York City).

These centers face chronic funding problems from an economy hostile to artistic and educational endeavors (a legacy of the Reagan years), and an even greater problem of passing two decades' worth of commitment and idealism onto the next generation of producers, media activists, and administrators. Yet, the presence of the Asian American voice and image on movie screens and through the airwaves have never been more assured. Where we go from here in sustaining a community of cultural organizations committed to "moving the image" of Asian Pacific Americans depends on how we assess the development of our efforts to date. What follows is a description and assessment of Asian American media arts organizations and their development from 1970 to the present.

Background—The Sixties

The genesis of any social movement begins with the influences that shape its artists, its leadership and directions. The Asian American media community emerged from the movements for racial and social justice and cultural affirmation of the 1960s. The institutions themselves—as media arts centers—were both unplanned and unprecedented. Mostly, Asian American media arts was developed by relatively small groups of diverse individuals from suburban Southern California to New York's Chinatown, from the campuses of Los Angeles City College to Harvard—who held two beliefs in common. The first was that being Asian American transcended the experience of being

WONG SINSAANG (1971)
Visual Communications

solely Chinese, Korean, or Japanese American. The second was a belief in the power of the media to effect social and cultural change, in response to the negative power of Asian stereotypes in the mainstream media. At this time, the tools of media production were becoming affordable and available for community and individual use in a way not possible earlier. Many foresaw the opportunity of replacing negative media stereotypes with more authentic and affirmative images.

What is a "Media Arts Center"?

The term is generally self-descriptive, and applies to several types of non-profit organizations which provide services to support media activity, generally in production, exhibition, distribution and advocacy. According to the Membership Directory of the National Alliance of Media Arts Centers, there are approximately one hundred twenty-five organizations in the United States that so define themselves. These centers serve constituencies of artists and producers working in film, video and radio, but they also help present these works to a larger audience. Some media arts centers, like the Community Film Workshop of Chicago, concentrate their efforts on one area of media activity, in this case, in film production training for minority youth. Others, such as the Film Department of the Museum of Modern Art, emphasize exhibition, distribution and film preservation, working on an international level with film archives and cinematheques in other countries. Whether connected to museum or university or not, media arts centers tend to support an alternative vision of media, or at least one that transcends the commercial Hollywood industry. The media arts, as opposed to the media industry, covers social issue documentaries, experimental film and video art with regional, gender, and multicultural diversity.

The media arts field is organized through mutual consent—on the part of the organizations listed above, and the hundreds of producers, filmmakers and video artists they represent. The rules of the game, in terms of grant support, are supplied by federal (the Arts and Humanities Endowments) and state funding agencies (such as the New York State Council on the Arts and the California Arts Council), private foundations (especially the MacArthur Foundation and the Rockefeller Foundation), and the public broadcasting system (through the Corporation for Public Broadcasting).

Asian American media arts centers should be viewed within the larger context of the field of media arts centers. After all, they share a common agenda of social and cultural change. More important, if this agenda is to be realized, they will have to work together to achieve it. But it is these very groups that also compete for limited funds from government agencies and private foundations. This paradox of interdependent competition is worked out in practice, as all intertribal relationships are, through unwritten protocol and obligations.

The Models—Visual Communications and Asian CineVision

In the beginning none of us know what we were doing—and that made for some difficult challenges. But that's also what made it so much fun.[1]

Robert Nakamura

In 1970, a small group of Asian Americans in Los Angeles came together to

RICK CHUN (left) AND DIANA YAMASHIRO (right)
VISUAL COMMUNICATIONS LIGHTING WORKSHOP

produce a photographic exhibit about the Japanese American internment during World War II. This was the first project by the group which began calling itself Visual Communications, or VC. The founders of VC, Robert Nakamura, Eddie Wong, Alan Ohashi, and Duane Kubo, had been deeply influenced by the civil rights and anti-war movements which had stimulated student and community activism. In the Japanese American community, community-based organizations such as Gidra and Storefront were established; at UCLA, a number of the key VC members went through the Ethno-Communications Program and made their first films, and were involved in developing the Asian American Studies Center.

Initially producing posters, leaflets and photographs for Asian American community groups, VC was incorporated as an independent non-profit organization in 1971. VC members recognized that these modest projects with their uncertain funding were inadequate to realize their larger goal of effective sustained social and cultural change. Non-profit status allowed VC to seek support from a broader set of funding sources, especially through publicly legislated programs such as the Comprehensive Employment and Training Act (CETA), and Emergency School Aid Act (ESAA). These programs provided key staff and production support early on; later, the Media Arts and Expansion Arts programs of the National Endowment for the Arts (NEA) became mainstays for VC's sustained development as an arts organization.

From 1972 to 1977 VC produced some ten films of increasing sophistication, including *Pieces of a Dream, Wataridori: Birds of Passage,* and *Cruisin' J-Town,* as well as a major photographic publication, *In Movement* (1974), and work in video. "It was not easy," Bob Nakamura recalls, "because the community at that time was really fragmented, with many different viewpoints and conceptions of what the Asian American community was and how people should serve it. The radical left and the conservatives of the community had very different ideas about the role of media. We were criticized by both sides."[2] Since there were no precedents for the films VC was beginning to make, people in the community felt proprietary about the content and treatment. Some criticized these early works based on their accuracy and historiography. Ironically, for some, the VC films were too technically proficient, too slick and too indebted to Hollywood and network television.

The pressure of being responsive and accountable to the community while at the same time trying to develop the craft of filmmaking continually challenges those in Asian American media. Steve Tatsukawa, the late and greatly missed VC administrative director once observed,

We have to fight the tendency of becoming isolated as filmmakers who happen to be Asian Americans. I think we like to see ourselves as Asian Americans who know how to make films. . . . Time and again we have sat down and said no, it's not just going to end in a production company that grinds out films for the sake of the dollar. We have some real stories that have to be told and some histories that have to be analyzed.[3]

VC thus defined and established an oppositional stance to commercial mainstream productions. In doing so, for the time being, they left unanswered the question of art-for-arts-sake, and media artists working in experimental genres that were more revelatory of personal vision than of community history.

As Visual Communications was becoming one important model of a media arts center, in 1976, a complementary organization was established in New York City: Asian CineVision. Founded by Peter Chow, Christine Choy and Tsui Hark, Asian CineVision was conceived originally as an organization to provide workshops to train the New York Chinatown community in basic video techniques, so that it, in turn, could produce half-hour video programs for the newly developed cable access channel on Manhattan Cable. The intent was to teach the community to produce programs to effect positive change in areas such as housing, redevelopment, and health care. In 1977, ACV-trained producers were creating a half hour of programming per week. By 1982 they were producing a nightly hour-long news program in Chinese. In time, however, ACV stepped away from the workshops, having found doing a daily video production and training facility too hard to maintain, especially since other media arts centers such as Downtown Community Television and Young Filmmakers (now Film/Video Arts) were able to fulfill this need adequately.

Peter Chow, ACV's Executive Director and guiding spirit, has long been a master of program diversification, and so ACV began to develop programs in exhibition, distribution, and information services. In 1978, ACV, with help from Daryl Chin and Danny Yung, organized its first Asian American Film Festival. The aim was to showcase independently produced films by Asian American filmmakers. The festival seemed to signal a coming of age for the 60s generation. More of an experiment than the inauguration of an event, few ACV staff members thought that there would, or could be, a second festival. The film festival is programmed by a committee whose selection process, stormy at times, has over the years helped to shape the definition of what the Asian American media arts are, and who is considered an Asian American media artist. This definition has ranged from the narrow to the non-specific: from the epigrammatic "films by, for and about Asian Americans," and "positive images and truthful portrayals of the Asian American experience," to experimental and personal works by artists like Fu-Ding Cheng, Gregg Araki and Trinh T. Minh-ha. The evolution to a more inclusive definition of Asian American media work indicates a steady maturation of the field, a growing assurance that once the basic history of exclusion and internment have been told we are free to tell more personal tales and follow other topics and impulses.

The festival was subsequently enlarged to include Asian films along with Asian American works, a move that acknowledged the cultural interconnectedness of Asian and Asian American work. It also enabled ACV to take advantage of Asian films in slack periods when Asian American works were scarce. Now in its thirteenth year, the Asian American International Film Festival tours to other cities around the country, although some sites occasionally supplement the selection with additional works.

Other key programs offered by ACV have included the Asian American Video Festival (now in its eighth year), two editions of the *Asian American Media Reference Guide,* and *Bridge* magazine, which up until 1986, when it was replaced by the more modest *CineVue,* presented an important mix of news, essays, film criticism, book reviews, photography and poetry from an "Asian American perspective." *Bridge,* published as an irregular quarterly, was expensive to produce but it offered a distinctive point of view and gave a coherent voice to the emerging Asian American media community.

For the Asian American media centers that followed in Boston, Seattle and Washington, D.C., Visual Communications and Asian CineVision have served as models and as sources of encouragement and support. The support has often been mutual. In 1980 VC produced *Hito Hata: Raise the Banner,* breaking ground as the first Asian American feature film. Unfortunately, the organization was faced with a substantial debt that threatened not only the film's completion but the future of the organization itself. Following the inception of the first Friends of Visual Communications support group in Los Angeles, numerous other ad hoc chapters came together in these and other major communities across the nation. It was not only an inspiring show of community support, but a catalyst in stimulating the formation of other groups.

Coast to Coast: The Network Grows

SEATTLE In Seattle, interest in the emerging Asian American media was concentrated in the offices of the *International Examiner,* where several staff writers and photographers, including Bill Blauvelt, Ken Mochizuki and Dean Wong, formed King Street Media.[4] Although incorporated separately as a non-profit organization, King Street has never emerged from the confines of the *Examiner* and in fact has never had a paid staff. But an informal organizational structure may have been the appropriate approach given the needs of the community and the interests of the members. King Street still manages to mount a film festival in order to broaden the exposure for Asian American films, and it also presents area premieres of significant Asian American features, such as *Dim Sum* (1985) and *Living on Tokyo Time* (1987), usually to benefit the *Examiner.* Their most ambitious project to date has been the production of *Beacon Hill Boys* in 1985. Co-directed by Blauvelt, Mochizuki, and Dean Hayasaka, this featurette (at forty-eight minutes) was a well received coming-of-age story of Japanese Americans in Seattle. The King Street members are currently at work on another screenplay and are also planning for another film festival.

BOSTON[5] The Asian American Resource Workshop was founded in Boston in 1979 by a group that included Mike Liu, Fred Ho, Ramsey Lieu, Irene Wong, and Albert Lau. Boston has many of the same elements found in New York City, albeit in a much smaller scale. It's an old Eastern city, within an urban context of diverse and turbulent ethnic groups, as well as a plethora of colleges and universities. So, Asian American Resource Workshop developed many of the same programs as ACV, including video workshops for the community, and film festivals and premieres. Later on, however, as chronic funding problems set in, the organization has modeled itself more on the lines of VC, which worked with AARW to develop a long range plan. Continual financial struggles and dismal funding prospects from the Massachusetts Council on the Arts and Humanities have kept AARW from developing as expected. Today, according to Helen Liu, the Workshop is in a "survival mode," concentrating on the provision of media services to the community and local colleges. Community workshops on video production are produced through contracts, as income generating services become vital to the organization's existence. Still AARW is the fourth largest Asian American media arts center in the country, which itself is a sobering fact.

WASHINGTON, D.C In Washington, D.C. the flame is being kept by a small group of true believers including Theo-dric Feng, Laura Chin, Lori Tsang and

"Time and time again we have sat down and said no, it's not just going to end in a production company that grinds out films for the sake of the dollar."
Steve
Tatsukawa

BEACON HILL BOYS (1985)
Dean Wong

Wendy Lim.[6] For more than ten years this group of volunteers have maintained an Asian American media presence in the nation's capital. Incorporated finally in 1985 as Asian American Arts and Media, Inc. (and known conversationally as Arts and Media) the group's efforts are impressive given the scarcity of resources and inherent limitations to organizational development. Arts and Media presents an annual film festival (a supplementation of ACV's touring festival), and activities and visual arts exhibits in conjunction with the Asian Pacific American Heritage Month. Theo Feng hosts "Gold Mountain," a weekly hour-long radio program covering Asian American political and cultural issues, on WPFW, a Pacifica Foundation station. Some of these activities are not necessarily Arts and Media projects but are undertaken by, inevitably, the same group of people. Because of the lack of Washington, D.C.'s foundations and corporations, the modestly budgeted D.C. Commission on the Arts and Humanities is the only source of public funds.

SAN FRANCISCO By 1979 the Asian American media arts field had a national network of organizations. In San Francisco, there was no formal media organization, although filmmakers and producers like Loni Ding, Felicia Lowe, Emiko Omori, Geraldine Kudaka, Christopher Chow and Curtis Choy had for years worked in and around the commercial and public spheres of television and film. Yet, a growing sense of frustration was developing there as well, especially with regard to equal access to public television (PBS) and radio. In response to more than a decade of criticism, the Corporation for Public Broadcasting, which has been created by Congress to channel public money to the public broadcasting system free of political pressure, responded by convening a national blue ribbon task force which produced a comprehensive report entitled "A Formula for Change." Its recommendations for inclusion of minority-produced programming and increased training opportunities for minorities in public broadcasting stations were initially acknowledged and then generally ignored. For the Asian American media community, the most significant result of these efforts was a growing sophistication in dealing with "the system" and resolve to claim a fair share of public broadcasting. These efforts culminated in a gathering of tribes: the first conference of Asian American filmmakers and producers held in Berkeley in1980. Organized by an ad hoc committee headed by Loni Ding, an independent television producer and instructor in the Ethnic Studies Department at UC Berkeley, the conference brought together Asian American producers and media activists from across the country. From the VC contingent decked out in Hawaiian shirts to the worldly-wise and slightly cynical group from New York, the Asian American media community was meeting face-to-face for the first time.

By the time the three-day conference had ended the groundwork had been laid for an organization which would acquire, package, and distribute television and radio programs on Asian American history and concerns. The new organization would also advocate against racist and stereotyped images of Asian Americans and support and encourage greater participation by Asian Americans in public broadcasting. Originally the organization that was to become NAATA (National Asian American Telecommunications Association) encompassed Pacific Islanders within its mandate to CPB. However, the effort splintered even before it was formally organized. Members of the Pacific Island media community argued for, and formed, a separate organization to provide relevant programming to the public broadcasting system.

NAATA, formally established late in 1980 in San Francisco with James

WPFW PROGRAMMER THEO-DRIC FENG (left);
NORMAN MINETA (right)

Yee as its founding executive director, was conceived as a national organization with a board made up of representatives from regional chapters. This structure has given way to a board of both local and national representation and a mix of national and local services and programs, including the television series (under the "Silk Screen" banner) and specials, like *The Color of Honor* (1987); sponsorship of original radio dramas such as "Quiet Thunder," "Juke Box," and "The Last Game Show"; "Cross Current" media distribution, and, more recently, workshops and exhibitions in the San Francisco Bay Area. NAATA has also played a highly visible advocate role in both the commercial and public film and broadcasting worlds, assuming a position against stereotyped depictions of Asian Americans in films like Michael Cimino's *Year of the Dragon* (1985).

NAATA's accomplishments, although significant, have always been tempered by the modest support provided by CPB[7] (roughly $135,000 per year throughout the 80s)—less money than is spent on the production of a single half-hour program on public broadcasting, or of a thirty-second commercial on network television. And yet this amount was supposed to provide for a significant and ongoing Asian American presence on public television and radio.

During the past year NAATA's Yee has been working with other independent media arts organizations to increase the amount of money for independent multicultural programming for public television. It now appears that the amount of funds for program development available specifically for Asian American works will double in the near future. In addition, sources and overall funding for independent production may also increase through the Independent Television Service. However, it is difficult to believe that all of these potential changes will, in fact, come to pass. The record to date suggests protracted struggle with the system.

Ten to the Twenty-first: Questions and Choices

What choices will we have to make in the next decade? Some are organization specific, though of a depressingly common genre: how to survive budgetarily. VC, ACV and NAATA have all participated in arts stabilization (so-called advancement) grants programs through the NEA and state arts agencies, yet still face ongoing budgetary problems. Worse, administrators find themselves spending more time seeking grants and contributions than they do in managing services to filmmakers and the community.

The question now arises, was it the ultimate goal of the Asian American media arts movement to get grants from Chemical Bank and Anheuser Busch? The Asian American media arts movement from its inception was an alternative movement developed in opposition to mainstream strategies and structures in the film and television industries.

Other challenges are how to continue to serve the ever-changing Asian American community (especially with recent immigrant groups from Southeast Asia, who have little in common with your typical highly-assimilated third-generation Asian American). This issue underscores the fact that the Asian American media arts field is fundamentally a political (rather than a cultural or ethnic-based) movement.

A related concern is how to attract and hold on to the next generation of filmmakers, producers, activists and administrators. Will the next generation be willing to accept lower salaries and career mobility for jobs of increasingly dubious social prestige?

CROSS CURRENT MEDIA (NAATA)

Each of the centers has and continues to struggle with the issue of Pan-Asian representation. Situated in L.A.'s Japanese American community, VC's Executive Director Linda Mabalot (herself a Filipino American) has struggled to diversify VC's board, staff and collaborators to include Chinese, Koreans, Filipinos and Pacific Islanders, while at the same time continuing to draw upon the tremendous support offered by the Japanese American community. In these efforts VC can call upon a history of working successfully with a variety of community organizations in workshops and exhibition programs.

In New York, Asian CineVision, originally a Chinatown group, has made concerted outreach efforts to include Indian and Filipino works in the film festival and publications. NAATA too, has diversified its board and staff and has struggled with the delicate issue of representation of and services to the Pacific Islander community ever since the initial splintering of the group in 1980. (The group originally recognized as representing the Pacific Island community by CPB is no longer functioning and a process is underway to replace it.) The Asian American media-arts-center field has also diversified from its original dominance by men to greater inclusion of women in key administrative and board governance positions.

Not all of its challenges lie within the inner circle. It has also become increasingly clear that the Asian American media arts centers may play a key role in the current cultural debate over "multiculturalism," whether it is the rhetoric about marginalized classes and ethnic communities or something more potent. As institutions, Asian American media arts centers must play an activist role on all levels of municipal, state, and federal arts funding. The recent attacks on the National Endowment for the Arts and the issue of federal funding for arts activities reflect both a continuation of a fight for freedom of expression and equity in support for the arts that is both decades old, and a harbinger of things to come.

NOTES

1. Interview with Robert Nakamura, *In Focus*, Vol. VI, No. 1, Winter 1990, 3.
2. *Ibid.*
3. Joe, Jeanne. "Visual Communications: A New Image on the Screen," *Neworld*, No. 6, 1979, 54.
4. Interview with Peter Chow, May 1990.
5. Interview with Dean Wong, June 1990.
6. Interview with Helen Lieu, June 1990.
7. Adequate support is relative. The entire Asian American media arts field is woefully under-capitalized. The three largest centers, VC, ACV and NAATA have budgets under $400,000 per year. The Asian American Resource Workshop has a cash budget of less than $50,000 per year, and Arts and Media and King Street have no permanent staff and individual project funding only.

FIFTH ANNUAL LOS ANGELES ASIAN PACIFIC AMERICAN
INTERNATIONAL FILM FESTIVAL PROGRAM,
(VISUAL COMMUNICATIONS AND UCLA)

MOVING THE IMAGE:
ASIAN AMERICAN
INDEPENDENT
FILMMAKING 1970-1990
RENEE TAJIMA

It was almost ten years ago. A small group of us perched on the rickety chairs at the old Collective for Living Cinema loft in Manhattan got a first glimpse at a low-budget, black-and-white feature by then experimental filmmaker, Wayne Wang. The appeal of *Chan Is Missing* (1981) went beyond its social relevance or the familiarity of the characters and themes. There was something original about the film, and something very Asian American.

You could barely talk about Asian American film as a genre then, or even grasp the individual sensibilities of the handful of filmmakers who had produced more than a single film: animator Arnie Wong, experimental filmmakers Taka Iimura and Al Wong, documentarians Christine Choy, Loni Ding, Sonny Izon, Jon Wing Lum, and the Visual Communications collective among them. An overview of the Asian American filmmakers who emerged in the 1970s would have looked more like a census count than aesthetic critique: most were Japanese or Chinese, college educated, lived in California or New York, earned low incomes. And most shared a passion for changing the way America looks at Asians.

To this day, whenever described as a group, Asian American independent filmmakers are made out to be saints or schoolteachers, rarely artists. Sociology passes for film criticism, and the work continues to be defined by thematic, not cinematic, significance. Asian American filmmakers have begun to transform the image of Asians but to what extent have we changed the way America sees?

The Eclectics of Culture and the Search for Asian American "Soul"

I believe that it is due time to start talking about Asian American filmmakers in a serious way as artists, and to reengage in the debate over our role in American culture. Asian American filmmaking has evolved parallel to a great cultural transformation. Increasingly, the definable center, white, male, heterosexual, is evaporating. Note the desperate, reactionary attacks on everything from 2 Live Crew to the National Endowment for the Arts. The mainstream press has been more sanguine, with *Time Magazine*, the harbinger of American social trends, sounding this alarm last April 9, 1990, "America's Changing Colors: What will the U.S. be like when whites are no longer the majority?" And artists and intellectuals are trying to make sense of the void at center with the notion of cultural multiplicity.

Asian Americans fit this new cultural demography in certain obvious ways. We're from a fast-growing ethnic minority, so eventually there will be more of us. But I also believe that we, along with other artists of color, can play a role in profound ways. By default of our "marginal" existence we understand first hand the meaning of cultural plurality. And we have learned to express this dichotomy as dimensionality, or, in Toni Cade Bambara's vision, "the Patois that breaks through" the conventions of English, French or Castillian Spanish, "when something vital must be expressed."

If, for example, I traced the conscious cultural references that Christine Choy and I drew upon for *Who Killed Vincent Chin?* (1988), it would include Akira Kurosawa's *Rashomon* (1951), the television police series "Hill Street Blues," and Motown. In our last film, *Best Hotel on Skid Row* (1990), it was Charles Bukowski and bebop. Coco Fusco, the critic and film curator, identified a similar hybrid sensibility among the Black British film workshops, the Sankofa Film and Video Collective and Black Audio Film Collective:

Theirs is a poetics of an era in which racial, cultural, and political transitions intersect. It is no surprise then, that their works contain references to sources as varied as Ralph Ellison and Louis Althusser, June Jordan and Jean-Luc Godard, Edward Braithwaite and C.L.R. James. On this very sensitive point I must insist that this is not a rejection of the goals of Black consciousness. This "eclecticism," aimed at theorizing the specificity of race, reflects the mixed cultural, historical, and intellectual heritage that shapes life in the Black diaspora.[1]

Fusco's defense of eclecticism is a crucial point for Asian Americans, for whom the development of a distinct, "national" culture has been elusive. The notion of plurality as the fabric of our own cultural identity contradicts our need for cohesion, our search for Asian American soul. In 1974, the editors of *Aiiieeeee! An Anthology of Asian American Writers* bemoaned the dualistic tendencies (East and West) in Asian American literature, and called for a singular and original literary voice. Like Wittman Ah Sing, Maxine Hong Kingston's *Tripmaster Monkey* (1988)—"Where's our jazz? Where's our blues? Where's our ain't-taking-no-shit-from-nobody street-strutting language?" Asian American artists have scrambled for an Asian equivalent to African American and Latino cultural forms, themselves hybridizations.

The answer, then, lies within Asian America itself, with cinema as mirror and provocateur. Louis Chu's novel, *Eat a Bowl of Tea* (1961), later turned into a movie (1989), is so rooted in Chinatown life that its pages literally sing with the distinct language of the Toisan bachelor community.[2] The same literate power is evident in Curtis Choy's emotionally-charged documentary, *The Fall of the I Hotel* (1983), and more poignantly, in Visual Communications' *Pieces of a Dream* (1974). By the same token, Wang's *Chan Is Missing*, on the surface, seems like a cultural hodgepodge, with traces of film noir, Italian neorealism, the languages spoken being English, Mandarin, Cantonese, a combination of two or more of the above, the title song from Rodgers & Hammerstein. It is eclectic, and it is essentially Asian American.

(Top) *WHO KILLED VINCENT CHIN?* (1988),
RENEE TAJIMA (left) AND CHRISTINE CHOY (right)
(Bottom) *THE FALL OF THE I HOTEL* (1983)
Jim Dong

Defining a Framework for Asian American Cinema

Can the eclectic nature of the Asian American cultural experience be reduced to a singular aesthetic? Film critic Clyde Taylor, probably one of the most knowledgeable observers of the various Third World cinemas, has proposed that the bourgeois western concept of the aesthetic is becoming an anachronism, and should be discarded altogether. However, given the need for some basis for looking at cinema culture, I will venture a broad framework for looking at Asian American cinema:

• a socially committed cinema;
• created by a people bound by 1) race; 2) interlocking cultural and historical relations; and 3) a common experience of western domination;
• characterized by diversity shaped through 1) national origin; and 2) the constant flux of new immigration flowing from a westernizing East into an easternizing West.

This framework addresses both the process of acculturation (not assimilation) as we have settled here; as well as the ever-moving tides of new cultural forms through Asian immigration. It takes into account our diversity, which is as varied as the Hmong, Koreans, Taiwanese Chinese, Mainland Chinese, Cuban Chinese, Pakistanis, Filipinos, Thai, and a dozen more, all bonded under the political term Asian American, and whose most potent commonality may be the fact of western domination. So in her one-woman performance, "Coming Into Passion: Song for a Sansei," Jude Narita does not create the composite Asian woman. Rather, she takes on the lives, attitudes, sensibilities of different Asian women as they are: a Vietnamese prostitute, a Filipina mail order bride, a shit-talking Sansei teenager, and a lilting Nisei secretary. The thread is sexism from without, survival from within.

Our heritage of aesthetic sensibilities from Asia are as varied, and has its own internal dynamic that continues today. Note the contemporary Kabuki artist, Ennosuke, who has incorporated elements of Chinese opera, even Russian folk dancing. In discussing his years with the Asian American International Film Festival, Daryl Chin noted,

We often got discussions of spare, ascetic, streamlined aesthetics, as if the haiku, Noh drama, and Ozu movies defined Asian aesthetics. But what about Indian sculpture, the Peking opera, and Cambodian dance, to mention only three examples of rather ornate forms of art? Kurosawa is still called the most Western of Japanese directors, as if the kinetic expressionism which characterized so much of his work, as in *Rashomon* (1951), *The Seven Samurai* (1954), *Throne of Blood* (1957), *Yojimbo* (1961), and *Sanjuro* (1962), had no correlation to traditions of Kabuki, Awaji puppetry, and Japanese drumming. What this means is that any definition of Asian-American (sic) aesthetics must be ipso facto partial, because the idea of Asian aesthetics must be pluralistic.[3]

Consider, then, the reality of our lives as diaspora people who have settled across America. Beyond the duality of East and West, many of us grew up at the demographic axis of mixed communities like Crenshaw, Queens or the northside of Chicago, as whites were on their way out and African Americans and Latinos were coming in. I remember being called a "Black-Jap" as a teenager, for the way I danced and the way I talked, feeling as much at home with the Delphonics as the Shigin; even closer to the Black Power movement than the Cultural Revolution. So it seems to me the natural order of things, as a filmmaker, is to use jazz and rhythm & blues in films about Asian Americans, as it is to draw from the style and sensibilities of the German-born Bukowski, who wrote about the neighborhood milieu where my mother grew up.

You can read the experience of cultural plurality in the poetry of Lawson Inada or Chicano writer Gary Soto; in the performances of Spider Women Theater—three Native American sisters who grew up in Red Hook, Brooklyn; the plays of Amerasian writer Velina Hasu Houston; you can see it in the lower Eastside paintings of Martin Wong; or hear it in the music of McCoy Tyner and the rhythms of the Texas Conjunto, with its Mexican, Eastern European, and country & western roots. While the modernist view of art has western culture disjoined into meaningless fragments, what is now referred to as multiculturalism tries to make sense of those fragments. And the plurality of cultural influences has always defined the Asian American experience, shaped as it is by a core of ethnic traditions, whether transmitted by family, community, or intellectual affinity. Tomas Ybarra-Frausto described this aesthetic development, "Rather than flowing from a monolithic, unifying aesthetic, our art forms arise from strategic necessities, what the Mexican writer Carlos Montavais has called *la cultura de la necesidad*—the culture of necessity. This implies fluid, multi-vocal exchanges between cultural traditions."[4]

The Other is Us

Given our explosive cultural heritage and future, will we articulate the meaning, history, and future of this experience ourselves, or will we let others take the lead? Beginning several years ago, artists of color who regularly make the speaking circuit were amused, then alarmed, to receive a deluge of invitations from academia and both alternative and mainstream cultural venues to speak on issues of "the representation of Other," "multiculturalism," and so forth. Our response was one of skepticism for institutions who had previously responded to the participation of people of color with, at best, benign neglect. And there was suspicion. This new interest was considerably oiled by new monies from public and private funders for audience development and eventually, for promoting multiculturalism.

For a number of years, we drifted through these conferences, sometimes with anger. I couldn't even understand the language they used. When asked to speak on a panel regarding the existence of a canon, my only response to the organizers was: "What's a canon?" Asian American filmmakers certainly weren't agonizing over questions of the psychoanalytic basis on the theory of the spectator. We were worried about financing our films, getting a decent airdate on PBS. And we were more than a little surprised to learn that "the Other" is us.

"Multiculturalism" is, itself, a term that seems to have fallen from the sky. As commonly used, it embraces (white) women and (white) gays and lesbians, as well as people of color. To what extent does this definition strengthen or dilute our own analysis of race and cultural oppression? Having lost the clarity with which we defined "minority-slash-Third World" struggles in the past, we have accepted this definition, almost by default. Regardless of the ultimate resolution of this debate, we have forfeited the debate itself—the process by which we shape the agenda ourselves, and in our own language.

How a Hundred Flowers Bloomed

I believe Asian American cinema has gone through two stages of development. The first was the early promise of the late 1960s and 1970s, when an urgent, idealistic brand of filmmaking embodied the energy of the Asian American political movement and sought to be a voice for Asian American people. It had its counterparts worldwide, in the movement for a Third Cinema, and its variations, led by activists from Havana to Little Tokyo, East Los Angeles to Manila, Detroit to London. At home, Asian American filmmakers were linked to a highly productive triad of artists-activists-scholars that infused the work with social meaning and a grounding in community life. While this political ethos gave Asian American cinema its birth and raison d'etre, Asian American filmmakers would ultimately reject the spectre of art by decree and, as it were, let a hundred flowers bloom.

This second stage, throughout the 1980s, was a period of institutionalization, pragmatism, and skills attainment, as filmmakers focused their sights on a mass audience. The tenor of the work was determined to a degree by the marketplace, and the marketplace was public television, still the most viable outlet for Asian American films. The political movement changed as well. These were the go-go years of the Reagan Age: activists began to focus on electoral politics, community groups became more professionalized, and it was even rumored that one Marxist-Leninist formation was scheming to buy out American Express. In the arts movement, in the midst of a dehomogenizing cultural shift, debate over notions of quality, art versus politics, content versus form, sharpened. Rather than to embrace this confusion, Asian American filmmakers tended to moderate it, taking tentative steps into narrative and feature filmmaking, paying more attention to our right of access than the meaning of access.

The 1960s & 1970s: Cultural Workers from Berkeley to Beijing

Asian American filmmaking during the late 1960s and 1970s was irreverent, even subversive. The Newsreel Collective, predecessor to Third World Newsreel, introduced its logo with a machine gun staccato. Visual Communications, borne out of the struggles against the Vietnam War and for ethnic studies, adopted the acronym "VC," as homage to the enemy of choice. It was an era in motion—the San Francisco State Strike, the Young Lords, the Black Power movement and the emergence of a new black cinema; the Chicano school blow-outs, the 1970 moratorium against the war, and the birth of the Chicano arts movement. The Asian American arts movement as a whole was fueled by this ethic, and driven by this energy, taking its cues from Beijing as much as Berkeley. My own early introductions to the scene consisted of essays on art and culture via Chairman Mao; not Sarris or even *Cahiers du Cinema* and *Screen*.

Particular characteristics in the Asian American film movement developed at this time:

1) As socially committed cinema, Asian American filmmaking had a dual heritage. It emerged in the same political climate and with similar ideology to African American, Latino and Native American filmmakers, influenced by variations on the movement for a Third Cinema in Latin America, and developed in parallel to American independents. And more specifically, the independent cinema was conceived as an organ of political/community activism

I TOLD YOU SO (1974)
Visual Communications

of the Asian American, parallel to ethnic studies, community health care, legal aid, and the like.

2) Early Asian American cinema was a direct result of affirmative action battles waged by people of color. Many of the filmmakers themselves came out of the student movement, and mirrored the predominance of Chinese and Japanese Americans. In the area of media education, a key development was the affirmative action program, Ethno Communications, at the University of California, Los Angeles. In the professional sphere, independent producers and media activists challenged segregation within the public television establishment, and some efforts at multicultural educational programming resulted.

3) Asian American media institutions took the form of community-based, activist-driven media arts centers that developed parallel to the Asian American movement—Asian CineVision (New York), King Street Workshop (Seattle), Third World Newsreel (New York) and Visual Communications (Los Angeles), later the Asian American Resource Workshop (Boston) and the Film News Now Foundation (New York).

The political basis of the early independents shaped the nature of their work. To an extent, it was a reactive cinema. Entitlement and affirmative action (in the media industry, access to the means of production), the redress of present and past injustices (stereotypes, yellowfacing, revisionist history), and advancing political struggles were on par with creative concerns. At the time, the cinema was still too young to steep itself in aesthetic considerations; it was enough to tell the stories, and record the images, of a people otherwise rendered invisible.

Oral History

Thematically, Asian American cinema chronicled the lives of ordinary people, not elites, and reconstructed their histories, drawing from the ideology and productivity of the Asian American studies movement. These topics ranged from the new immigrant experience, as in *The Filipino Immigrant* (1974) and *The New Wife* (1978) to the perspectives of young Asian Americans in *To Be Me: Tony Quon* (1974) and *The Dragon Wore Tennis Shoes* (1975).

Many of these earlier films took the form of documentary oral history. The 1960s–1970s was crucial to Asian American history, as the Manong, Issei, bachelor-society sojourners and other pioneers were beginning to age. Filmmakers and scholars alike were in a race to beat the chronological clock. Thus, the only filmed interview of the Nisei actor, Yukio Shimoda, conducted just before his death in 1981 by writers Akemi Kikumura and Karen Ishizuka, formed the basis of *Yukio Shimoda: An Asian American Actor* (1985) which filmmakers John Esaki and Amy Kato completed several years later.

Among the most prolific sources of pioneer histories was the public television documentary series under the direction of executive producer Noel Sonny Izon entitled "Pearls"—aptly named because the stories uncovered were treasures for young Asian American filmmakers: *Emi* (1978), Michael Toshiyuki Uno's chronicle of a Nisei woman's pilgrimage back to the World War II relocation camp where she spent her teenage years; Uno's *Fujikawa* (1979) which traces the contributions of Japanese Americans in Southern California's fishing industry through a tuna fisherman named Fred Fujikawa, and Deborah Bock's portrait of Al Masigat, a 74-year-old Filipino housing activist, in the documentary *Pinoy* (1979).

"Pearls," and its predecessor "Pacific Bridges," were a part of the new breed of multicultural educational programming, much of which was a direct result of lobbying by Asian/Pacific, African American, Latino and Native American groups for a greater presence in public television. "Pearls" itself was not groundbreaking in the tradition of "Black Journal," the WNET-produced public television series that initiated the careers of William Greaves, St. Clair Bourne, Stan Lathan, and others. But the cumulative impact of these new multicultural programs was strong: they produced the likes of Renee Cho and Jim Yee from WGBH's Rebop; Loni Ding and Michael Chin via "Bean Sprouts"; early funding for Visual Communications came from the Office of Education through the Emergency School Assistance Act (ESAA) Program.

As educational programming, the political scope of "Pearls" was restricted. It did, however, succeed in portraying Asian American culture and working class life: By elevating oral history and positioning the filmmaker as a committed, partisan observer, Asian American filmmakers went against the grain of standard journalistic practice.

Building a Cultural Mythology

Lest Yellows continue to live and have their being in this fog of false consciousness, the task that lies before us continues to be the proper recovery of Asian American mythology—that is, history, culture, and sensibility.[5]

Benjamin Tong, *Amerasia Journal* (1989)

Beyond affirmation of the image, Asian American filmmakers began to do just that—to make the leap from the realm of documentary history to mythmaking. There have always been mainstream critics who minimized the capacity for artistic ingenuity in people of color, and are notoriously color-blind to the distinction between recording reality and creating art.

But it is the embrace of the imagination that brings real life to the level of cultural mythology—the element that fires Luis Valdez's *Zoot Suit* and David Henry Hwang's *F.O.B.*, the reason why Mine Okubo's World War II internment camp sketches articulated, rather than recorded, the era. And so early Asian American cinema was at its best when it captured the pulse of the awakening Asian American movement, and began to forge a new style and attitude on film. The gritty Chinatown documentaries, fast and furious in style, captured San Francisco's burgeoning "Chonk" Chinese American street culture in Curtis Choy's *Dupont Guy: The Schiz of Grant Avenue* (1975); in *Save Chinatown* (1973), Jon Wing Lum fuses provocateur filmmaking with the Philadelphia Chinatown community's fight against redevelopment; and Christine Choy's documentary about community struggles on New York's lower Eastside, *From Spikes to Spindles* (1976), expresses the confluence of Third World political culture.

Early Asian American cinema released rather than contained the raw energy that infected young Asian Americans, both politically and artistically at the time. One epic production from that time is *The Fall of The I Hotel*, completed by Curtis Choy in 1983, but begun seven years before by Choy and his former partner Christopher Chow. Behind the camera, scores of Asian American artists and activists are listed on the credits (nine cinematographers, eight sound recordists, five interviewers). Before the lens, *Fall of the I Hotel* documents one of the most remarkable moments in movement history.

DUPONT GUY: THE SCHIZ OF GRANT AVENUE (1976)
Chonk Moonhunter

In the ongoing struggle for neighborhood control, and in the cultural mythology of the Asian American movement, the battle for the International Hotel stands out. Choy's documentary recorded the dramatic confrontation between the city's real estate interests and the hotel's elderly Filipino residents. It culminated on August 4, 1977, when the remaining residents were forcibly removed in a pre-dawn raid by over three hundred city marshals. Choy's cameras captured the eviction and the moving demonstration by thousands of protestors who formed a human wall around the hotel. As collective memory, *The Fall of the I Hotel* is poetic and powerful. In one beautifully composed sequence, a camera travels through the lonely corridors of the hotel, lit only by a bare bulb and moving to the cadence of Al Robles' poem to the manong.

manong, the rice harvest is ready
come out of your room
let the ifugao women cook *bangkodo*
over the little fires, balancing pots
sunk in a bed of tribal ashes

The camera reaches a window and then looks down on startling scenes of thousands chanting "We won't move." The film culminates with mounted police storming the human barricades that had mobilized overnight, through a remarkable feat of community organization that tried to protect the hotel. On one door a sign is posted: "Felix Ayson: Deaf. In case of emergency, help him out first." And we wonder what happened to Felix Ayson.

Two short classics from Visual Communications that capture the cultural motion of the movement are *Cruisin' J-Town* (1976) and *I Told You So* (1974). Based on poet Lawson Inada's poem by the same name, *I Told You So* is a street allegory of downtown Fresno, its graffiti, the local bars, the Nisei barbershop, told to the rhythm of the poet's work. It is a journey back to Inada's youth, growing up in a Chicano neighborhood and knocking around his aunt's Fresno Fish Market, where she asks, "All this identity thing. What is it you're looking for?"

Cruisin' J-Town, a documentary on the jazz-fusion band, Hiroshima, is probably the closest thing so far to the definitive Sansei film, apart from *Beacon Hill Boys* (1985). Heavily influenced by Afro-Asian-Latin culture, Hiroshima is largely comprised of Sansei musicians who grew up among these melodies and rhythms. The film documented the musical and political influences that shaped the original Hiroshima sound, with the koto (a string instrument) and taiko drums at the heart of the band, and Asian America's socio-political milieu at its soul.

These early films drew on the sense of beauty, organization of space, and way of seeing in Asian American life. In composing interviews, Christine Choy, who is also a cinematographer, searches for and celebrates the clutter of Chinese American households to contextualize the subject. Like John Akomfrah of the Black Audio Film Workshop, who uses ornate and stylized backdrops to elevate the interview frame, Choy's composition employs a complex interplay of light and objects in the backdrop. The camera, however, stays up-close probing the interior life of the subject resulting in a masterful economy of a single frame. In Visual Communications' beautifully crafted *Pieces of a Dream* (1974), a documentary on the Sacramento Delta, the cam-

(Top) *CRUISIN' J-TOWN* (1976)
Visual Communications
(Bottom) *PIECES OF A DREAM* (1974)
Visual Communications

THE FALL OF THE I HOTEL (1983)
Crystal Huie

era caresses apples lining a conveyor belt, the contents of an old man's bureau—snapshots of his brothers back in the Phillipines, a carton of Quaker Oats, an English language book.

This visual lyricism is most pronounced in the work of Robert Nakamura, a VC founder. *Wataridori: Birds of Passage* (1976) describes the collective history of the Issei (first-generation Japanese Americans). In it, Nakamura conveys the beauty that Issei and Nisei managed to nurture from any piece of earth, whether the Imperial Valley, or the lifeless expanses of Heart Mountain and Tule Lake. See, also, Nakamura's lyrical *Conversations: Before the War/After the War* (1986) a narrative documentary on World War II relocation camps.

Experimental Films

During this early period, animation and experimental films also covered the front, shaped by the alternative political and social culture of the time, such as *Tourist Bus Go Home* (1969), *To Serve the People* (1979), and *Acapulco Gold* (1972), a hilarious animation piece by the irrepressible Arnie Wong. The avant garde, in particular, has been largely overlooked by observers of Asian American cinema, including myself. The notable exception is critic Daryl Chin, from whom I draw much of my references to experimental films in this section.

Conceptual artists like Taka Iimura, however, were already known in the avant garde by this time. Iimura has remained one of the most prolific, beginning with *Eye Rape, Dada62, Junk,* and *Iro,* made in Japan as early as 1962, that combined formal concerns of poetry and surrealism. Iimura's sensibilities are closer to the European avant garde; but his approach to the *eiga* (reflected cinema) is based on a fascination for the physical qualities of this western invention, through a Japanese perspective. As Iimura explains in the essay "On 'Reflected Cinema'":

I recall a lantern which I saw at a village festival in Japan in my childhood. A lantern covered with screens on which shadows of paper fishes revolved. It was the first time I saw a "movie." In fact, the word "reflected picture," I believe, is deeply rooted in the traditional shadow-picture which had (and has) existed in the East long before movies were invented. In Chinese, "movie" is literally called "electric shadow picture." That explains where movies came from for them. But in Japan, the term "reflected picture" seems to put more emphasis on a state.[6]

The Contradictions of Anti-Slick

In formal terms, Asian American films of the 1960s and 1970s were often raw by necessity and even, consciously so. Political filmmakers scorned the notion of "perfect cinema" that Julio García Espinosa, director of the Cuban Film Institute, described in his 1969 essay "For An Imperfect Cinema." "Nowadays perfect cinema—technically and artistically masterful—is almost always reactionary cinema," wrote García Espinosa. This anti-slick ideology influenced the arts movement as a whole, and is evident in the poster art created out of Japan Art Media in San Francisco, the design and prose style of *Gidra,* the Brechtian style in political theater groups like El Teatro Campesino, the new literature influenced by Amiri Baraka/Leroi Jones, Frank Chin, and others, and the driven power of Hiroshima's early sound, in unrecorded cuts like

"China," before their style was neutered by a producer and a label. Therefore, it is a mistake to attribute the rough-edged quality of early Asian American cinema as technically haphazard, or immature alone. Filmmakers grasped these new Asian American cultural forms in their raw state, and they moved swiftly towards building it whole.

Certain contradictions emerged from the political ideology of the cinema's first decade, which influenced the field during the 1980s. First, the struggle for entitlement was inherent to the movement. Victories that were won in the 1980s such as access to funding and mainstream venues had an effect of co-opting the work. Second was the notion of filmmaking as social change—versus the artist as individual—which extended to the production process itself. Through collective principles, filmmakers challenged the elitist, hierarchical basis of cinema practice. But there were inherent dangers in the ideological conception of these films, and in some cases, they were unsuccessful in execution.[7]

Entitlement

Asian American filmmakers demanded access to government grants, public television carriage, theaters, film festivals, film schools, library collections. Asian American filmmakers were small fish in a small pool, and even the Film Fund was considered a bastion to conquer. I can remember our inaugural reception at the PBS Program Faire in 1981. So that we could introduce the newly-formed National Asian American Telecommunications Association to program directors in style, we snuck cartons of *lo mein* and six-packs of Tsingdao into the Washington Sheraton. We couldn't afford the in-house catering costs. Hell, we couldn't even afford the cost of admission, and Steve Tatsukawa's lone registration pass multiplied severalfold, as if by immaculate conception.

These were gatekeepers to mainstream acceptance, and we wanted in. But the new structures of finance and distribution would change the nature of the work. A number of factors converged at the juncture of the 1970s and 1980s which moved the Asian American cinema closer to the mainstream. First, Asian American cinema needed to broaden its audience and base of support to survive. Ironically, the guerrilla filmmaking ideal of the Newsreel-Students for a Democratic Society era, often perpetuated middle class elitism. "Trust-fund babies" were in abundance. True to the art world, poor and working-class people could not afford to make art and live on air. During her years as executive director of the Pacifica Foundation, Sharon Maeda was often criticized by those in the community radio foundation who distrusted her solicitations of corporate funders. But Maeda wanted sufficient funds for salaries, so that women of color could afford to work in community radio. Although the bulk of Asian American filmmakers came from middle-class backgrounds, few had the independent wealth and access to resources to work as full-time artists without subsidies.

In the final analysis, the power of the image was not enough, even in a marketplace in which Asian Americans were the consumers. The Asian American community itself could not, and would not provide the sufficient financial basis to support production. There was a political schism between the youthful filmmakers and their parents' generation, who represented the community establishment (JACL, CCBA, etc.), uncool assimilationist tendencies, and controlled the concentration of wealth in the community.

Our audiences also needed a way to see the work. During the late 1970s, independent filmmakers were beginning to create new distribution venues for their work. In this sense, *Hito Hata* (1980) was a groundbreaking event. Visual Communications devised its own barnstorming strategy, by working with coalitions of local community organizations to sponsor fundraising screenings of the film. They did this at sites, from San Jose to Washington, D.C., and by the end of the tour, Visual Communications had literally forged an entire grassroots media network across the country. Individuals and organizations became involved in Asian American cinema as never before, and these broad coalitions undoubtedly strengthened the redress and reparations efforts that began crystallizing about that time. Today, this barnstorming strategy is still in force, although taken to a broader professional level by the Asian American media arts centers who have taken the lead in programming.

Noteworthy also is the coalescence of the Film News Now Foundation, a multicultural service and production center based in New York City which came into being in the 1980s. The FNNF, an offshoot of Third World Newsreel, assists film and videomakers of all backgrounds, from African Americans to Asians, Latinos, Native Americans, Palestinians, and European Americans.

The 1980s: Quality Time

Years before, in their 1969 essay "Toward a Third Cinema," Cuban filmmakers Fernando Solanas and Octavio Getino critiqued the nature of "permitted protest" intrinsic to the Second Cinema, or alternative film production:

This alternative signified a step forward inasmuch as it demanded that the filmmaker be free to express himself in non-standard language and inasmuch as it was an attempt at cultural decolonization. But such attempts have already reached, or are about to reach, the outer limits of what the system permits. The Second Cinema filmmaker has remained "trapped inside the fortress," as Godard put it, or is on his way to becoming trapped.[8]

This is a good description of Asian American filmmaking during the 1980s, a period of formal and technical improvement for filmmakers now even more beholden to the structures of mainstream media production. Barnstorming and the nontheatrical market provided exposure for the work to target audiences, but filmmakers quickly realized that the television and theatrical markets were the viable frameworks for financing production, and reaching respectable numbers. During this juncture at the end of the 1970s and beginning of the 1980s a number of developments made possible an Asian American push towards the mainstream: 1) Two national conferences and the birth of NAATA laid the groundwork for coordinated advocacy to funders and PBS; 2) public funders shifted priorities to general audiences; 3) the first wave of Asian American filmmakers were reaching a level of maturity, and were ready to take on more ambitious projects; 4) a second generation of quasi-"yuppie" independents emerged. This is a group I would include myself in, along with Arthur Dong, Lisa Hsia, Mira Nair, and Lise Yasui. Like their college peers who stormed Wall Street in the early 1980s these filmmakers were pragmatic and entrepreneurial in their approach to production; 5) Ronald Reagan is elected President of the United States of

America. Ironically, Asian Americans would make their greatest strides towards entitlement under the anti-entitlement president.

Asian American cinema had always been socially committed, not revolutionary. By 1980 the Asian American movement itself had changed. It broadened: The Chol Soo Lee case, the redress and reparations movement, and the Vincent Chin case crossed the lines of class, generation, ethnicity, and geography in the greater Asian American community. And the movement became more institutionalized: arts centers, legal aid, public health centers, and advocacy groups got offices, professional staffs, and boards of directors. Certain activists, who ten years before got out of the classroom and into the factories, were now getting out of the factories and into business school.

As Asian American cinema became more market-driven, filmmakers paid attention to technical accomplishment. Anti-slick was dead. Three styles emerged which characterized the 1980s: 1) documentaries made for public television; 2) low-budget feature films with limited theatrical release; 3) film school product with considerable technical promise, and a diversity of themes.

Documentaries

The overwhelming sensibility of Asian American documentarians is to position themselves from within. The greatest achievement of the Asian American documentary may be its intimacy. Cameras rarely stray far from the subject, and there is little of the visual remove of a wide-angle lens, or the attitude of remove of cinema veritists and old-style broadcast journalists. This empathy is evident in the personal diary films which developed parallel to and merging with the women's documentary genre. The first to make an impact was *China: Land of My Father* (1979), a chronicle of Felicia Lowe's poignant return to her family village in Canton, and an anecdote to the Sinophile frenzy that followed normalization. Given the standard of Asian American documentaries at the time, *Land of My Father* was refreshingly well-paced and coherent. It was followed, seven years later, by Lisa Hsia's *Made in China*, a journey of cultural awakening that begins with her parents' first date at a Harvard-Wellesley mixer, extends to the homes of distant cousins in Beijing.

The personal diary films are remarkably tight and engaging in execution. As social statements, they are nonconfrontational, but illuminate a different depth from the more aggressive, investigative style of conventional journalism.

The construction of closely held, empathetic Asian American worlds sometimes eluded direct confrontation with white America. Films about the Japanese American experience, for example, have conveyed the breadth and depth of the internee experience, but are almost void of testimony from the white architects and proponents of World War II relocation, many of whom are dying off with the Issei. Who are they? How did they think? What were their motivations?

By the end of the decade, Asian American independents were producing technically accomplished documentaries for the Public Broadcasting Service that are on par with any others: Loni Ding's *Nisei Soldier* (1983), Arthur Dong's *Forbidden City* (1989), and Lise Yasui's *Family Gathering* (1988) for the series "The American Experience"; and Steven Okazaki's *Days of Waiting* (1990) for the series "P.O.V." (*Who Killed Vincent Chin?* (1988) also aired on "P.O.V.") The stable of PBS producers have largely been a continuum of film-

DAYS OF WAITING (1990)
Mouchette Films

makers who came out of multicultural education and local public television producers—Deborah Bock, Renee Cho, Loni Ding, Felicia Lowe, Steven Okazaki, among them—and the new crop of second wave independents. Of the first generation of political filmmakers, only Christine Choy and Bob Nakamura have moved into PBS production. Curtis Choy, Jon Wing Lum, and Michael Chin (*Inside Chinatown*, with David Goldstein, 1975) have concentrated on technical specialties; and Visual Communications' Duane Kubo and Eddie Wong left filmmaking, though Wong recently completed a video documentary on Chinese American music.

Although socially conscious, Asian American documentaries reflect the constraints of television conventions and tastes, positioned largely in the realm of history, cultural documentaries, and personal forms. Let me add that my own work has embraced these approaches. My last documentary, *Americajin no Tainichikanjo no Tatemae to Honne* (1990), literally, "America's True Feelings Toward Japan," produced for Fuji Television, dealt with the Asian American experience through diary form and history; as was *Yellow Tale Blues* (1990), a collaboration with Christine Choy. Japanese American filmmakers, in particular, seem stuck in reverse. Perhaps it is a function of catharsis, as the Nikkei assemble the various pieces of the story in order to release itself of the whole. Thus, we have examined the legal angle in *Unfinished Business*, a Nisei perspective in *Emi*, the three-generational Japanese American experience in *Conversations*, the Amerasian experience in *Family Gathering*, and the white experience in *Days of Waiting*. But by relegating Japanese American life to historical artifact, we are not confronting racism today; and we are failing to confront the tremendous changes in our own cultural identity.

Crossing Gender Lines

For Asian American directors, gender divisions are not cut and dried. There are few directly feminist films by Asian American women, and some of the best films about women have been made by Asian American men. Male centrality is not the norm. In Steve Okazaki's *Survivors* (1982), the searing document of Japanese American victims of the atomic attack over Hiroshima and Nagasaki, again it is the Nisei/Kibei women who shape the emotional core. His documentary short, *The Only Language She Knows* (1983), is a portrait of the rocky relationships between Chinese American mothers and daughters. The film is funny and incisive, engined by Okazaki's economy of style and Lim's recreations of her mother and herself. This theme is repeated in Wayne Wang's *Dim Sum*, the 1984 feature about the love and hate relationship between an American-born Chinese and her immigrant mother. Then you have Arthur Dong's *Lotus* (1987), which exposes the feudal basis of women's exploitation through footbinding.

In formal terms, there is also cross-pollination. The personal documentary is known to be the realm of women filmmakers, but Asian American men have always used this approach, both in diary form and autobiographical form. From Visual Communications, Eddie Wong's *Wong Sinsaang* (1971) and Bob Nakamura's *Wataridori* profiled the filmmakers' immigrant fathers. And there is no particular gender affiliation in subject matter—just as Arthur Dong profiles his mother in *Sewing Woman*, Lori Tsang portrays her father's life in her intriguing first effort, *Chinaman's Choice*.

Asian American women documentarians have produced films about

FORBIDDEN CITY (1989)
Arthur Dong

Asian women's experiences, but few of these are expressly feminist films or filmmakers. Two exceptions are Trinh T. Minh-ha and Mira Nair, who are both consistent in grappling with the issue of sexual exploitation in their films, although they couldn't be more different in approach. Nair's *India Cabaret* (1985), a biting portrait of nightclub dancers in suburban Bombay, Nair places these "polluted women" within the broader scheme of Indian sexual politics, in which male domination renders every wife a whore, and every man a john. Her cameras had considerable access, following the dancers everywhere: at home, primping backstage, or performing on the floor to an Indian version of "Black Magic Woman." The film was attacked by some feminists for being voyeuristic, a bewildering label at best. The dance scenes are titillating at first, but stop short of exploitation. As a visual thread, these scenes gradually come to express monotony, it's a job after all, and the underlying meaning of the women's lives comes into sharp focus.

Vietnamese filmmaker Trinh T. Minh-ha renegotiates the hierarchical basis of cinematic language itself. The work has a compelling theoretical base, and has sparked considerable excitement among those familiar with semiotics, and debates on representation—but some befuddlement among those who are not. Her latest film, *Surname Viet Given Name Nam* (1989), steeped as it is in Vietnamese music, literatures, and lives, has its own intrinsic poetry which doesn't need as much theoretical translation. A bifurcated film within a film, Trinh first reconstructs the history of Vietnamese women's resistance through scripted voices—sort of a lilting version of Santiago Alvarez's *Seventy-Nine Springtimes of Ho Chi Minh* (1969)—then reveals the lives of those Vietnamese immigrant women who played these roles. Like the Black British Workshops, Trinh's work is theoretically elegant and aesthetically challenging. I only wish they would lighten up a little. Trinh may be the only filmmaker alive who could render the campy footage from a local Miss Vietnam beauty pageant into a humorless artifact of cultural deconstruction.

Notably, Nair and Trinh are more closely linked to Third World Cinema than to that of the Asian American movement. In its first period of development, the Asian American cinema reflected the political sensibilities of the broader movement. But to say that Asian American filmmaking never developed its own feminist genre is akin to those critics of Japanese cinema who claim the *benshi* tradition eclipsed the evolution of a narrative base. Asian American cinema, as it reflects sexual politics with the Asian American community, has its own particular development, and needs to be looked at on its own terms.

During the 1980s, however, a third wave of Asian women directors has emerged who have addressed Asian/Asian American sexual politics in dramatic shorts. All were trained in film schools, especially at UCLA. Kayo Hatta's appealing short, *Otemba* (1988), is a girl's-eye view of the final days of her mother's pregnancy as her father, owner of a Little Tokyo karaoke bar, hopes and prays for the birth of a boy. In Hei Sook Park's uneven drama, *Mija* (1989), a Korean American divorcee grapples with the alienation of life in a Koreatown halfway house, and Hiroko Yamazaki's *Juxta* (1989) explores the conflicts of Japanese war brides and their racially-mixed children. The most sophisticated of this group is Pam Tom's *Two Lies* (1989), a crafted and stylized piece that manages to attack western concepts of beauty—and Asian women's self-hatred—on a number of levels. The film's premise is simple: Again, a girl's view of the foibles of adulthood, this time her mother's eyelid surgery. There

(Top) *JUXTA* (1989)
Hiroko Yamazaki
(Bottom) *TWO LIES* (1989)
Pamela Tom

is no clunky didacticism to the narrative. As a tale of Asian womanhood, Tom surrounds the drama in Americana, reminiscent of *Paris, Texas* (1984), Wim Wenders' perspective of the outsider.

Dramatic Imperative and Crafting a New Language

In any developing cinema, the narrative is the next level of sophistication after the documentary. During the 1980s, independents as a whole moved towards dramatic production—a function of the maturing field and the decade's cultural politics—dominated by the economies of entertainment, and of scale. Some Asian American documentary filmmakers tried their hand at dramatic shorts, but they were mostly unremarkable efforts, such as Bob Nakamura's *Fool's Dance* (1983), Christine Choy's *Fei Tien: Goddess in Flight* (1983), *Permanent Wave* (1986), produced by myself, and Arthur Dong's *Lotus* (1987). More intriguing were these same filmmakers' push to open up the documentary form, incorporating narrative and non-documentary elements with documentary realism. Given the new atmosphere of experimentation and personal exploration, the 1980s was also a crucial period in the development of individual filmmakers.

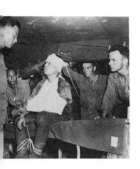

At the heart of these experiments is Montavais's strategy of necessity: for example, how to recreate the past now that the key players are no longer living? Some early efforts were awkward in execution, especially when dramatic recreations were combined with the documentary like so many apples and oranges. Three examples of this approach are San Francisco-based filmmakers Steve Okazaki's *Unfinished Business* (1984), Loni Ding's *Color of Honor* (1987), and Felicia Lowe's *Carved in Silence* (1987). One problem may be the visual contrast between the qualities of dramatic lighting, which can achieve an exquisite look—especially true in cinematographer Emiko Omori's narrative camerawork, in contrast to the raw quality of 16mm documentary images. It is the same problem with films that combine 16mm footage with video, without regards to any aesthetic logic. Perhaps taking these factors into account, Okazaki's later film, *Days of Waiting* (1990), combined various formats but achieved a greater proficiency in visual unity.

In Arthur Dong's *Sewing Woman* (1983), for instance, the elegance of the narrative text elevates the documentary realism of the film. In this case, the protagonist may still be living, but her recollections are articulated through a fictionalized script based on oral histories. On the surface, *Sewing Woman* is a simple biographical story of filmmaker Arthur Dong's mother, told ostensibly in her own words. The deft construction of filmed elements—archival footage from prewar China, family snapshots, and home movies—combined with the straight-talking eloquence of Lorraine, Dong's script moves the film beyond the realm of oral history.

A second aesthetic "problem" Asian American filmmakers have tackled is how to articulate to a general audience, an experience lived and spoken in another tongue? Or, beyond the debate over subtitles versus voiceovers, how do we speak to each other in a multilingual culture? In *Chan is Missing*, Wayne Wang lets the myriad of Chinatown/Chonk/Chinese dialects work organically, as the "Spanglish" of the Nuorican writers.

Multimedia Strategies

Long before performance artists like Laurie Anderson rediscovered multimedia strategies, Asian and African cultures fused storytelling and music

(Top) *THE COLOR OF HONOR* (1989)
Loni Ding
(Bottom) *CARVED IN SILENCE* (1987)
Felicia Lowe

with silent movie projection in Korea, Japan, India, and Nigeria. These raconteurs improvised to the films, sometimes creating a narrative that had nothing to do with the original story on screen. In Japan, the *benshi* were so strong a union, they were able to force theater owners to turn the volume off when talkies came in. In 1982, Korean American poet Walter Lew revived the *pyonsa*, using his own narrative and Sessue Hayakawa's 1924 silent feature, *The Dragon Painter*. Collaborating with filmmaker Lewis Klahr, he then renegotiated the tradition with the performance piece, "Movieteller, Part I: Ch'un Hyang"—expanded this year to "Movieteller, Part II: Kogi Eso"—which incorporates the Korean dance, Salp'uri, Sanjo music played on the kayaggum, a string instrument, William Powell in *Mr. Peabody and the Mermaid* (1948), and Super-8 footage Lew shot himself in Korea. Lew draws upon the *pyonsa* tradition in both form and spirit. During the Japanese invasion over fifty years ago, according to Lew, movie theaters were among the only places that Koreans were allowed to assemble by their Japanese occupiers. The pyonsa turned them into political forums, showing seemingly innocuous films like *Ben-Hur* (1926, 1959), but appropriating its scenes of Jewish rebellion as a symbol of Korean resistance.

The appropriation and reconstruction of images has its western equivalent to the silent era as well. During the 1920s, Joris Ivens' Dutch film society, Filmliga, borrowed newsreels from conspirant projectionists over weekends, then recut the establishment-line footage to produce an altered film with a leftist message. When Taka Iimura (*Film Strips, Number 1 and 2*, 1969) or Trinh T. Minh-ha, twenty years later, renegotiates scenes of Vietnam, or when the Black Audio Film Collective reinterprets the BBC's television newsreels—the use of media images goes beyond social critique because the media industry itself embodies racial hegemony and power. And the media industry has been Asian America's nemesis and obsession.

The Feature Film

The 1980s was launched with the resounding success of *Chan Is Missing*. Its release coincided with the popularity of Maxine Hong Kingston's *Woman Warrior* (1976) and David Henry Hwang's burgeoning career as a playwright, making it seem like big things were on the horizon. For the first time, a critical mass of Asian American actors with cinema, as well as theater, experience had evolved: veterans like Lisa Lu, Pat Morita, Mako, Nobu McCarthy, Victor Wong now joined by new talent, Marc Hayashi, Amy Hill, Hong Kong actress Cora Miao, Kelvin Han Yee. There were newly bankable cultural properties—Kingston's work, Amy Tan's *The Joy Luck Club* (1989); and there was a new crop of writers such as Hwang, Marina Gonzalez, Philip Kan Gotanda, Karen Ishizuka, Jessica Hagedorn, Genny Lim, and Spencer Nakasako, among them. This convergence of factors made Asian American feature filmmaking during the 1980s promising, but in reality, feature products were limited to the art house circuit. Wayne Wang and Peter Wang alone accounted for the majority of these films. All of the features have been produced by male filmmakers, with the exception of Mira Nair's neorealist drama of abandoned youth, *Salaam Bombay* (1988), and Shirley Sun's portrait of an *American in China, Iron and Silk* (1990).

Feature filmmaking has been the greatest hurdle for filmmakers of color, because it is at once a risky creative and business venture, and the industry has been resistant to investment. At a conference of black independents two

MOVIETELLER, PART II: KOGI ESO (1990)
Walter Lew

years ago, veteran documentary maker William Greaves told this story:

> When I was studying with Hans Richter, a young man came over to my house. We talked about our aspiration to become film directors. I had been assured that the path to become a documentary film producer was the right one. He, on the other hand, seemed anxious to get on with the business of making features. His name was Stanley Kubrick. My choice of the documentary as opposed to the feature film can be explained by the fact that I am more interested in documentaries. But this is a rationalization. The simple fact was that Kubrick was white and I was black. The motion picture field is one of the most fiercely competitive enterprises. The talented Kubrick could take a gamble and hope to succeed. I couldn't.[9]

Once Asian American filmmakers have overcome the hurdles of production, they are dependent on the vagaries of the theatrical market. Distribution woes seems to have plagued David Rathod's *West Is West* (1988), a funny tale of culture shock and crosscultural discovery in San Francisco's Tenderloin district. In it, Ashotosh Gowariker plays a young Indian student named Vikram, who finds himself stranded in a seedy hotel run by a Mrs. Shah (Pearl Padamsee), and pursued by immigration agents. Rathod has devised a classic pairing in the upper-class kid, whose impeccable manners and a good heart have little currency in America, and the wily Mrs. Shah, a queen bee standing guard over her hotel. *West Is West* is witty and appealing, but its distribution trail seems to have ended with festival and showcase releases.

What Language Do We Speak?

In this short period of time—about twenty years—the Asian American film movement has proceeded at an accelerated pace. We've had eight Academy Award nominees, a winner of the Cannes Camera D'Or (Mira Nair, *Salaam Bombay*), and a handful of theatrical releases, even an Asian American vanity film (Patrick Chu, *Illusory Thoughts*). James Wong Howe received Oscars in 1956 for *The Rose Tattoo* and in 1963 for *Hud*. Okazaki's *Days of Waiting* garnered an Oscar in 1991. But we have reached a glass ceiling, a barrier forged by continuing racism in the industry, and hoisted by our own failure to leap beyond the public television heaven we've come to inhabit. It is unclear whether or not any Asian American independents will be able to cross the threshhold, as Spike Lee or John Sayles did. I mention these two, because they embody an element of creative, even political daring, as well as a broad audience appeal. A film like *Do the Right Thing* (1989), for example, reflects the political manifesto to provoke and entertain. It moved the debate over the complexity of racial conflict in a primarily Black and white, but also Latino and Asian world; and it sharpened the battle lines. Therefore, by invoking Spike Lee, I'm not talking box office alone, but a reaffirmation of our earliest ideals as Asian American filmmakers—to create an original cinema that would reach, and appeal to the people. Will Asian American cinema stagnate during the coming decade—churning out new and better educational market programming and occasional art house hits—or will we emerge from the minor leagues?

A handful of filmmakers, like Nair—whose work-in-progress *Mississippi Masala* casts Denzel Washington in a transatlantic production shot in Uganda

WEST IS WEST (1988)
Jim Block

and Mississippi—have begun to chip away at the glass ceiling. Foremost among them is Wayne Wang, who continues to be one of the most consistently exciting independent filmmakers. His work bears a distinct, personal signature—visually stylized, a wry intellect, stronger on concept than in narrative—but he is rarely predictable. Imagine following *Eat a Bowl of Tea*, a mild romantic comedy that resembles a Chinatown version of *Barefoot in the Park* with *Life Is Cheap...but Toilet Paper is Expensive* (1990), codirected and written by Spencer Nakasako, a collision course of a film that could be subtitled "A Guide to Hong Kong on Ten 'Ludes a Day," and has the added distinction of an "X" rating from the Motion Pictures Association.

The only other feature filmmaker to approach Wang in prolificacy is Peter Wang, an actor who nearly stole the show in *Chan Is Missing* with his rendition of a samurai chef. As a filmmaker, Wang's work has been uneven. He first appeared on the independent scene in 1984 with *A Great Wall*, the captivating story of a Chinese American family's trip home to the People's Republic. In contrast to Wayne Wang, Peter Wang is primarily a storyteller who stumbled with the high concept *Laserman* (1988), a comedy thriller about a laser scientist living in the bicultural blur and technosheen of downtown New York. Here again, Peter Wang is wryly effective as an eccentric, self-deprecating police detective. *Laserman* was ambitious in conception, but less successful in execution, with its meandering storyline. It also made Wang infinitely more interesting as a filmmaker, especially in light of the conventional delights of *A Great Wall* and his new coming-of-age tale, *First Date* (1989).

It is the element of risk-taking that sets *Laserman* and *Life Is Cheap* apart—along with the filmmakers who are moving forward the documentary and narrative form—especially in the 1980s, as Asian American filmmaking in general entered a relative comfort zone. These two films also represent an intriguing crosscultural free-for-all: Tossing into the celluloid stage a mix of cinematic influences from film noir to Jackie Chan, evoking an Americanized China (Hong Kong) on the one hand; and a Sinophile America (New York) on the other—and allowing all the pieces to land where they may. Although uneven in execution, both have the same raw energy and freshness that characterized the Asian American films made fifteen and twenty years ago, like the rambunctious *Dupont Guy* (1976). But much of the fire in these early films has been replaced by the cool embrace of television, sometimes the remove of history. Along the way, Asian American films have gained in technical standards, narrative cohesion, and basic watchability. We have learned the master's language, but have we sacrificed our own?

Something should be said about the tumult over "quality," with which we were baptized at the start of the decade. The debate has been an undercurrent to these new cinema practices, but we have never really resolved the heart of the matter. At the time, the word "quality" became synonymous with exclusion for artists of color. Our work was labeled primitive, unaccomplished, immature, amateurish and sociological. To some extent, we swallowed the reactionary definition whole, and set about sharpening our technical skills and rethinking the beauty of form, rather than building our own cultural forms. In truth, quality derives from the esthetic emotion inherent to a work of art. So when filmmakers refocus the Asian American way of seeing through a camera's lens, or locate the poetry in real life stories, that is quality.

THE LASERMAN (1988)
Peter Wang

It is likely that much of the angrier, and aesthetically daring work is being produced on video today, such as Shu Lea Cheang's brilliantly conceived *Color Schemes* (1989), a three-monitor rumination on racial identity installed in the most common of crosscultural venues—a laundromat. Bruce and Norman Yonemoto, whose films were once staples at the Asian American Film Festival (*Garage Sales*, 1975) switched gears early, going on to make one of the first video features, *Green Card* (1982).

There remains a strain of underground filmmaking, from new directors like Gregg Araki, whose low-budget feature *Three Bewildered People in the Night* (1987) is a bleak and clever picture of the adolescent twilight; and Jon Moritsugu, director of *My Degeneration* (1989), an extended rock 'n roll anthem to the juvenile and the grotesque. Angst-ridden to be sure, but there is little that is subversive or even outrageous about these films. In *My Degeneration*, for example, girl group lead singer Amanda may be heavy in love with a hog's head named Livingston. But she only goes so far as to manage a few caresses of the porker's snout, never crossing the line that John Waters would have obliterated in a minute.

The Future

The Japanese American experience, and the weight of historical artifact, may be a lesson for the cinema as a whole. Asian American filmmakers may be moving away from the community-based culture that infused its early development. Furthermore, the continued monopoly of Chinese and Japanese American filmmakers means we have failed to nurture talent from the other immigrant populations—such as Filipino, Korean, Laotian, Pakistani, Thai, et al—the newer communities being the most vital cultural centers in Asian America. A tremendous support system of advocacy and mentorship has evolved over the years, but its benefits have been distributed largely within our own ranks. Our own political prejudices may have played a part in this neglect. Unlike the Chinese, East Indian, Filipino, and Japanese sojourner of the first century of Asian immigration, many immigrants of the last twenty years have come from far different political circumstances. They may have been too rabidly anti-communist and pro-American for our tastes, or at least, intent on buying into the American Dream that we scorned in our parents' generation. As the nature of the Asian American community has changed, we cannot remain stagnant in our outlook.

Ironically, many filmmakers from the newer communities are being nurtured at film schools, and not the Asian American media arts centers. From New York University, there is Fruto Corre, director of the hilarious Imelda Marco send-up, *Women of Waray Waray* (1990); from USC, Charles Ignacio, who wrote and directed the contemporary gothic tale, *Deans' List* (1987); Supachai Surongsain, director-writer of the first Thai American independent film, *Pak Bueng On Fire* (1987) studied at UCLA. The slow matriculation into prestigious film schools accelerated during the 1980s, and these students have produced some of the best short, narrative work in the last ten years, not all of which lies within the thematic boundaries of Asian experience: They include NYU graduates Stephen Ning, director of the affectionate coming-of-age story, *Freckled Rice* (1983), Orinne J.T. Takagi's bitingly funny *Community Plot* (1984), and LiPo Ching's deftly crafted comedy, *One Sunday Afternoon* (1988); and from the American Film Institute, Susan Inouye's professionally executed *Solo* (1989).

(Top) *GREEN CARD: AN AMERICAN ROMANCE* (1982) Kira Perov
FRECKLED RICE (1988) Stephen Ning
(Bottom) *SOLO* (1989) Susan Inouye

Filmmakers trained at these institutions will undoubtedly play a major role in Asian American cinema during the 1990s. And the nature of film training will slowly change as well. Filmmakers like Ayoka Chenzira, Christine Choy, Haile Gerima, and Bob Nakamura are now teaching on the college level, and you can bet the "canon" of cinema practice they expose to their students is far different from the Eurocentricism that has dominated media education. However, if film schools are the conduit of the future, how are we nurturing talent from poor and working class backgrounds? Film schools are exclusionary in a number of ways, foremost being the expense. In the rough and ready days of anti-slick cinema, a young filmmaker could learn on the job. Now that production occurs on a professional level, you have to come to the location with proven skills. For professional training, Third World Newsreel remains the only 16mm film workshop directed towards people of color; Visual Communications teaches in Super-8, Asian CineVision in video, and Film News Now Foundation in screenwriting alone.

What is the future of Asian American film? Of cinema "on the margin" as a whole? Right now the debate is sharpening: read it in the *Black Film Review*, which has been publishing essays by Zeinabu Davis, David Nicholson, Clyde Taylor and others on the future of African American cinema. Or see it in *August 29*, the new play by the Los Angeles Theater Company's Latino Theatre Lab, which ostensibly documents the Chicano Moratorium and murder of Ruben Salazar, but in fact, questions the direction of Chicano art and politics—"the spirit of the movimiento"—under the spectre of assimilation.

As we steady our gaze towards the next twenty years, we may not really have to look too far. Artists of color sit squarely in the midst of cultural upheaval. And when all the dust settles, we may very well arrive, if not at the center, as the links in a new cultural matrix. We are concentrated in the country's metropolitan centers, in the belly of cultural production. We are facing constant infusions of wealth from the Pacific Rim via direct investment and new immigrants, and these new immigrants, rich or poor, are a potent source of cultural vitality.

How will we move forward from here? Twenty years ago, Asian American cinema was borne out of a lucid and pragmatic social and political ideal. Along the way, we may have bought into the conventional wisdom, relegating our place in America to the marginalized and ghettoized, and positioning our cultural products accordingly. It may now be time to look back, in order to start looking at the state of Asian Americanness in a new way, in the new world.

NOTES

1. Coco Fusco, "A Black Avant-Garde," in *Young British & Black: A Monograph on the Work of the Sankofa Film Video Collective and Black Audio Film Collective* (Buffalo: Hallwalls/Contemporary Arts Center), 20.
2. Louis Chu, *Eat A Bowl of Tea* (New York: Lyle Stuart, 1961, reprinted by the University of Washington Press).
3. Daryl Chin, "Film Forums: The Asian American Case, *CineVue* 1:3 (1986), 9.
4. Tomas Ybarra Frausto, speech at "Show the Right Thing: A National Conference on Multicultural Film & Video Exhibition," New York University, September 1989.
5. Benjamin Tong, statement in "Public Record," *Amerasia Journal* 15:1 (1989), 154.
6. Taka Iimura, "On Reflected Cinema," *A Note on the Program*, (New York: The Japan Society, 1978).
7. Third World Newsreel—which split off from New York Newsreel in 1974—and Visual Communications operated as production collectives during the 1970s. Individual credits were not

listed on screen, and there was considerable mobility in production tasks. In conceiving *Mississippi Triangle* (1983), a documentary on relations between African Americans, whites, and Chinese in the Mississippi Delta, Choy took this precept a step further. Three separate co-directors and production teams—Alan Seigel with a white crew, a black crew led by Worth Long, and Choy's Asian crew—documented their respective communities. The material was then interwoven into a meandering, 110-minute analysis of race and class in the Delta.

The making of Visual Communication's *Hito Hata: Raise the Banner* (1980) was cinema by ideal in epic form. Hailed as the first Asian American feature film (Hayakawa's 1924 silent, *The Dragon Painter* was yet to be rediscovered by archivist Stephen Gong), *Hito Hata* was to be the definitive Japanese American story, involving the collective vision of a cadre of filmmakers, community activists, featuring the most promising cast of Asian American actors since *Flower Drum Song*. With a compilation of oral histories, the production team fashioned a script about an Issei bachelor named Oda, facing the threat of eviction from his Little Tokyo home by city redevelopers. Oda's life provides a vehicle for retelling Japanese American history: a textbook approach that diluted the narrative effect. But the film's ambitious conception and script by committee sealed its fate, perhaps even before the production began.

8. Fernando Solanos and Octavio Getino, "Towards a Third Cinema," reprinted in Michael Chanan, editor, *Twenty-five Years of the New Latin American Cinema* (London: British Film Institute, 1983).

9. William Greaves, quoted in John Williams, "Black Filmmaking in the 1990s: A Pioneering Event," *The Independent Film & Video Monthly*, December 1988, 18.

BACK TO REAL
ASIAN AMERICAN
FILMMAKING
JOHN ESAKI

An Asian American director I worked for a few years back kept two books handy on the set during the production of a feature-length Chinese American drama. The director periodically referred to these two volumes for inspiration: Donald Richie's biography of Yasuhiro Ozu, the Japanese film director considered by Richie to be the "most Japanese of Japanese directors"; and *Screenplay*, Syd Field's popular, formula-laden instruction manual for writing "professional," Hollywood screenplays.

The film that ultimately resulted from this marriage of Asian and American cultural and commercial influences was well-received by audiences and critics—both mainstream and Asian American alike. The images were framed with the simplicity and formal elegance reminiscent of the Japanese master, and the plot wound its way to a satisfying, if somewhat predictable, emotional resolution. After viewing the finished film, however, I could not escape the nagging conclusion that although the art admittedly had been artfully executed, an essence of the vital spirit and unique character qualities of the Asian American people on whose lives the film was based had been artfully eluded. Form—in homage to Syd and Yasuhiro—had triumphed, but, disappointingly, the content had been made less vibrant.

Having been privileged (and in a sense, cursed!) to participate in the making of Asian Pacific American films as a technician, I have felt that gnawing disappointment often enough to suspect the existence of an immutable cinematic law: film crew members are eternally doomed to the hell of knowing too well the yawning gap between creative ambition and practical fulfilment. Asian Pacific American audiences, starved for films truly representative of their own experiences, understandably have been tolerant of these shortcomings, as have our critics, who, perhaps, eager to demonstrate their intellectual command of cinematic language and history, have preferred discussing style and form in favor of the more mundane issues of content. Film workers, on the other hand, are a pragmatic, less forgiving breed.

The gripes of Asian American grips and gaffers, costumers, camera assistants and Nagra jockeys—essentially the working class of film crews—represent a primal, emotional response to the disparities between the vitality of Asian Pacific American reality and the studied, occasionally pretentious, artifice that has surfaced in some recent major films. The startling image in a recent Asian American feature film of an elderly Japanese American with hair more resembling Billy Idol with a bad dye job than any Nisei uncle I ever knew is symptomatic of this troubling development. This film's director once patiently explained to me why he would not employ a particular Asian American cinematographer because of his lighting style, yet allowed a critical and jarringly inaccurate detail of Asian American life to be committed to film (not so incidentally, perhaps, by a non-Asian American director of photography).

I wonder if such an oversight could have been committed had the director been a bit more obsessive about content than about creating Cinematic Art?

There is tremendous expressive potential yet untapped in the Asian Pacific American experience. As Asian Pacific American media enters its third decade, it would be productive for our filmmakers to recall the earliest of our filmmaking efforts. In those first, completely unprecedented works lies the direction to a future in which the incomparable richness and growing complexities of our communities can be more effectively—and distinctively—portrayed. That is through a return to less formulaic, less derivative, more genuinely personal and cultural aesthetic choices.

At a discussion following a recent retrospective screening of a half dozen of the first Asian American works produced in the early 1970s by student filmmakers from the seminal Ethno-Communications Program at UCLA, several members of the audience marveled at the vitality of the films from those formative years—particularly in comparison to work produced currently. These films express an exuberance about the Asian American experience at a direct, visceral, emotional level.

A motorcycle gang cruises the streets of L.A. in *Yellow Brotherhood* (1970), a film by Brian Maeda. The "choppers" are identical to the ones made American icons by the 1969 film *Easy Rider*. Maeda's camera rides along with these intimidating, long-haired, mustachioed bikers, testing a contemporary audience's tolerance for bouncing, vertiginous handheld shots, but, nevertheless, directly communicating the rough intensity and immediacy of the experience through an integrated, fully appropriate camera style.

In Danny Kwan's film, *Homecoming Game* (1970), the terse, often droll dialogue between members of a vintage sixties commune rivals the inventiveness of many a Hollywood screenwriter for humor and character development. Scenes of a living-room party at which participants coolly dance "The Jerk," and of a fervent political activist preparing the group for a demonstration, provide a very tangible, recognizable sense of a distinctive era in Asian American history and the compelling folk who marked that era with lasting significance.

The presence of the filmmaker as first person observer is a vital component of these films. In the climactic sequence of *Manzanar* (1970), the first film created by Robert A. Nakamura, the camera darts frantically, searching through the desert brush in a frenzy of erratic movement. Reprinted from its original Super 8mm format to a 16mm print, the film's images jerk and skip with each primitive tape splice of the original reversal film, yet the raw, unpolished qualities of *Manzanar* are extraordinarily compelling—and fully appropriate to communicate the emotional content of the subject: Nakamura's own bitter memory of life in a desolate desert as a young boy in an American concentration camp thirty years before. The colors of the film stock have shifted and faded with age to a reddish monochrome, but like vintage bordeaux, this film's essences have grown in complexity and significance over time.

These films have retained their impact on viewers because of the immediacy with which the content is communicated. The viewer never gets the sense of a form or style imposed upon the content, but rather that the form has emerged from the filmmaker's obsession with—and thorough involvement in—the subject matter.

Out-of-focus shots are ordinarily edited out of a film, yet the presence of such shots in Eddie Wong's poignant black and white portrait of his laundryman father, *Wong Sinsaang* (1970), actually enhance the impact of the film, contributing a sense of expressive urgency to the filmmaker's efforts. Here, given the choice of editing for content or precision of style, Wong wisely opted for content. His images of the elder Wong—working the steam presses, bantering with customers and practicing *tai chi*—may occasionally be soft but the film as a whole is undeniably sharp in its perceptive observance of an immigrant's complex responses to life in America.

These early films are exclusively documentaries, but the approach to filmmaking that they embody clearly is applicable to dramas as demonstrated by Wayne Wang's landmark *Chan Is Missing* (1981). This independently-produced feature captured the energy and distinctive qualities of Chinese American life through the inspired use of non-actors such as Laureen Chew and the inimitable settings of San Francisco Chinatown known so intimately by Wang and his documentary-trained cinematographer Michael Chin. The spare style highlighted the quirky, yet fully believable characters and gave audiences an unvarnished look at the vitality and uniqueness of Asian America. This point was lost upon a few members of Hollywood's old guard Asian Americans, who, at a preview screening in Los Angeles, I recall, were unimpressed by *Chan*'s lack of technical polish. Regrettably, in spite of the eventual critical and box office successes of *Chan Is Missing*, this Hollywood preoccupation with style at the expense of content still remains the most formidable obstacle to the progress of Asian Pacific American filmmaking.

The economic lure and the seductions of prestige held forth by the filmmaking industry in Los Angeles are difficult to resist. (I have personally witnessed the most hardboiled and intellectually rigorous New York filmmakers go "ga-ga" at the prospect of fondling an Oscar statuette.) Imagine the power of this seduction to the most recent generation of Asian Pacific Americans emerging from the film schools armed with the latest creative technology. The initial student productions of Pam Tom, Kayo Hatta and Dan Tirtawinata—nurtured by the relatively industry-free creative environment at UCLA—have clearly demonstrated commitments to Asian Pacific thematic material coupled with their distinctive filmmaking talents. The Asian Pacific community can only hope that they can resist the lures of Hollywood-style filmmaking.

The answer to these powerful distractions, I believe, is in confidence—in our own stories, our own experiences and our own perceptions of those experiences. Yasuhiro Ozu's way of seeing the world and recording it on film were right for him, as were, respectively, the visions of Ousemene Sembene, Ingmar Bergman and Truffaut and Scorsese. Only by believing in the compelling nature of our lives as Asian Pacific Americans and by trusting in our own creative ways of seeing those lives and framing them on film can we forge a true Asian Pacific American cinema.

Our cinema began with great promise back two decades ago. As we enter our third decade, a hopeful sign is Wayne Wang's recently declared return to "guerrilla filmmaking." Described in a recent article as "raw, dirty, satirical, violent, funny and honest," Wang's new film *Life Is Cheap . . . but Toilet Paper Is Expensive* (1990), seems to indicate a return to the kind of idiosyncratic filmmaking revealed in *Chan Is Missing*. Significant is Wang's collaboration with Spencer Nakasako, certainly one of the most idiosyncratic, direct, and nonpretentious filmmakers—and characters—on the Asian American media scene today. The future for Asian Pacific American filmmaking is looking more real.

CONVERSATIONS: AN EXPERIMENT IN COMMUNITY-BASED FILMMAKING

Karen Ishizuka and Robert A. Nakamura

Equipped with an abundance of passion and determination on one hand, community-based filmmakers are always faced with a paucity of funds on the other. Coupled with an unconscious desire to rival the production value of *The Godfather* (1972), the task of completing a meaningful, well-crafted film seems even more challenging. Too often we get caught in the independent filmmaker's syndrome of spending more time and energy trying to raise more funds and emulating big budgeted looks on bargain-basement means rather than on what we want to say and how we're going to say it. Of course, there are many ways of scaling down production costs—some good, some not so good. ("Ask your cast and crew to eat a big breakfast before coming to the set," states the book *Feature Filmmaking at Used Car Prices*.) And a comfortable budget is always desirable—don't mistake this essay as saying poorer is better— or holier.

When we received a small grant to produce *Conversations: Before the War/After the War* (1986), we went through the trite but true stages. Elation—at getting a grant, no matter how small; Anticipation—another chance to go to Cannes; and Depression—over how we're going to make do with short money. This time (I'm mad as hell and I'm not going to take it any longer), we decided to take the bull by the horns, invert the situation and turn our liabilities into strengths. After some thought, we realized that what community-based filmmakers are blessed with is the passion and persis- tence of our communities. Without a doubt, our stories and our people are our greatest strengths. And so we decided to focus on that rather than bells and whistles and let this focus guide our filmmaking.

One decision was to use non-actors. With all due respects to our fine SAG actors, they can be very expensive. Even when they are willing to work for minimum, and most are, there are agents and SAG to deal and negotiate with. (We've actually been told by an overzealous agent, "I'll see to it you'll never work in this town again!") Our decision was not entirely motivated by budget. We knew there were very charismatic and downright gutsy people in our community who would be willing, get a kick out of participating, and do a great job.

Conversations was based on Karen's play, *The Truth of the Matter*, and hence the characters were already developed. We chose our actors based on their appropriateness for the role—their look and feel for the character. Then we adjusted the characters with the non-actors in mind, incorporated their own histories, personalities, and abilities into the character, and wrote lengthy character sketches for each. We went over these characters with each community actor very thoroughly and a modified script was written.

Although the community actors were provided the extensive character profile as well as a written script, they were all encouraged to improvise. This they did to varying degrees, thereby providing an unexpected level of verisimilitude that was very exciting. One community actor used only the bare outline of her character, relying almost totally on her own feelings and actual experiences. We don't think this was done deliberately, rather that it was highly unconscious and organic and hence akin to psycho-drama. Another melded his own experiences with those of his father and for a magical time became one person. In hermeneutical fashion, his father's stories were simply not retold but, being part of his psychic inheritance, came through him and hence in the telling became his own. By having community people play a character, and not themselves, and yet encouraging them to bring forth their own personal stories and experiences, they were able to disclose very real emotions and private feelings without revealing themselves. (Of course, self-disclosure is certainly attainable in traditional documentary format depending on the person featured and usually burning a lot of film to capture the decisive moment or being very lucky.) We found this method to be very exciting and successful in terms of our goals of maximizing content (the psychological impact of the World War II internment on personhood) and not have our hands tied by budget.

We sought to create moving (vs. still) psychological portraits that provided insight into who people are—not at any one period of their lives (or sitting), but over a period of time—in this case, who they were before the war and how that experience affected who they became after the war. A fourth character in the film was the spirit of the camps themselves as epitomized by the ruins of Manzanar, one of the ten camps, located in the Owens Valley, California. In live-action footage, the remains of Manzanar were interspersed in the film in between the living portraits like a haunting presence in the lives of the three people, wrapping them in its barbed wire of the mind, even forty years later.

Some people loved the film, some hated it. It defied many conventions—talking heads; blurring the lines between the drama and documentary; preferring black and white over color. We took a risk in an effort to explore new ways of working; as we all must.

Teshome Gabriel, one of Bob's colleagues in the Film and Television Department at UCLA, helps put our efforts into a larger conceptual framework when he calls the emergence of such alternative ways of working "a response by minority filmmakers to an historic situation that demands a new outlook towards film practice . . . (this approach) creates provocative works precisely because they portray their own world, a microcosm of American culture, within its proper aesthetic, cultural and historical context. Here you have the dimension of the minority cinematic act demanding to be examined on its own terms."*

*From the introduction to a retrospective of Independent Black American Cinema held at UCLA in February 1984, titled, " American Black Film Practice: Towards a Conceptual Framework," by Professor Teshome Gabriel.

CONVERSATIONS:
BEFORE THE WAR/AFTER THE WAR (1986)
Generation Films, Inc.

Nobody rules us.
We rule ourselves.
Omai Fa'atasi
Coming together to survive.

OMAI FA'ATASI

Visual Communications (1979)

Van Troi Pang

About Myself
1) Born July 17, 1971, in San Francisco, CA;
2) Chinese & Japanese—5th-generation A.B.C.; 4th-generation Buddhahead;
3) Van Troi—named after South Vietnamese revolutionary martyr Nguyen Van Troi;
4) Currently residing in "Nueva York." Attending community college, studying liberal arts; I haven't decided on a major yet.
5) Active member of E.C.A.S.U. (East Coast Asian Student Union);
6) Hobbies—Martial Arts (Kali, Arnis, Pilipino Escrima & Indonesian Pencak Silat), reading, drawing, and hangin' out with friends;
7) Ambition—Do the right thing for the community & go kick it in Hawaii!

Reason for doing *Mochi Monster*

Well, I was 13 years old back then. I suppose I took Mar's introduction to animation class because I wanted to learn some of the process of making cartoons from watching Saturday morning cartoons. I remember having a lot of fun in that course doing experimental works in "stop-motion," "still-motion," "cell animation," and I forget what you call it when you "directly draw on the film."

My final project in the course was *Mochi Monster* (1985). I don't know what I initially intended to get across with the two-minute flick. Looking back at it now, you can construe a whole lotta things out of it. Community, cultural, environmental, social issues . . . you name it! I guess that's why all the VC folks call it a "cult classic."

I guess for a long time I've carried a great sense of pride and joy about being Asian and so it comes out that way in whatever I do. *Mochi Monster* was no different. Even at age 13, you look at television or the movies and you find that there is little offered that has any relevance, especially to a person of color. This is the reason *Mochi Monster* came out the way it did. I wanted to do something that showed where I was coming from. I figure any person who does any form of art tries to do the same.

That's about all I can mention on behalf of *Mochi Monster*. It's been so long! Anywayz, thanks VC! Also, I'd like to wish my bro Maceo, who's recuperating from an injury in Japan, well!

OMAI FA'TASE (1971)
Visual Communications

About the picture:

This is a sketch to commemorate my grandfather, Daisho Miyagawa, who passed away last year. This picture is based on a photograph taken of him when he was 19, the same age as I am now. I remember a while ago I asked my mother, "Why don't Asian Americans have specific heroes like Marcus Garvey, Harriet Tubman, Geronimo, Gregorio Cortez, or Malcolm X? I mean, I know Asian people worked the sugar plantations of Hawaii, built the railroads, started unions and made all kinds of agricultural accomplishments collectively, but how come there aren't really any specific names that stick out?" She replied, "Just because we don't know about them doesn't mean they don't exist."

At least I was proud to know of Carlos Bulosan because of his autobiography *America Is in the Heart*, and then of course Bruce Lee, the brother who showed Asian people can kick ass, but who else can be pointed out as figures, who we as Asian people in America can really draw inspiration from? This has lead me to look at my own roots.

My grandfather was a guy who did a lot during his lifetime despite a disability he had in one of his legs since the age of seven. A few things that I can mention about him was that he was part of a movement (before WWII and before the camps) that was against the U.S. sending scrap metal to Japan which in turn was used to build weapons against other peoples in Asia; also he worked in the Alaskan fishing canneries in the 30s and helped to unionize the workers there (my mom has got this other cool picture of him in those days with two manongs and they all have this "don't mess with us" kinda look) and for a period of time he was a journalist for the *New York Nichibei*.

I guess what I'm trying to get at is he was a real cool guy for what he did, for who he was even though he was so humble about it. I found a hero who wasn't try'n to be one. That's the true kind. PEACE!

MOCHI MONSTER (1985)
Van Troi Pang

GRANDFATHER'S PORTRAIT
Van Troi Pang (1990)

STRATEGIES OF AN ASIAN AMERICAN FILMMAKER
LONI DING

Missing Images: Lost and Found

MI noticed him sitting on the end of the row, this elderly Chinese man in his seventies maybe. He looked like one of those bachelor men I imagine having spent most of his life working the Chinatown restaurants, thinking someday he'd get back to visit his village in Toishan. All afternoon he'd been sitting there in the auditorium watching the English lessons on television, over and over. "Sut Yung Ying Yee"—basic practical English—a T.V. series produced by a collaboration between the local Westinghouse station and the Chinese community, was continuously replaying three sample programs at the community screening. It featured a bilingual approach (Cantonese/English), with a Chinese host and many community volunteers acting out the vignettes of practical scenes from life—getting on the bus, shopping for shoes, seeing the doctor, etc. All the roles—bus driver, sales clerk, doctor—were played by Asians.

"How do you like the lessons?" I asked.

"Pretty good . . . not bad," he answered, and went on to say a few more things, swinging into more English than Cantonese.

I was puzzled because these lessons were very beginning stuff. "You speak English pretty well. . . ."

"Yeh, I don't need them."

"But you've been here all afternoon . . . and I've seen you really watching them."

"Well . . . I just like to see the faces."

Fifty-plus years in America, and all of it in Chinatown, you'd think he'd had enough of seeing Chinese faces. What's so special about seeing them on T.V.?

That was 1970, with an elderly immigrant, "long-time Californ." Sixteen years later, something similar happened with a student at UC Berkeley. I heard a knock on my office door. There she was, standing with an open box of take-out food, chopsticks sticking out of the top.

"It's lunchtime . . . I have this Chinese food and I thought you might like to share it."

She was a mass communications major, who'd grown up in San Jose. All semester I hadn't heard much from her in class, but here she was ready to share her chopsticks. Real intimate. I was surprised. Something was definitely up. Taking the box obediently—no sudden moves or the bird might fly away—I mumbled my thanks, hid my amazement in silent eating, and waited.

"I went to see the movie, *Dim Sum* (1985) last night."

"Umm humm . . ." (more silent eating).

"I don't know why, but almost from the first moment when the show started, I started to cry . . . and I cried off and on throughout the whole movie. I don't really know why. Her mother isn't really like my mother, and I'm not in her situation . . . my mom is not after me to get married. But everything in the movie is familiar . . . the people and the way things look. . . ." It is the real image you don't know you need and you're missing . . . until one day it's there.

It is somehow not enough that we've lived among a group of people, and see them every day in life. Something essential is missing when that existence is not also a confirmed public existence. The subtext of media absence is that the absent group "doesn't count," or is somehow unacceptable. And psychologically we know it affects our sense of self, our feeling of being agents who act upon the world.

Images may not always have been so important in the days before the power of contemporary media. It may also be that the absence of authentic media images of women and workers, too, is equally significant to their sense of identity. But no one doubts the critical role of media in defining public images of minorities.

Television imagery is particularly critical in this way, not only as a pervasive formative influence on the young, but as the public institution present in the home of almost every family. It may be junk on the T.V. but it's junk that—along with consumer goods and the public schools—we share in common with "every other American." Television is the contemporary, publicly accepted record of faces and voices. To be absent in T.V. imagery is a special kind of "non-existence" or way of being "non-American."

Making Mass Media

Almost all my work has been for television, designed for reaching a mass audience. In doing that, I've made certain assumptions about the audience. I assume, for example, that they carry somewhere in their minds three common misrepresentations of Asian Americans: the common stereotypes of Asians as perpetual foreigners; as resigned, silent victims; and most recently, as successful "model minorities" who "contribute to America."

I have tried not to counter these misrepresentations directly, but rather to address the three kinds of stereotypes in my overall project design . . . to "show the opposite" rather than to "explain, argue and oppose."

For the problem of absence, the main work is to create presence. My preferred approach is to displace stereotypes by creating vital images of Asian Americans as real human beings, with individual faces, voices, and personal histories that we come to know and care about.

They would not be the Americans whose differences are dissolved in the "melting pot," but people speaking with the distinctive accents and rhythms of their real individual and family histories; neither looking nor sounding like the "typical American."

Authentic images of minorities do not abound. For ourselves too, we have a need for the objectifying record. We think we know what we look and sound like, until we're surprised or shocked by hearing our actual voices on a tape recorder, or seeing our physical selves in moving images.

LONI DING
Robert Kaufman

The Camera's Gaze

My works have often been celebrations of ordinary people and celebrations of particular communities.

"Ordinary people" of no particular position—not heroes, stars, celebrities, scoundrels, criminals, or monsters—are yet capable of doing extraordinary things. Individually and collectively they can have the power to engage us: to hold our interest, draw us nearer, fascinate, instruct, and charm us.

Possibly they have this power because we empower them with our attention. Someone once startled me with the proposal that if you were to gaze at anybody long enough, you could become enamoured with them. Like the primal bonding of mother to infant, even one "so ugly that only a mother could love" (which still leaves the mystery, why this attachment is so wondrously blind and unreasoning). Perhaps the gaze of the camera does the same, in the hands of someone who turns towards the camera subject with respect. The question is not raised, "Is this person worthy of my attention?"

He/she exists, and the camera muses in his/her direction.

In Robert Nakamura's _Wataridori_ (1976), portraits of three Issei, I vividly remember a moment when his camera slowly moved along the tools on his father's work table. It was like a meditation about his Issei father's life. A few scenes later his father is driving in his car, singing a Japanese song to himself. The camera just sits on him and its quiet gaze makes us love this man.

More recently there was a scene in a documentary _La Offrenda_ (1989) by filmmaker Lourdes Portillo, about Mexican traditional beliefs and practices concerning the dead, and how one communes with them.

A member of the crew asks a villager amidst a mass of burning candles, "Can you really see the souls?"

"Yes. With that apparatus (points to his camera), you can see them."

Indeed. The camera sees the soul.

A human gaze is empowering; equally empowering is the camera's gaze.

Casting the Storytellers

I think selecting your on-camera personality is akin to answering the question, whose face is mine, whose face could be mine?

The very "ordinariness" of our camera subjects is their humanity, which affirms and extends ours; their ability to do extraordinary things when called upon resonates in us stirrings about our own possibilities. The experience would be very different, I believe, with images of "celebrities and heroes," who can put us into states of passive sycophany, anxious envy, and aggressive ambition. Those kinds of images of "heroes" take something away from us.

Whether a film is fiction or documentary, I see it as storytelling. On-camera persons—actors or interviewees—are chosen for their ability to be convincingly themselves. I have looked for camera subjects not to show an exemplary character (charismatic, articulate, handsome or talented), but to show diversity and a representative, credible character. On _Island of Secret Memories_ (1987), the boy cast to play the lead, Joe, was considered by some to be "pudgy" and "nerdy"; so why not find someone more handsome, stylish or thinner? In _Bean Sprouts_ (1978) a man was cast for the role of a father who some complained fitted the stereotype of the immigrant father—stern, serious and traditional. But in each case, the actors "worked" in their roles because they projected conviction about themselves, and by the end of the scene, they'd won us over.

To me it is particularly important to put Asians on camera who don't sound or feel only like vehicles for information or ideas in the sense that they've got the appropriate formal credentials, or satisfy journalistic conventions. I'd rather put on people who have personal vividness and credibility as human beings, because Asian Americans are invisible or missing from the media in exactly that way—as human beings.

Finding Emblematic Images

Besides images of credible human beings who are given the aura of the camera's gaze, I have been looking to find what might be called emblematic images. These are the "true images" that have power because they embody a central theme or contradiction of the story being told.

Nisei Soldier (1984), for example, has as its central contradiction the issue of inequality and the Japanese American soldier's struggle to obtain a future equality. Studying the footage at the National Archives, I saw many images flicker by of officers pinning medals on Nisei soldiers in some military ceremony. Typically, in these scenes, the soldier's eyes were downcast, his body language humble. But one image caught my eye: the Nisei soldier looked up, met his general's eye as they shook hands. In a profile view of the two men facing each other, they leaned forward with vitality and mutuality, smiling at each other; and the viewer is witness to a fleeting instance of rare equality achieved. The image is emblematic because it embodies the issue of equality. It became a freeze-frame in the film.

The Interview as Communion

At its best, the interview may be like the vision of the angels presented in Wim Wenders' film, *Wings of Desire* (1987). Wenders' angel, as an agent of God visiting among earthly mortals, has the power to cause what is really in one's heart to be said out loud. Whenever the angel appears, merely by standing nearby, the person is able to reveal what he/she truly feels at the deepest level.

I think an interviewer's presence can be a form of communion that can cause much the same thing to happen. In ordinary life when undergoing an experience, what one says to one's self or to family and friends at the time is not necessarily significant, and yet the experience may be profound and critical.

Years later, in remembering these moments, the recounting may begin as a long dry session of banal surface details, matter of factly told. But if the interviewer waits out the silences and maintains a close and expectant inner ear, asking the questions that spring from a confidence that there is "something more," then somehow, that "something" often emerges, and floodgates of emotional truth open. The initial recounts are then more like a prelude, a circling before you find home.

This should not sound like therapy because that is not the purpose. The purpose is to uncover and present a human story. But the person interviewed is not being "used just to tell a story," nor "mined" as an "information source"—as with journalism—but instead is offered a vehicle through the film to be a tribal storyteller, to present himself/herself as a central character playing out the drama revealed.

Life Choices

Filmmaking and television production was for me a late choice in life, having

"Consider the experience of thinking we know what we look and sound like, until the shock of hearing our actual voices on a tape recorder, or of seeing our physical selves in the moving image."

taught college sociology and having done community organizing for a number of years. I was also married and a late mother with a daughter and son both under three when I started in media.

In the 60s, I had left the University in Berkeley to work in organizing against the Vietnam war, and then later, in community organizing for grassroots culture and arts programs in the neighborhoods of San Francisco. In 1969, I started in media, and have remained with it now for twenty years. The shows I chose to do were largely in response to some of the key community and social issues of the times, and in turn, community participation was inseparable from their production.

My first producing/directing assignment was "Sut Yung Ying Yee" in 1969-70, a T.V. language series of sixty-five half-hour programs for teaching survival English to Chinese immigrants. The series was sparkplugged by a relatively new civil rights organization, Chinese for Affirmative Action, at that time a little volunteer organization operating out of a closet-sized room with cardboard desks.

Open Studio (1970-1977), was a community access production and broadcast service established at KQED, the local public T.V. station in San Francisco, which democratized the means by which communities all over the Bay Area could present their own concerns and interests and define their own images. Any community group or organization from the nine Bay Area counties could apply to do a half-hour program of their choice, collaborating with Open Studio staff producers and station crew. The program would then be aired on KQED—in prime time. This service was constantly in danger of cutbacks, so communities of great diversity—Asians, Black, Latino, elderly, library users, etc.—would annually circle the station with picket signs to demand that Open Studio continue to produce programs with them and air these programs at the prime time hours then in practice.

Open Studio was based on the outrageous idea that the public television station should serve all the communities reached by its signal (an FCC concern at that time), rather than cater just to its relatively affluent subscribers, or pick programming reflecting only the tastes and standards of the station's largely white male corporate management, with its ruling class style and pervasive Anglo-Saxon bias.

Open Studio lasted seven years before being discontinued by the station, and produced over 700 shows. After producing and studio-directing over 250 of them myself (of varied formats—talk shows, multi-camera drama, dance, music, live remotes, etc.), I honed my craft and came away from the experience with several convictions. One was that there was no show of any format or subject I would not tackle. The other was that a producer must also do political organizing as well as production, or you may be squeezed out of the budget and out of air time.

The Open Studio experience also left me with the solid conviction that working closely with non-media people from the community as partners, no matter how inexperienced they may be in media work, always results in more vitality, substance, and heart.

"The Great Wall is Coming"

The last show I produced at KQED was "600 Millenia: China's History Unearthed" (1976), a 90-minute PBS special on the international tour of the exhibition of archeological finds from the People's Republic of China. Nineteen seventy-five was still a very politically sensitive time in which people spoke of "Red China," and the "Bamboo Curtain." The film documented the first official U.S.–China cultural exchange, and heralded the coming normalization of relations between the two countries.

I knew little about Chinese archeology or Chinese art history, especially since this was a collection that spanned from Peking man's jaw and Neolithic pottery to works of the fourteenth century Yuan dynasty of Kublai Khan. Though daunting to a reasonably modest person, I figured that advisers and a writer could take care of the art history—what I wanted to bring was a significant social and community approach. For one thing, the exhibition was coming to San Francisco, the largest Chinese community outside Asia.

One elderly Chinatown bachelor capsulized it: "All these years I have not managed to go home to visit my village. I wanted to see the Great Wall. But now the Great Wall is coming to see me. I am so happy."

For the general American public as well, "the Great Wall was coming." The collection was a visitation from the immense legacy of ancient China, packaged and sent forth on a global journey by the government of "Red China." The juxtaposition was irresistible.

I wanted to show the PRC government digging up, restoring, and displaying for the public the archeological finds, which they no longer allowed to be looted or taken out of the country by foreign collectors. The story of this collection would include the artisans and craftsmen who created the works and the type of society that existed during the creation of the artifacts.

Besides showing the collection itself, the local Chinese community would be shown getting ready for the coming exhibition, the wide diversity of people standing in the long lines, the comments of viewers as they went through the collection, etc. And I noticed some foreign-born Chinese, Mandarin speakers, in the lines at night, who caught my eye because they were wearing dark glasses. (Maybe in the daytime, but at night, going to a museum?) I decided they were Taiwan supporters who didn't want to be seen, but couldn't resist coming either.

Clearly, my approach was not going to be, "God, look at the gorgeous patina on the bronzes."

So I passionately pursued getting the permission from the Chinese government (only a "Liaison Office" in Washington, D.C. at that time) and the funding of Bank of America, to do "600 Millennia," little suspecting that I was in for several memorable political lessons.

War Stories and Strategies

"There's nothing you can do, Loni. They have you over a barrel. You are coming up against the ruling class of San Francisco."

My former boss at the T.V. station—not otherwise a particularly political person—was explaining to me why I was having so much trouble doing the PBS special on the archeological collection from China.

He was referring to a Byzantine series of maneuvers which included a vigorous objection to me, as producer, by the elite city museum authority; the concurrence of the station's chair of the board, not wanting to break class rank; and my being saved only by the insistence of China's cultural attaché that "Miss Ding enjoys our support."

The museum's objection to me was not racial, but class based. They recognized that I was not going to use an "art for art's sake" approach, but rather

BEAN SPROUTS (1978)
Loni Ding

intended to include other elements that might "sully" the "most important exhibition we have had." They regarded the crowds of people coming to see the exhibit, people who normally never visit their museum, with condescension, if not contempt. The fact that this important collection was under the control of curators from socialist China was another source of uneasiness.

The museum authorities were deeply offended by my approach, and managed to find fault with the tiniest detail of my every move, blown into mountainous proportions, and expressed in a series of memos to the president of the station, no less. "The Museum" made it clear that this producer was "totally unacceptable."

I believe, had I been a white producer of elite culture, or an Asian-born producer of reliable class background, there would have been no problem. But an American-born Chinese ("ABC") is not an elegant flower of the Orient, a Shanghai princess who speaks English with a British accent, but a garden variety "minority," more like a weed, a stubborn weed.

What I had behind me was the support of the community, my production resume, the support of the chief curator from China, and the permission of China's liaison office in Washington, D.C.

The museum was adamant: if the unacceptable producer was not removed, KQED would not be permitted to film the collection in their museum. This would be very embarrassing to the station's Bank of America funding, the big color spread the national *TV Guide* was offering to do, etc. At this point, the KQED chair of the board, a wealthy *grande dame* who was a member of the same club as the trustees of the museum, devised a solution. She wrote a letter apologizing to the museum for the behavior of "this young producer who obviously doesn't quite understand," asking for their extreme indulgence, to give her another chance "for the sake of her professional advancement"; that KQED 's ability to do the program was, of course, completely dependent on the museum's good graces and willingness to accept the producer. The KQED chair concluded the letter by saying, "And to assure you that we are all in complete agreement on these matters, I am asking Loni to read and mail this letter to you. . . ."

I did what I had to do in cold blood and mailed the letter. I realized I was being asked to deliver my own head on a platter to the museum. (The Chinese authorities would still have to write another letter later, insisting that the museum cooperate with me, at which point the museum finally gave in.)

I showed the betraying letter to my boss before mailing. He had also been my trainer in broadcasting production and engineering and was an honorable man. He read it, and was silent for a long time. Finally, with a voice quivering with emotion he whispered, "You are up against the ruling class of this city." He advised me to just cooperate, no matter how onerous.

My boss's advice, given in a sympathetic but resigned tone meant to console, contrasted with the very different kind of advice given me by Mr. Mai, chief curator from China, who was accompanying the archeological collection on its world tour. I told Mr. Mai that his help and that of the Washington, D.C. liaison office had now made it possible for me to proceed.

Flattering me by confiding in Cantonese, Mr. Mai said: "Well, now you have overcome all obstacles, and finally be allowed to come into the museum in the evening to film. Congratulations. I want to offer some advice."

"Yes, of course," I chirped, my spirits restored, pencil poised earnestly to take notes.

"When you finally come here to the museum to film the collection, you will be working through the night."

"Yes."

"You and your crew will get hungry, but there will be no restaurants open. So you must bring your own food for your crew."

"Yes."

"When you bring food for your crew, you must also bring food for the security guards and anyone else who works here. It will not cost you very much. But it will help them understand you, and make your work easier."

It was humbling that someone from far away told me about something so close to home and so simple. His advice, of course, was part of an entire political outlook: to expect to struggle; to keep looking for solutions within my control, more than likely something simple, close at hand; and to rely on people "from the ground up." There have been many times I have turned to whoever was closest, often someone of no particular status or technical relevance—the switchboard operator, the custodian, security guard, waitress, passerby, etc.—for some critical information and cooperation. By now it has become second nature to go forward with this approach.

Everything I've done since has been as an independent producer. "Bean Sprouts" in 1980 was the first national children's T.V. series starting from a community base which portrayed the dramas of ethnic identity of Chinese American children ages nine to twelve with a multicultural approach.

The Necessity for an Oppositional Stance

It is difficult for some to grasp the necessity of taking an oppositional stance, which is at the same time not accusatory. Accusations only trigger defensiveness where the other person stops listening, or feels "guilty," a feeling notable for its fuzziness and short life span.

I remember while visiting once at Syracuse University, a particular graduate student in broadcasting from Asia. After a seminar screening of "Bean Sprouts," he raised his hand and asked: "I am Chinese too, but why are you Asian Americans so defensive?" Not only an incredibly rude question to a guest, I thought, but a question not unlike, "Aren't you being too sensitive?" or "What is it you people really want?" He was upper class and from Singapore. I had to point out—and remind myself again—that Asian Asian is not Asian American; in Singapore he is not a racial or ethnic minority (indeed, he belongs to a privileged class), and the experience of all people of color in America, historically and currently, inevitably comes down to: defending, challenging, opposing, and re-defining on our own terms. Image-making just happens to be my particular arena.

The Gatekeepers

"The Gatekeeper" is a figure familiar to any producer of minority or "alternative" films and programs. Everywhere you turn, gatekeepers are ready to question your being funded, have doubts about the content, and stall and postpone the distribution or broadcast of your film to your audience. That was my prototype experience with the PBS children's series "Bean Sprouts."

"Do you know what was my first impression of you?" a PBS program manager at PBS headquarters asked me. "You and I had all these phone calls about how to get 'Bean Sprouts' on the regular national schedule, but we had not actually met. As I walked down the hall toward you I thought you

THE COLOR OF HONOR (1987)
Loni Ding

reminded me of one of those figures you see on the prow of old sailing ships."

So it shows, after all. I thought I was being pretty cool, but she's spotted my real feelings: ". . . in for a fight . . . uphill, heading into the wind." It did finally take the drumbeat of one year of organized national letter writing from Asian Amerians and media friends across the country to get "Bean Sprouts" on PBS. And then we could never be sure how powerfully the community response counted because PBS also underwent basic restructuring and changes in top level personnel at about the same time.

But we followed an abiding principle: take nothing for granted and give it our best shot.

We have to always assume some form of resistance by persons in authority is likely, and plan our strategy and call upon our friends, collaborators and allies as needed. Only people who take power and privilege for granted assume otherwise.

Collective Organizing for Media Access

While I was at Open Studio, the black producers put together a proposal for a national black television series and presented it to KQED. The proposal had to be rewritten many times to meet various station management objections, but it finally reached the desk of the station's top official. This gentleman conceded that the proposal was now finally "okay," but felt there was a more serious problem: "if we got funded we'd have to do it, and I don't think I want the first national production under my regime to be a Black series."

The political fight never goes away, personally and collectively. There is a need for organizing in a collective way.

When I first went into media in the late 60s, communities (Asian, Black and Latino in San Francisco) were regularly meeting with all the local television station managements to critique and advocate for better coverage for their communities and for more "authentic" representation in the media. These actions were legally supported by the "community ascertainment" provisions of the FCC rules then in effect, which required stations to consult with communities and develop a plan based on community findings before they could get their profitable television licenses renewed by the FCC.

Now the situation is different. The ascertainment requirement was nullified by Reaganite policies, and communities no longer use the 60s protest and pressure tactics with the same effectiveness. No longer do picket lines circle the station in protest of threatened program service cutbacks, as they did in the late 60s and early 70s.

The last ten years have seen a renewal of active political organizing, this time by producers and cultural organizations themselves, for greater diversity in television protection and programming. National media coalitions have been formed to engage in collective advocacy. Many saw the need for a new national television programming service that was structurally independent enough to offer diverse, innovative and controversial fare. NAATA and Pacific Educational Network were formed in 1980, joining the other racial/ethnic consortia funded earlier: the Black, Native American, and Latino Public Broadcasting Consortia.

The embryo that led to the birth of NAATA was the first national conference of Asian and Pacific American producers, held in July 1980 in Berkeley. The CPB official in charge of funding the gathering tried to strike a pre-emptive bargain: he would agree to fund the conference if organizers would agree in advance not to use the meeting as the standard first step for asking for an Asian American consortium (like NAATA). In his opinion the other existing minority consortia (Black, Native American, and Latino) were not a good idea, and he didn't want to see a new one created. We got the conference funded, promising him nothing, and submitted the proposal that formed NAATA the following year.

All the consortia were funded with extremely modest public broadcasting money for acquiring more ethnically representative programs to offer the 300-plus stations of the Public Broadcasting System (PBS) across the nation. This is an audience of no small potential, and worth a fight to gain more accessibility.

It took the 1979 report of a national task force commissioned by the Corporation for Public Broadcasting (CPB), "A Formula for Change," to tell what several earlier reports also commissioned by them already found, and which everyone knew: that public broadcasting, in hiring, training, and programming, was totally lacking in commitment to racial, cultural and class diversity.

Left to themselves, and using public monies, they would continue to import dramas on the British upper class, and program those endless nature and science shows (the brain, primates, etc.) which the big corporations are pleased to partially fund and buy expensive ads to associate with their names, and which at their best have been called, "splendidly safe."

The very practical and specific recommendations of "A Formula for Change" to overhaul minority programming in public broadcasting ended on the same shelf as earlier reports, and it took more than ten years of national coalition building in the independent filmmaking community, lots of media press work, visits, letters, and phone calls to lobby congressmen and their aides for legislative changes, and testifying before congressional subcommittees—to finally bring about the most promising congressionally mandated changes we have to date.

As of 1990 we have the Independent Television Service (ITVS), a new non-profit entity created by the community of independent producers, and funded at six million a year. It operates within public broadcasting, but is autonomous, with its own policy board, and is committed to diversity and innovation, with the intention of helping "to reinvent how television serves the public."

Under the same legislation in 1990, an additional three million was set aside for improvement in minority programming under the guidance of a Multicultural Programming Service board (MPS). However, the MPS board is seriously flawed in not being an independent body, remaining formally under the control of CPB, with no power to select its own future board members, as does the ITVS. In naming the new MPS board, the nominating committee served notice that the lack of autonomy was perceived as a serious, perhaps fatal flaw, and that "the matter cannot be considered closed."

A struggle will have to continue to move the MPS board into the next stage of independence from CPB, and to lobby for a much higher level of funding than the three million now allotted for all the designated ethnic groups, Asian, Black, Native American, Latino, and Pacific Islander.

Personally, I have found no way to avoid political involvement in the "Formula for Change" report; helping to create NAATA; testifying before congressional subcommittees; or helping to do the networking and lobbying work for the ITVS and MPS. I believe that independent minority producers them-

"The experience of all people of color in America... comes down to defending, challenging, opposing, and re-defining on our own terms."

selves—and not just media organizations—need to be involved to help fight for the dollars and independence to bring forth their visions. Nobody else will do it for us.

Looking Ahead—Stretching the Documentary Genre

The right to tell our stories has largely been won—although it seems that right has to be continually reasserted. As a producer, I have become more and more interested in developing new forms, new ways of telling the story. Mainly, I have been looking for more subjectivity, and searching for the first-person voice. To present the historical past with this type of subjectivity and voice, I've been exploring the use of devices like metaphors, surrealism and tableaux.

For example, with *The Color of Honor* (1987-1989) the central metaphor is one of uncovering a buried past. The film's opening image shows a first-generation Japanese father and his Nisei son digging in their California backyard, searching for a crate of Japanese possessions the family hastily buried on the eve of their forced removal by the U.S. government forty years earlier. A montage of torn pictures, from family albums and historical archives, begins to appear and grows throughout the film, each piece a torn fragment of the diaspora not quite acknowledged, filling in the holes as the story unfolds. By the end of the film, the overall mosaic is a metaphor for the collective portrayal of that generation.

Also in *The Color of Honor*, a Nisei woman speaks of how ordinary scenes can trigger a haunting memory. She recalls the group of young volunteers for the Army from her internment camp posing for their group portrait, "sitting in the desert in their Sunday best." We use the location of a California desert in a somewhat surreal manner: the triggering image is a row of empty folding chairs seen set out in the midst of nowhere.

A tableau is conceived as a still life or scene where objects are brought together that might not ordinarily be arranged in that particular way. They are not "re-creations" or simulations of the past, as in naturalistic "flashbacks" or docu-drama, but are stylized representations of subjective reflections and memories. The tableaux materialize interpretations and are evocations of significant feelings and states of mind made visible.

In *Island of Secret Memories* (1987), the program on Chinese detention on Angel Island, eleven-year-old Joe imagines the bed his grandfather occupied in the barracks. He enters the tableau and sits on the bed, handling the various personal items lying there (historical artifacts): a bottle of Chinese pills, a Chinese-English dictionary, a pair of spectacles. As he tries on the glasses, he "sees" another tableau from the past: an interrogation in progress, played in limbo—a young Chinese male being questioned by the immigration officer, posing the actual questions used by the immigration protocol of the time. The tableau is stylized; we hear only the questions of the interrogator and see the mute petitioner. Only as the scene ends with the tableau dissolving to a matching black-and-white archival picture of exactly the same kind of interrogation, do we hear him speak: a single word ringing, "No!" The echoing resonance bridges the historical images that follow, showing the ways in which the Chinese of that time protested and resisted their unjust detention on Angel Island. I look forward to utilizing these and other techniques that weave together the fictional, non-fictional, and experimental to create a more subjective and first-person voice.

THE COLOR OF HONOR (1987)
Loni Ding

CHRISTINE CHOY

Christine Choy

Dear V.C. (Viet Cong),

Q: Your intention or purpose:

A: My intention is simple, I don't like to think too much so I make movies instead. Purpose? Not much either, just want to be a fun storyteller about the Great American Tragedies and the decline of the human race.

Q: The issues addressed or choice confronted:

A: All my films are reflections of this "jack-ass" society from the bottom up. Everyone hates poor people, Black or white, some whites love Blacks, very few Blacks love whites, Asians or Asian Americans are sandwiched in-between. But when there is money, they all mix together nicely. Nice is not necessarily kind.

I am not nice or kind, my issues are crude, there ain't much money in my type of films, funders always tell me there isn't much of an audience for this type of film, but they are wrong. When I show my films, there are always three types of people: one Black, one white and one other.

Q: The specific technical/aesthetic and conceptual resolution:

A: I don't like movies, I don't like T.V. shows, I hate those half-assed movie deals. All those directors, producers, agents, cocksuckers, porno genera- tors are all pretenders. I don't read *American Films*, *Variety*, *Screen* (on or off). There are too many movie magazines or magazines semi-interested in movies, and all of them are TRASH so they can sell. They are shit, but look what happens? Here I am sitting here writing this for your "magazine," what comes around goes around.

"Technically" speaking, I am a very simple person (in the head). I like to use minimal lighting to save electricity and my energy, for the light cases are designed for gorillas. I use $5.00 practical light bulbs, one tungsten, two day-light bulbs. That's all. My advice to emerging filmmakers is practical, fast film stock, fast lens, lots of quantity, forget about quality.

I shoot, record sound, fix lights, interview people, which doesn't leave me with much to do as a director. As a producer, I simply push one pile of papers onto another pile of papers, occasionally rotating the stock to fresh ones up front.

"Aesthetically" speaking, I'm pure and still a virgin, not letting myself get influenced by Hollywood or the "Avant Garde" movement. It's a "Choy" style, an image mover and shaker.

"Conceptually," as an Asian American, oriental, third world, woman of color, crazy, "nonsuccessful," successful professional, unprofessional, under-class, working class, middle class (yet to be called upper class). Look where my concepts come from, right between my legs.

Be Cool.

CENTER THE MARGINS
RICHARD FUNG

When I look at mainstream Western movies and at television, I see that the imaging of gay people and of Asians is mutually exclusive. In other words, I see (a few) gay men and lesbians and (a few) Asians but I don't see gay or lesbian Asians. At the same time, there is a great deal of similarity in the way that the two groups figure in popular media.

Both Asians and gay people are used primarily as signs—as simple shorthand when the director wants to conjure up a particular atmosphere or induce a certain reaction from the audience. Asians can invoke mystery, humour or danger. A gay character can be loathsome, ridiculous, bizarre or pathetic. With the increasing impact of the Asian American and the gay and lesbian movements, we are now witnessing an increasing use of gay as well as Asian characters, especially in television. Unfortunately, while these characters integrate the "look" of the program, they are seldom the center of the story. Or else their portrayals continue as extensions of long-circulating stereotypes and associations in the dominant culture.

Early European accounts of Asia were filled with horror and fascination with the apparently libertine nature of sexual relations. Sixteenth-century Italian missionary, and scholar Matteo Ricci bitterly wrote of China:

That which most shows the misery of the people is that no less the natural lusts they practice unnatural ones that reverse the order of things: and this is not forbidden by law, nor thought to be illicit, nor even a cause for shame.[1]

According to cultural historian Jonathan D. Spence, Ricci's outrage simply reflected a Jesuit preoccupation established by "the Apostle of the Indies" himself, Francis Xavier, who in 1549 wrote of the Japanese Buddhist clergy that "the priests are drawn to sins against nature and don't deny it, they acknowledge it openly. This evil furthermore is so public, so clear to all, men and women, young and old, and they are so used to seeing it that they are neither depressed nor horrified."[2]

In early Canadian law, precautions were taken to protect white women from the unbridled libidos of Asian men. In 1912, the Saskatchewan legislature disallowed the employment of white women in businesses owned or managed by Chinese. This was followed by similar legislation in Ontario and in British Columbia.[3]

As Asian American archivist Stephen Gong describes the career of Sessue Hayakawa, the imaging of the Hollywood silent-movie star relates to this early vision of Asians as sexually unmanageable and threatening.[4] In contemporary popular consciousness, there continues an association, especially of Southeast Asia, with sexual commerce and accessibility—for the foreigner at least. Most recent mainstream cinema, however, owes more to another seemingly contradictory discourse; one that finds its rationale in Eugenics, and has its most current distillation in theories such as those of psychologist Philippe Rushton. According to Rushton, Asians are more intelligent and less sexual than whites, who are in turn brighter and less sexual that Blacks. Sexuality is measured by a wide variety of variables such as penis size, frequency of intercourse, and fertility.[5] Rushton's methods are shoddy as his conclusions are racist, yet teaching at one of Canada's most prestigious universities, his course has become framed as a struggle for academic freedom and he has gained supporters on both sides of the border.

Renee Tajima has written about the figuring of East Asian women in Hollywood, as falling into a dragon lady/lotus blossom dichotomy.[6] In fact, Asian women have long been featured in Western representation for the pleasure of the white man's eye. Asian men, on the other hand, have not often been portrayed in sexual terms at all. Asian male characters tend either to be brainy wimps or else martial arts ascetics. The one commonality of both men and women is that neither is represented as sexual agent—desiring as opposed to desirable (or undesirable), the subject in the cinematic gaze.

So if Hollywood cannot bring itself to represent Asians with sexual drive, how can we expect the representation of homosexual drive? A gay or lesbian Asian character would require more investment in character and writing that would detract focus from the white protagonist. Even *Mishima* (1985), a film about an "avowed" homosexual, managed to effectively skirt the issue.

For their part, Asian filmmakers working in North America have not successfully managed to raise the question of homosexuality either. In the selective world of feature filmmaking Wayne Wang has consistently attempted to deepen the representations of Asians on the large screen. Whether it is the negotiation of the adult couple to sleep together in the face of parental supervision in *Dim Sum* (1984) or the central theme of impotence in *Eat A Bowl of Tea* (1989), sexuality is a discernable focal point in all of Wang's films. Except for a well intentioned but formulaic reference to lesbianism in the experimental drama *Life Is Cheap* (1990), however, gay characters have not peopled his Chinatown landscape thus far.

In *The Displaced View* (1988), Sansei director Midi Onodera probes the more subtle effects of the internment of Japanese Canadians during World War II. Her innovative docu-fiction moves between the perspectives of three generations of women in one family. The third generation character is a lesbian, but since the word is never used and there are no dramatized sequences which illustrate her sexual orientation, it is left somewhat up to the viewer's acuity to decode the clues in the spoken text. In "Then/Now" (1989), Onodera's made-for-T.V. drama, the relationship between a Japanese Canadian woman and her father is temporarily torn apart by her need to set her own terms on their relationship. This includes her career as a writer and her love for a woman. Unfortunately, censorship from the upper echelons of the

> 'If Hollywood cannot bring itself to represent Asians with sexual drive, how can we expect the representation of homosexual drive?"

network bureaucracy deleted or distorted almost all of the lesbian reference, so that the actual nature of the relationship between the two women remains an enigma. At this time Onodera remains perhaps the only Asian lesbian film-maker in North America who deals with the issue of her sexuality in her work.

There are at least several reasons for the virtual absence of gay and les-bian Asians on the North American screen. Assuming that gay Asian repre-sentation would come primarily from gay Asian producers (though this is not necessarily so), it must first be recognized that there are relatively few Asian producers in North America in the first place. Some, like Los Angeles inde-pendent filmmaker Gregg Araki, touch on sexual politics without a specific Asian reference; others do not address questions of sexuality at all. The fact that both Midi Onodera and I work in Canada probably has a great deal to do with the overtly homophobic climate in the United States, carried from Reagan into the Bush years and characterized by a hysterical attempt on the part of a right wing, both radical and established, to prop up what they see as a shifting status quo.

Since to make films or videotapes about gay or lesbian subject matter is to invite scrutiny of one's own sexual orientation, at least one of the major fac-tors for the absences relates to the general issue of "coming out" for gays and lesbians of color. In the context of North American racism, families and com-munities can have particular significance for Asians in affirming identity. So while white gays and lesbians can avoid personalized homophobia by separating from their families or formative communities and still see them-selves reflected in the society around them, their Asian counterparts do not always share this mobility and often find their sexual/emotional and racial/cultural identities in conflict. Generally, the more one is dependent on one's ethnic community, the more difficult it is to come out and risk losing support. This of course puts more of a burden on immigrants and Asians without financial mobility, especially those with less facility in English.

This process became apparent to me in producing *Orientations*, a 1984 videotape on gay and lesbian Asians, for which a major hurdle was finding a range of people who were willing to appear on camera. Middle-class, educated, young, North American-born men were easy to convince, but the working-class, older, immigrant men (and especially women) that I knew, felt that they had too much at stake to risk the exposure. Of course the ab-sences in the tape reinforce a false image of who gay people are.

If asked to articulate the reasons for the relative lack of gay and lesbian visibility in most Asian communities (and in saying this I realize that there are exceptions), many people would say that the communities are too traditional to deal with this issue. I have heard this cited by gay people as a reason for not coming out, by parents for not telling the rest of the family, and by our "leaders" for protecting the communities from discord—in other words en-forcing censorship.

Behind the Mask, an AIDS educational videotape aimed at the Asian Pacific communities, is very comprehensive ethnically and linguistically, as well as in its representation of the various issues at stake—except for homophobia. In fact, while it features interviews with obviously gay people, the tape never mentions the "g" word once! Right from the start, the AIDS epidemic has been represented as a "gay" disease. In order to reach out to heterosexuals, it has been deemed necessary to banish the gay reference altogether. This does nothing to displace the fact that AIDS is taboo precisely

ORIENTATIONS (1984)
Richard Fung

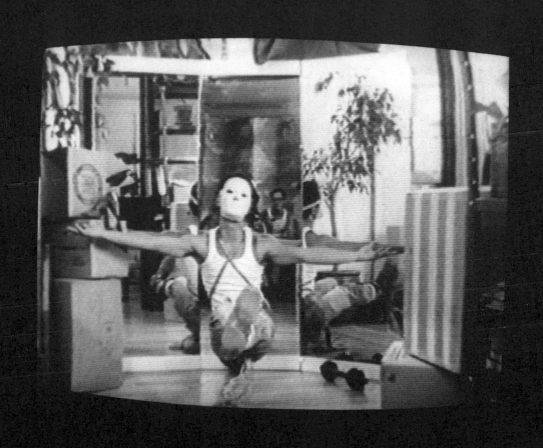

because it is associated with homosexuality, but it does reinforce the notion of homosexuality as shameful and unspeakable. There is no way out of this impasse without confronting the demon of homophobia head on. Sidestepping the issue fails to take into account that one cannot transcend homophobia any more than one can transcend racism.

The notion of the "traditionalness" of the Asian communities has also been used as a reason for gay and lesbian Asians not to come out. However, from my decade of working with gay and lesbian Asians, the proportion of rejection and acceptance for those who do choose to come out to their families is not significantly different to those for white people. Yet whereas white homophobia is not interpreted to say anything about whiteness, there is a way in which Asian homophobia is assigned meaning. I am not implying that the fears, hatreds and anxieties that Asian communities feel about same sex love (or sex) are not sometimes "different" from those of European cultural background. The first concern for my own mother for instance, who is herself third generation Western born, centered around who would take care of me when I got old, a Confucian preoccupation. I do feel, however, that the idea that the homophobia of an Asian is somehow "worse" than that of a white person, or that it says something about Asianness, feeds into a racist discourse. In a similar analysis, both Angela Davis and bell hooks have deconstructed the notion among white feminists that the sexism of black men is again somehow more significant than that of white men.

The notion of Asian societies and overseas communities as "traditional" also fixes them as static and unevolving. In the racism and flux of Western society, it is the tendency of emigrants and their descendents to look towards the homeland for spiritual affirmation and constancy. In our need to assert identity we eliminate complexity, homogenize and fall back on totalizing and essentialist visions of "home." Not that one should ignore history or acquiese to the Eurocentrism of North American culture. But there are always dangers of romanticization in any recuperation of other times or places.

Further, the invocation of tradition as an excuse for not confronting homophobia in the Asian communities, implicitly suggests the fallacy that homophobia is absent from European tradition and "mainstream" contemporary society. The fact that middle-class white lesbians and gays may have a certain amount of mobility to avoid direct confrontation with homophobia, should not be taken to mean that they do not experience oppression, or to discount the actual effects of the gay and lesbian liberation movements.

It must however also be acknowledged that the notion of tradition is contested ground. Gay and lesbian Asians are also quick to point out the existence, indeed the sometime celebration, of same sex love in Asian history. But to what extent the dalliances of samurai and page described by Saikaku Ihara, the Chinese legends of the cut sleeves and the shared peach, or the many Amazon romances relate to cruising down the Castro, Church and Wellesley or the Michigan Women's Music Festival, is a hotly debated topic in gay academia.

Ironically, it is from Asia itself that we have seen the few representations of Asian gay characters in cinema; in *Macho Dancer* (1988) from veteran Filipino director and political activist Lino Brocka and *The Outsider* (1986), based on the Taiwanese novel by Pai, Hsien-Jung and in the Thai films such as *The Last Song* (1986) and *I am A Man* (1988). Problematic because of their coyness or their sometimes oppressive morality, these films nevertheless acknowledge a homosexual presence in the societies in which they are made.

In my own video work in the area, I have seen the most important task as the representation of gay and lesbian Asians as subjects, both on the screen and especially as the viewer. I believe that it is imperative to start with a clear idea about audience. This in turn shapes the content of the piece. Many Asian or gay and lesbian tapes and films are still guided by notions of "positive images." To the extent to which positive images are a response to negative stereotypes, it is a limited strategy in that it takes its cue from what the white man or what the straight man thinks. Reaching out with alternative images for a mainstream is valuable but we can become so obsessed with how others might interpret what we have to say that we can cast our own Asian or gay audiences into passivity.

In the process of making work for an intended audience that is gay and Asian, I have felt myself freed to touch on issues that are neither important nor attractive to other communities (the so-called mainstream) but of pressing interest for many gay viewers. How do we want to take up drag or role playing? Must we always talk about race in relation to white people? How do we relate to our Black, Latino and Native American brothers and sisters? How do we relate to other Asian men and women in sexual or emotional terms; is integration always the ideal?

I do not think that it is possible to create innocent images of Asians either; to ignore the overbearing history of Hollywood and of television, we must somehow learn to place ourselves at the centre of our own cultural practice, and not at the margins. (Re)creating ourselves in our own terms requires constant reevaluation of the master narratives that have bracketed our lives. For this we need to understand the history and language of images, we must grasp this language and make it our own.

> "Many Asian or gay and lesbian tapes and films are still guided by notions of 'positive images.'"

NOTES

1. Fonti Ricciani. Pasquale M. D'Elia, S.J., ed. *Storia dell'Introduzione del Christianesimo in Cina*. (The annotated version of Matteo Ricci's original manuscript of the Historia) Rome, 1942-1949, vol.1 pg. 98, as quoted in *The Memory Palace of Matteo Ricci*, Jonathan D. Spence (New York: Penguin Books, 1984), 220.
2. Joseph-Marie Cros, *Saint Francois*, vol. 2, pg. 12, quoted in Spence, 224.
3. Peter S. Li, *The Chinese in Canada*, (New York: Oxford University Press, 1988), 29.
4. Stephen Gong "Zen Warrior of the Celluloid (Silent) Years: The Art of Sessue Hayakawa, *Bridge*, Vol.8, No.2, Winter 1982-83, 37 – 41.
5. As an example of Rushton's work, see "Race Versus Social Class Difference in Sexual Behavior: A Follow-up Test of the r/k Dimension," *Journal of Research in Personality* 22, (1988), 259.
6. Renee Tajima "Lotus Blossoms Don't Bleed: Images of Asian Women" *The Anthology of Asian American Film and Video* (Third World Newsreel), n.d.: 28-33.

gregg araki

I must admit I was pretty bewildered when first asked to produce this piece. As a (relatively) young, somewhat reckless "guerrilla" filmmaker with two features to my (dis?) credit, *three bewildered people in the night* (1987) and *the long weekend (o' despair)* (1989), I've never really sat down and waxed intellectual over the "aesthetic/critical issues" which concern me. Filmmaking is a much more intuitive, privatized, ultimately mysterious thing to me; I get a movie complete with scenes/images/sound/music/etc., growing tumorlike in my head, then spend the next several years inexorably killing myself translating it to celluloid. I don't think about the process so much as just "do" it (which my nastier detractors would say is an inherent problem in my work). Since I completed my first two pictures virtually by myself—without a crew or behind-the-camera collaborator of any sort—I suppose I was fortunate in that I never had to communicate "What This Film Is About" to anyone but my usually baffled cast.

Recently, however, two challenges—this article and teaching a seminar course at UC Santa Barbara on the very slippery subject of "Independent/Guerrilla/Underground/American New Wave/Neorealist Cinema"—have forced me to concretize, tack down some of my more ephemeral, amorphous, fly-by-night ideas. I suppose as good a place as any to start is with the basic, fundamental issue at hand—the whole concept of "What Independent Cinema Is" and how it differs from the Mainstream Hollywood Product besides budgetary size and non-union paychecks.

One of the sharper students in my class pointed out that independence doesn't seem to come about naturally, all by itself. Rather, it is generally a reaction to the political/cultural/formal/aesthetic restraints of the Status Quo. I know this to be true at least in my case: *three bewildered people* was very much a damn-the-torpedoes, fuck-Hollywood-and-all-it-represents (and won't represent) endeavor. In fact, my production company, desperate pictures ltd, was pretty much founded on this anti-Hollywood tenet. And *the long weekend* was the result of a double-whammy inspiration—my personal observations of the complete fuckedupness of my hopelessly lost generation and the abhorrence I felt towards the smug, yuppily-ever-after, "don't worry be happy"ism of Lawrence Kasdan's baby boomer epic *The Big Chill* (1983).

I've been a loudmouthed critic of two recent "independent" productions, *Sex, Lies and Fatuous Bourgeois Posturing* and *Metropolitan*, both of which I see as indicative of an alarming trend within The Movement (which, to my mind, doesn't really exist outside of a scattered handful of filmmakers doing a project here and there with no money). In their convention-gagged, T.V.-movie way, they obsess over the very same white, middle-class, majority-oriented content that any lamebrained studio picture or T.V. show has already done to death a million times over. To my addled mind: Any "Independent" Film that reinforces and buys into the values of the Mainstream is an opportunity wasted (desperate dogmatic axiom no. 66b).

There is a genuine need for the under- and mis-represented to identify themselves via the cinema machine. The world really doesn't need any more wannabe hack Hollywood directors (how many John Badhams does it take to screw in a fucking light bulb anyway?). However, the totalitarian dominance of White Male Heterosexual Cinema should not be used as an excuse to let all "minority" films/filmmakers/media critics off the hook.

As a gay Asian American, I consider myself a card-carrying (albeit controversial) member of two, count 'em two, "oppressed" subcultural groups, and I've been screened on the circuit under both "umbrellas." While, like any struggling independent, I'm always grateful to have my work shown/ seen/discussed, I've found that the response to my films within those contingents is often, surprisingly, more hostile and xenophobic than even that of the Mainstream. *long weekend* got some of the most vehemently spiteful reviews I've ever received when it was shown at the gay festival in San Francisco last year—most critics simply attacked the film (and me personally) for not painting a more constructive "positive gay image"—i.e., not criticizing the film for what it was (or what it was trying to represent), rather chastising me because it wasn't the movie they wanted to see. My reviews in the straight press—even *Daily Variety* for God's sake—have been much more open-minded and receptive. Ironically, I've found "my" subcultures to be more repressive, more straightjacketing, more tunnel-visioned than the Majority culture which they so relentlessly and demonstratively attack.

This is my purely personal view (which undoubtedly is going to get me into even more trouble than I'm already in) but I feel that gays who listen to disco, wear Castro-clone moustache-levis uniforms and spout old 70s gaylib Stonewall rhetoric and Asian Americans who eat sushi, take their shoes off in the house and only make films about the camps and fortune cookie factories are like blacks who love rap music, wear Nikes and eat fried chicken. They are subscribing to and ultimately wholeheartedly embracing the very restrictive stereotypes that the White Patriarchal hegemony foists upon us. There is room, in fact there is a dire need, for difference within our claustrophobic little elitist clubhouses. The pitfalls of generic stagnancy in gay, Asian American, and independent cinema(s) are not being avoided. Lackadaisical conformity and formulaic toeing of the "politically correct" line are celebrated by audiences, critics and programmers alike. Like Paramount and Universal, the so-called "Other" Cinemas have gotten lazy, complacent and retrogressive in their outlook.

The word "new" figures prominently in virtually all the catch-phrases of radical film movements throughout history (various countries' "New Waves," "New American," "New German"—and cheating a bit—"Neorealism"). And it is that word which ultimately provides the key: new and/or different via form and/or content. A lame, sentimental coming-of-age story or typical, propagandistic documentary blowing its own horn of "Independence" is a sheep in wolf's clothing: it's still trite, pat, conventional—regardless of the nationality or sexual orientation of its subject and/or maker.

What The Movement (which again, does not exist) really needs are those formal/political/thematic challengers of the Status Quo (and by Status Quo, I'm not just referring to the usual heterosexist WASP one, but also to the equally stale Status Quos found within the gay, Asian, Black, feminist, independent, one-eyed pygmy subcultures). I'm talking about the next generation of Godards, Fassbinders, Derek Jarmans who push the envelope, who are not satisfied with the "Good Story Well Told" Bullshit that Mainstreams of all stripes and colors unabashedly endorse.

Pretty much any bonehead can see that there's a genuine crisis now: with the insidious cancer of censorship creepily spreading throughout the arts, with the collapse of most alternative distribution/exhibition arteries, with funding sources harder to find than a suitable kidney transplant donor, Independent Cinema is on its deathbed and in desperate need of a transfusion, not more pablum crammed through its IV tubes. And embarrassed as I am to quote a bunch of smelly, hairy hippies from the 60s, desperate pictures' dogmatic slogan/love potion no. 9 is: "If you're not part of the solution, you're part of the problem."

"OF LIFE AND PERVERSITY": WAYNE WANG SPEAKS
JANICE SAKAMOTO

Wayne Wang was born in Hong Kong in 1949, named after John Wayne, the star of American Western movies. At the age of eighteen, he moved to California to study painting, and in 1973 he received a masters degree in film and television from the California College of Arts and Crafts. After graduating, Wang did some directorial work in Hong Kong, but soon returned to America in 1975 where he temporarily gave up filmmaking to become involved in community programs that helped Asian immigrants adjust to life in the U.S.

With the help of two grants from the American Film Institute and the National Endowment for the Arts, Wang completed his first film feature, *Chan Is Missing* (1981), shot in 16mm black-and-white for less than $25,000. A critical and popular hit at the 1982 Filmex in Los Angeles and the New Directors/New Film series in New York, *Chan* was described as "the first yin-yang mystery film." It was blown up to 35mm and went on to a successful national release.

In 1985, Wang began working on the script for *Dim Sum: A Little Bit of Heart*, a film that allowed him to explore both the specific conflicts of the Chinese American experience and the no-win situations common to all families.

Whereas *Chan* was mostly about men, *Dim Sum* was very much about women—mothers, daughters, sisters, and friends. Both films treat their characters with humanity, affection and humor, and provide enlightenment on some of life's most complex human relationships. Wang's *Eat A Bowl of Tea* (1989), based on the novel by Louis Chu, was set in New York's Chinatown in the late 40s-early 50s. Wang's latest film is *Life Is Cheap . . . but Toilet Paper Is Expensive*. Wang currently resides in San Francisco with his wife, actress Cora Miao.

S. How do you look at the past decade? What have Asian Americans accomplished in film and what is your vision for the 1990s?

W. I thought the 80s was pretty good in terms of breaking the ground with a lot of different kinds of Asian American films out there, speaking specifically of theatrical releases, between Peter Wang, Steven Okazaki, Michael Uno, myself. There's a lot out there but there could be a lot more if we can have ten more younger filmmakers who break out and do their work . . . that's sort of the emphasis I felt pretty strongly about in looking back at the 80s.

There is a whole new generation of kids who did not come out of the 60s or 70s, who may be doing films that may not directly relate to Asians but somehow have a sensibility that relates to themselves growing up as Chinese or Japanese. It may not be specifically ethnic related, but it doesn't matter. Maybe they have a view about film itself that is very different than storytelling which I am always a believer of, because of MTV and other influences.

For me, we've kind of done our share of telling about our history although there's a lot more to be done. If we do deal with that history, it should be done with a new perspective rather than the same kind of things we've been doing through the 60s, 70s and 80s...looking at different poignant ways that make all that stuff more relevant now. Those are the things that are important for the 90s too.

S. With the theatrical release of *Eat A Bowl of Tea, The Wash* (1988), and *Living on Tokyo Time* (1987), do you feel there is a growing recognition by the industry of Asian American films?

W. The industry doesn't give a fuck. The industry sees Asian films as nonprofit films. They just won't make money for them. Audiences are not big enough to make it worthwhile for them. Basically, that's the bottom line. If you have a film that's Japanese, Chinese, or your characters are predominantly Asian, it's immediately against you.

For example, *The Joy Luck Club* [Wayne's next feature film] was a huge best seller, yet it was almost impossible to convince people that this is going to be a mainstream popular movie. It's built on a lot of credit because of the book, but still it's been difficult because there are so few Caucasian characters in it. It's still labeled an "Asian film." It was a tough process.

S. What would you advise to younger filmmakers who want to produce theatrically successful films?

W. I think to be really realistic, if they want to make it in the industry, they shouldn't make Asian-related films. If they wrote *Sex, Lies, and Videotapes* and perhaps put one Asian character in it, that's probably a better way to start. Once they have the power, it's probably a little easier to go back and do Asian stuff. And I'm not saying that young filmmakers shouldn't (produce Asian American films) because in the end you have to follow your heart, material that is close to you, that you are driven by and that you can make a wonderful film out of.

S. You're originally from Hong Kong and attended film school in the U.S. In 1976 you temporarily put your film career on hold to work with Chinese immigrants in San Francisco Chinatown and subsequently produced three films (*Chan is Missing, Dim Sum,* and *Eat A Bowl of Tea*) dealing with the Chinese American experience. What prompted you in this direction?

W. When I was going to college, I felt I didn't do justice to my own Asian or Chinese upbringing so I went into dealing with that in the late 60s and began working in Chinatown which really changed the second half of my life. That's why the films that I have done are related to Chinese Americans or Chinese or Hong Kong. I have this perspective where I see what Chinese Americans go through and what immigrants go through. I can straddle those two worlds.

This is the material that has always been closest to me. At the same time, I'm very "Americanized" and can also do films like *Slam Dance* (1987).

So there's a part of me that wants to do purely American material and I haven't quite fulfilled that kind of drive yet. My interest is to do an American mainstream film, which doesn't mean just white middle-class America. I'm interested in other minorities and how other Americans live and what their stories are.

S. Do you feel *Tea* was an overall successful film?

W. I don't know if it was that successful. It basically wasn't promoted very well because Columbia halfheartedly put it out there. *Tea* is the most polished and most mainstream of all the different things I've done.

S. What do you want to accomplish in your films, both artistically and socially?

W. I want to make interesting films about people, their stories. Spence (Nakasako) and I are working on some things that are eventually going to be non-Asian. We're getting stories about Asians and dubbing the Asian faces and making them white or Latino or whatever and I think in the end those stories are the same, about people, about the ironies of life. The color of the face may make a difference but in a lot of instances it could be anyone who is poor, or rich, or anyone who is trying to go through life.

S. How do you feel your films will stand out from Hollywood directors?

W. The reason I was fascinated in *Eat A Bowl* was the perversity that this good-looking guy couldn't get it up. And his father is just crazy. And in the end someone's ear got chopped off in a very black way. Perhaps one of the failures of *Eat A Bowl of Tea* was that it was too tame. There were a lot of elements in there but the tone and mood were milked down for a certain audience. Life is cheap. That kind of irony of life and perversity is what I'm interested in.

S. What are the future challenges for Asian American filmmakers?

W. Not enough work has been done on the historical stuff such as Angel Island and which I feel we're ready to do. The three films that I've done I've consciously avoided Caucasian characters or other minority groups. I've just dealt with the Chinese.

Now we can deal with things that are a little more complicated. For instance, there are more interracial couples these days. Asian women with Jewish men. There could be some fascinating stories that could be told. And they're difficult to write. One of the things I feel we're lacking and still developing is the craft of writing good material for Asian Americans. There are very few people who are writing or writing strong stuff.

> "*The reason I was fascinated in* Eat A Bowl of Tea *was the perversity that this good-looking guy couldn't get it up.*"

With a pen, our country was
divided in two;
    in a blood bath, united.
By rights of conquest, the
victors painted
    their dais with crimson;
by loss of freedom,
    the vanquished dyed the
sea in blood.
So we left on little wooden
boats to search for
    life in a graveyard, for
sweet liberty
    in the salty sea.

QUÁCH QUỲNH-HOA

Vạt Nắng, 1990

UNTIL THE DAY

UNTIL THE DAY BREAKS: NATIONALISTIC FILM AND VIDEO MOVEMENT IN KOREA

Hye Jung Park

I went to Seoul, Korea for three weeks in April this year. The time that I had was meaningful and unforgettable. Last time when I visited Korea, in 1987, my purpose in visiting was just to see family and friends, and to have fun. However, this time was different. I went there full of excitement but at the same with a full burden of assignments.

Through my eight years' stay in the United States, I had developed a new awareness about the Third World media through my college education. I realized how the image of the Third World countries is reflected in the U.S. media. It is a totally distorted, ugly face which consists of disasters, floods, wars, poverty and so on. In spite of that, all the world is completely dependent on the U.S. news agencies in getting information about the others. The effect of western media is like a flood that we cannot control.

I started to realize that the problem Korea has is not just ours but that the other Third World countries have the problem in common—the conflict between the oppressor and the oppressed. I felt the necessity of solidarity for these oppressed countries to change this deformed world system. To share and unite together, it is necessary to know the facts about each other. How much do we know about each other? Do people know why Korean students and workers are demonstrating? Do we know what is going on in our neighbor country? How about El Salvador? South Africa?

I tried to figure out a possible solution to align each other. How about using video and film? Yes, that's it. Let's use media! Let's exchange information! The best way of educating and informing each other is showing the reality with visual resources. It could be subjective but I had a strong confidence that it would work.

Coincidentally, I found out that Korea's independent filmmaking became active since 1987, and had played a significant role in the cultural movement. Despite the oppression, those brave young filmmakers were producing nationalistic film and video continuously. The purpose of the national film movement is to save people who have been badly affected by Hollywood-style western cultural domination. The nationalistic film appeared to put nationalistic content in an art form to enrich people's culture. The issues of the films vary but have one underlying theme— they pursue reunification and democratization of Korea. When I started to receive videos and films about the labor movement and farmers',

SURNAME VIET GIVEN NAME NAM (1989)
Trinh T. Minh-ha

KOREAN DEMONSTRATORS ON VIDEO
Hye Jung Park

students', teachers' movements documentaries and features, I was moved by these valuable resources. Those tapes on my shelves are not video tapes. They are the voice and life of our oppressed people who are struggling to build a better world. What shall I do with those videos? How can I make them useful for my country and the other oppressed countries?

In the fall of 1989, when Shu Lea proposed to work together on the project, *The Revolution Will Be Televised: Social Movements in Asia*, I replied "yes" right away. It seemed that this opportunity was given to us. However, it was hard to communicate with film groups in Korea by letters or telephone. We did not know each other's situation, or of what was going on. I could not sit and explain everything to them, and I also was curious about the group's incredible activity.

Finally, I decided to go to Korea in April this year. From the day of arrival, I visited all independent media groups. Those young fellows were producing tapes without proper equipment. They were running around with VHS home video cameras to the rallies and meetings, running the risk. I asked them, "How do you edit?" They said, "We sneak into the University Communication Department. It is not easy." However, they didn't seem discouraged but were working militantly with strong commitment.

By accident, when I was in Korea, the second feature film screening, *Night Before the Strike*, was being censored by the government. The film dealt with the labor workers' struggle and life for the freedom of workers. When the small theater tried to show it, the government gave an order to arrest the owner of the theater and the head of the film group. In spite of the oppression, movement groups decided to screen it. College students collaborated with them and finally the film was shown at different college auditoriums in different provinces.

I remember a rainy afternoon on April 12, Yeonsei University. Student volunteers as guards surrounded the auditorium to protect the audience from the armed police. I was in the middle of a crowd of two thousand. My heart was beating from standing on the line. "Am I going to be arrested?" I looked at the people next to me. They seemed not to mind what would happen to them in the near future.

In the dark auditorium, what you could hear was the big crowd's heavy breathing. The film started. We laughed, shouted, and cried while we were watching the film. At that time, we were united. We were one. The end of the film was really touching and people were still in their seats for the time being. Suddenly, one young fellow jumped up on the stage and shouted, "Let's sing 'Song for the Militant Workers!'" I was singing but also crying. I was proud of the film and these singing people under the suppressing situation. The mixed feelings of sadness and happiness were indescribable.

When I came out of the auditorium, it was dark and still rainy. The student guards huddled around a small fire warming themselves.

I felt like talking to them loudly saying, "Hey friends, let's not be frustrated with the situation. Aren't you proud of our film? Aren't you proud of our brave people who run the risk to do the right thing? We are not alone. We have our alliance in the world. Let's struggle for true democracy hand in hand with all the oppressed people in the world until the day breaks! Let them hear and see us!"

THAILAND – NOT TAIWAN:
A PLAY IN ONE ACT
NICKY TAMRONG

CAST OF CHARACTERS

NICKY TAMRONG, a man in his early thirties
TEERANEETEE TAMRONGWEENIJCHAI, a man in his early thirties

SCENE

On top of a tall building in New York City

TIME

Fall, 1987

SCENE 1

SETTING:
We are on the top of a tall building in New York City. It is quite empty but the place is dusty. There are many chairs scattered all over the place and many papers on the floor.
AT RISE:
Morning. Offstage music of the new age is heard from a radio from the room below. TT and NICKY are standing by the edge of the building looking over New York City's landscape.

NICKY

You want to jump? Don't you have anything to do besides trying to jump out of the building? I thought you are a director, why are you committing suicide easily? Do something, make a documentary about your nationality.

TT

What's about it? I have nothing to say. That is why I want to commit suicide.

NICKY

Let's start from your name. How long did it take to get this very long name?

TT

I don't want to talk about my name. Nobody will be interested.

NICKY

How about your country? I like Thai food. I like spicy food.

TT

How come when anybody want to talk to me all they say is they like my food and how much they enjoy it. I don't want to talk just that. Do you know the difference between Thailand and Taiwan?

NICKY

What? Is there a difference? What do you mean?

TT

You know like Austria and Australia.

NICKY

I know that. Everybody should know that. We learn that in first grade.

TT

So you know the difference between Thailand and Taiwan? Do you?

NICKY

I thought they are the same. Is there a difference? Really. Maybe I should do more research. Maybe I should talk to people about it.

TT

You know people always ask me where I came from and when I answered them that I came from Thailand, they thought it's Taiwan. They said the country sells cheap stuff and fake products. And they thought Taiwan is in Thailand and vice versa and they both are Chinese. One of them said Thailand is in New Jersey. Or Thailand is in Chinatown. Most thought they were the same place. I got to do something, there are so many subtle humors in this.

NICKY

I don't think you can do a documentary focusing on a topic like that. Nobody cares. Nobody thinks it's important to their life. It doesn't affect them directly. What else can you say? It's a one dimension topic.

TT

I'm not making a conventional documentary. I'm making an absurd comedy out of the confusion of people that could not distinguish the difference between the two. My point is to show how people don't pay attention to details in life. You can't judge only by the sound of it. It may sound the same to you because you already have that narrow and one-sided mind. All I'm saying is I shouldn't have a first focus, I should go out in the field and look for that confusion in people. If you ask them what Thai people eat for breakfast, they probably say I don't know or maybe rice and soy sauce.

NICKY

I still don't see your point. I think you will waste your time and money if you don't do any research first. It's a very important process, because you never know what you will get. Don't go out and shoot, you are not going to get any good responses. You must do research and have lists of questions you want to ask and lists of answers you want to reply. You can't go out there naked.

TT

I don't think I'm going to commit suicide anymore. Thanks a lot for saving my life. I will prove to you that confusion and ignorance and stereotypes of each other are out there all the time. I will make a tape that reminds people that there is a need in recognizing each other's background and nobody should take anybody for granted. Nobody should make anybody better than others. If Thailand is Taiwan, it's not because they both make shoes and eat rice. Can you tell me from here where Thailand and Taiwan are?

NICKY (points his finger to the sky)

I thought they are the same. It's over there somewhere in the Pacific.

BOLD OMISSIONS
AND MINUTE DEPICTIONS

TRINH T. MINH-HA

Thanks to Ayi Kwei Armah, I know the screens of life you have left us: *veils that rise in front of us, framing the world in neat pieces. Until we have grown tall enough to look over the next veil, we believe the little we see is all there is to see. From veil to veil, the bitter taste of surprise in disfranchisement keeps on renewing. But again and again, we hold fast to what our eyes perceive; again and again we fool ourselves, convinced at each step, that we have grown wise.* Recently, in a casual conversation, two visiting writers from Martinique and Guadeloupe remarked with a certain bewilderment that the question of migration was again enjoying a great vogue in the States and that "they all talk about identity and marginality." Finding myself deeply implied in this "they" despite the fact that my friends tacitly included me on their side while talking, I was suddenly hit by a brief but sharp feeling of confusion as to where my identity lay, lied. Since, they, in this context, pointed both to the trendy Euro-American intellectuals eager to recycle strands of subversion and to those for whom the migrant's condition continued to be an everyday reality and an ongoing border struggle, it was difficult to react quickly without speaking simply for or against. Caught between two fixed closures—American and Asian—I was at the same time grateful to be treated as an outsider to the passing trends of discursive thought in North America, and repelled by my friend's apparent refusal to identify (even strategically) with the fight against marginalization. However, their remark did have a strong destabilizing effect. I was assaulted by intense skepticism as I realized the intricacy of my own participation in what had been indirectly pointed to here as a spurious, fashionable preoccupation of the West raised up for the sake of western vanguardism and its desire to conserve itself as sovereign subject of radical knowledge. For the above writers, the word "marginality" clearly did not make sense, nor did its juxtaposition with the notion of "identity" seem any more revealing. They thus reacted to its use with astonishment, if not with sarcasm: "What marginality? Marginal in relation to whom? To where? To what?"

Perhaps vindicating and interrogating identity takes on a peculiarly active significance with displacement and migration. It becomes inevitable with the questioning of established power relations, or with the daily meddling with the hegemonic culture. For those who feel settled at home in their land (or in other lands) where racial issues are not an everyday challenge, perhaps self-retrieval and self-apprehension are achieved without yielding to the urge to assimilate, to reject, or to fight for a space where identity is fearlessly constructed across difference. A familiar story of "learning in America" is, for example, the one lived by artist Wen Yi Hou when she left Mainland China to further her education in the States:

I became aware of my minority status in America . . . . I asked people there [at the University of California, San Diego], "Why did the school select me?" They said when they saw my slides, they were surprised by my paintings. They were modern and very Western. How could that happen in Red China? I was surprised that shortly after I started the program, I was asked why my paintings were not traditional Chinese paintings. I was depressed. I did not have any value as a Chinese artist in their minds. My feelings of worthlessness as an artist intensified in San Diego. There was a group of American graduate students who talked about the Eastern influence on Western art. I was in the seminar, but no one talked to me or looked at me. I worried about how they could talk about Eastern cultures and yet they would not even look at a person from the East. I was the subject of the lecture but was excluded.[1]

Hear how the story happened again; watch the scenario of disfranchisement repeat itself across generations; smell the poison taking effect in the lives of those who dare mix while differing. The predicament of crossing boundaries cannot be merely rejected or accepted. It has to be confronted in its controversies. There is indeed little hope of speaking this simultaneously outside-inside actuality into existence in simple, polarizing black and white terms. The challenge of the hyphenated reality lies in the hyphen itself: the becoming Asian-American; the realm in-between, where predetermined rules cannot fully apply. Presumedly, the real Chinese artist should abide by Chinese aesthetics, the authenticity of which is naturally defined on *their* (Euro-American) terms. After all, who would dispute the fact that western influence should be challenged in its global domination? But again, who ever hesitates to take the license to decide what is Western and what is Eastern in this context? Indeed, no statements about the negative nature of such influence could be more dogmatic than those often made by Euro-Americans for the benefit of their non-western proteges. "Yes, the white world is still a pretty dark one for the man of color," noted Ezekiel Mphahlele.[2] It is always mind-boggling to recognize how readily opposed liberal Westerners are to any discrimination in the public treatment of people of color while remaining blind to it in more individualized relationships or when dealing with difference on a one-to-one basis.

A lesson learnt from the failure of Negritude is that any attempt at pegging things and reclaiming a denied heritage to construct a positive identity should remain at its best, diacritical and strategical, rather than dogmatic and originary. (The term *negritude*, created by poet Aime Cesaire to denote a quality common to the thought and behaviour of black people, was championed in the fifties by the Society of African Culture in Paris as a concept capable of defining and exalting the negroness of artistic activity.) Racial and sexual discrimination are based on assumptions of biological essences, and with such an affirmation as "Emotion is completely Negro as reason is Greek" (Leopold Sedar Senghor), Negritude, like "Feminitude" (or reactive feminism) ends up trapping itself in what remains primarily a defensive stance. *In my struggle to overcome the artistic difficulty that arises when one is angry most of the time and when one's sense of values is continually being challenged by the ruling class, I have never thought of calling my negritude to my aid, except when writing protest material. But is not this elementary—shall I call it "underdoggery?"—that Senghor is talking about? Even he must know, however, that his philosophy will contain his art only up to a point: it won't chain his art for long (Mphalele).*[3]

If Negritude tended to oversimplify and to reentrench black values in its assertion, it was mainly because it indulged heavily in binary oppositional thinking. As Wole Soyinka put it, it resulted from the adoption of "the Manichean tradition of European thought," therefore borrowing "from the very component of its racist syllogism."[4] However, as a Vietnamese proverb says, "Bound to be round is the dweller in a calabash/Bound to be long is the dweller in a tube." Separatism as a strategy, not as an end point, is at times necessary for the emergence of a framework that promotes and entitles second-class citizens to articulate problems related to their condition. Highly privileged are those who can happily afford to remain comfortable in the protected world of their own, which neither seems to carry any ambiguity nor does it need to question itself in its mores and measures—its utter narrowness despite its global material expansion. When the footprints made by the shoes are not readily confused with the shoes themselves, what Negritude has also achieved can never be belittled. Due to it, the creation of a multicultural alliance with the world's dispossessed became possible. It is in having to confront and defy hegemonic values on an everyday basis, in other words, in assuming the between-world dilemma, that one understands both the predicament and the potency of the hyphen. Here, becoming Asian-American affirms itself at once as a transient and constant state: one is born over and over again as hyphen rather than as fixed entity, thereby refusing to settle down in one (tubicolous) world or another. The hyphenated condition certainly does not limit itself to a duality between two cultural heritages. It leads, on the one hand, to an active "search of our mother's gardens" (Alice Walker)—the consciousness of "root values" or of a certain Asianness—and on the other hand, to a heightened awareness of other "minority" sensitivities, hence of a Third World solidarity, and by extension, of the nature of oppression. Unavoidably, the step backward is constantly also a step forward. The multi-dimensional necessity of being both here(s) and there(s) implies a more radical ability to shuttle between frontiers and to cut across ethnic allegiances while assuming a specific and contingent legacy.

Cultural difference is not a totemic object. It does not always announce itself to the onlooker; sometimes it stands out conspicuously, most of the time it tends to escape the commodifying eye. Its visibility depends on how much one is willing to inquire into the anomalous character of the familiar, and how engaged one remains to the politics of continuous doubling, reversing and displacing in marginality as well as to the necessity of changing both oneself-as-other and other-as-oneself. *Fervently, we have wanted to belong somewhere at the same time that we have often wanted to run away. We reached out for something, and when by chance grasped it, we often found that it wasn't what we wanted at all. There is one part of us that is always lost and searching. It is an echo of a cry that was a longing for warmth and safety. And through our adolescent fantasies, and however our adult reasoning may disguise it, the search continues*

"Bound to be round is the dweller in a calabash / Bound to be long is the dweller in a tube."

SURNAME VIET GIVEN NAME NAM (1989)
Trinh T. Minh-Ha

(Mai-mai Sze).[5] The quest for this other in us can hardly be a simple return to the past or to the time-honored values of our ancestors. Changes are inevitably implied in the process of restoring the cultural lineage, which combines the lore of the past with the lore of the complex present in its histories of migrations. As soon as we learn to be "Asians in America"—that is to come to a rest in a place supposedly always there, waiting to be discovered—we also recognize that we can't simply be Asians any longer. The fight has to focus on our physical and political whereabouts, so that "here in San Francisco/there is Saigon/their locks of mouths/damming the Pacific!" (Stella Wong).[6] Listening to new sounds in the attempt to articulate a specific and transcultural between-world reality requires again that the step backward be simultaneously a step forward. As Al Robles puts forth in these lines: "A Filipino fisherman once said/that looking for your roots/will get you all tangled up/ with the dead past.../If the mind bothers with the roots/It'll forget all about the weeds. . . ."[7]

I am not a painter who has come to America to paint China. I am a painter from China who came to America to continue painting.

Why paint? People need to paint and painting needs people.

Wen Yi Hou[8]

What is Chinese in America? An artistic event is often presented as a thought, a feeling that has found its form in its formless nature. To paint is to continue painting. The becoming is not a becoming something; it remains active and intransitive. While, for example, for Thomas Mann "a spiritual— that is, significant—phenomenon is 'significant' precisely because it exceeds its own limits," for Andrei Tarkovsky the film image as acute observation of life is linked to the Japanese *haiku*, which he wrote, "cultivates its images in such a way that they mean nothing beyond themselves, and at the same time express so much that it is not possible to catch their final meaning...the great function of the artistic image is to be a detector of infinity...(and to give) the beholder as simultaneous experience of the most complex, contradictory, sometimes even mutually exclusive feelings."[9] People need to paint and painting needs people for, in this mutual need, they both exceed their limits as people and as painting. This is the challenge of the hyphen. Chinese artist Shih-T'ao (1630–C.A. 1717–1720) evolved his philosophy of painting around the fundamental notions of "the form of the formless" and "the sound of the soundless."[10]

The basic urge to manifest (not to arrest) the Formless in form seems, indeed, to be what Tarkovsky yearns for through the many words he uses to explicate an aesthetics that remains implicitly admirative of the *haiku* as well as of other Asian sources, such as Kurosawa's poetic approach in his *Macbeth*. What Tarkovsky tries to retain and "make it incarnate, new each time," is the Formless, or as he said it, the life principle itself, *unique* in each moment of life. Thus, form is not intended to express form but rather, formlessness. The non-consumable relationship between form and formlessness or between art and life defies every binarist attempt at reducing it to the old dichotomy of form and content. In Tarkovsky's definition, "the image is not a certain *meaning*, expressed by the director, but an entire world reflected as in a drop of water."[11]

Transformation requires a certain freedom to modify, appropriate and reappropriate without being trapped in imitation. Chinese traditional arts, for example, do not speak so much of beauty or of aesthetic, as of the spirit—the *ch'i*. What can be taught and assimilated, indeed, is technical knowledge; not the *ch'i*—the principle of life that is unique to each artistic movement, event, manifestation; or the breath that sustains all processes of movement and change. To excel only in the mechanics of a language, be it verbal, visual, or musical, is to excel in imitation—the part that can be formulated, hence enclosed in formulas. Form as formulas can only express form; it cannot free itself from the form-content divide. However, a film can be made the way a tale is spun by many storytellers. Nothing is explained, everything is evoked. When explanations were requested, the storyteller would pause, listen carefully, and after due consideration, repeat exactly the passage relevant to the question. No more, no less. Here, there is no necessity to reduce the plural meaning of the story to some flat explanatory answer, and the questioner is invited to listen again more mindfully to what he or she has missed. Since form cannot be separated from content—the form of the story being (integral to) the story itself—there is no other way to say it without reforming it (that is, unintentionally modifying, augmenting, or narrowing it). One of the characteristics of Shih-T'ao's principles in painting is precisely the *yugen*, translated as "subtle profundity" or "deep reserve." The quality emphasized here is the ability to imply, rather than to expose something in its entirety; to suggest and evoke, rather that to delineate laboriously. "Such works," wrote Shih-T'ao, "enable us to imagine the depth of content within them and to feel infinite reverberations, something that is not possible with detail painted minutely and distinctly."[12]

The realm of a film is that of a mediating elsewhere, albeit one deeply rooted in reality. It seeks the truth of reality, or the *ch'i* of life's fictions, but is neither dream nor reality. Its meaning is never simply true or false. For, it is thanks to its falsity (recreation through the mediation of the cinematic apparatus) that a truth is made perceptible to the spectator. In confusing meaning with truth or imposing it as truth, a form of literalism, of narrow-mindness and of ensuing terrorism is accorded the name of "realism." Such glaring "misnaming" in film history ultimately serves to mask the process in filmmaking by which meaning is fixed and formulas are prescribed. Thereby, the oppressive cinematic conventions that serve the ideology in power are naturalized, and representation, lacking *yugen*, no longer vibrates; it ceases to be political, while meaning becomes merely a pawn in the game of power. *The stereotype is not a simplification because it is a false representation of a given reality. It is a simplification because it is an arrested, fixed form of representation . . .*[13] To disturb the comfort, the security, the fanaticism of meaning is a critical task that allows film to partake in the politics of everyday life as well as in the challenge of the dominant ideology of world cinema.

One of the ways by which feminism defines itself as a politics of everyday life, thereby breaking down the barriers separating the public and private spheres of activity, is precisely to continue redefining the nature and boundaries of the political in relation to the personal. Much has been said concerning the "misuse" of the personal in attempts to radicalize consciousness. And much has also been voiced on how sexual politics can lead straight to identity politics, which tends to collapse the personal and the political instead of maintaining the tension between the two so that, in the absence of the one or the other, the state of depoliticization that occurs can no longer go unnoticed. Still, feminism continues to be a political critique of society and what it has contributed is the possibility of a new way of understanding subjectivity, a radically different aesthetic, a rewriting of culture in which women are addressed as social and political subjects. As bell hooks remarks, "to begin revisioning we must acknowledge the need to examine the self from a new, critical standpoint. Such a perspective, while it would insist on the self as site for politicization, would equally insist that simply describing one's experience of exploitation or oppression is not to become politicized. It is not sufficient to know the personal but to know—to speak it in a different way."[14]

Listening to new sounds, speaking in a different way, manifesting the Formless. There would be no "new," no "different" possible if it were not for the Formless, which is the source of all forms. The belief that there can exist such a thing as an outside foreign to the inside, an objective, unmediated reality about which one can have knowledge once and for all, has been repeatedly challenged by feminist critics. For centuries, this belief has most perniciously served to reduce the world to the dominant's own image, and the fight against "realism" is, in fact, not a denial of reality and of meaning, but rather, a determination to keep meaning creative, hence to challenge the fixity of realism as a style and an arrested form of representation. Claire Johnston argued in her famous essay on "Women's Cinema As Counter Cinema":

> Within a sexist ideology and a male-dominated cinema, woman is presented as what she represents for man. . . . What the camera in fact grasps is the "natural" world of the dominant ideology. . . . Any revolutionary strategy must challenge the depiction of reality: it is not enough to discuss the oppression of women within the text of the film: the language of the cinema/the depiction of reality must also be interrogated, so that a break between ideology and text is affected.[15]

Realism as one form of representation defined by a specific attitude toward reality is widely validated to perpetuate the illusion of a stable world (even when it depicts sickness, poverty and war), in which the same "how-to-do's" are confidently standardized and prescribed for different realities. Gaps and cracks of the systems of filmmaking and filmviewing are carefully made invisible so that the flow of events can continue to provide the spectator with a sense of gradual, linear acquisition of knowledge. This is the way the West envisions forms for centuries. If eighteenth-century Chinese artists used to judge Westerners' skill in engraved illustrations as "nothing but artisanry" and their methods "good only for creating likeness," the "Chinese image" long remained an example of what the Western painter should avoid, since it was viewed as being deficient in three-dimensionality. It was not until the twentieth century, when the rejection of illusionism spread among artists of the West that the nonillusionistic art of the Chinese started to "make sense" to them. History abounds with instances where, for example, established representational devices used by early Europeans for picture-maps to display or isolate the object of study in its most readable and informative aspect, were adopted by the Chinese for purposes other than legibility and information. The illusionism of exactitude in representation and of three-dimensionality on a two-dimensional medium could hardly be what the Chinese would search for at the time, no matter how intrigued they could be with the Euro-

"As soon as we learn to be 'Asians in America...' we also recognize that we can't simply be Asians any longer."

pean pictures. Not only did they consider the Europeans to be quite incapable of depicting landscape (rocks, trees, rivers, mountains, which demanded more than illusionistic technique), but they also did not accept these pictures as true representations of real scenes.[16] Imitation of the forms of nature (or rather, the viewing of nature as arrested forms) had apparently little to do with manifestation of the *ch'i* and the Formless that is life or the source of all forms. In working with the sense of the unknown instead of repressing it, in bringing infinity within sight, traditional Chinese arts choose to suggest always more than what they represent. Thus, "if one wishes to paint a high mountain, one should not paint every part, or it will not seem high; when mist and haze encircle its haunches, then it seems tall."[17]

The work of the mountain does not lie just with the mountain, but with its quiescence . . . the work of the water does not lie just with the water, but with its movement. Moreover, the work of antiquity does not lie with just antiquity, but with its freedom from error. The work of the present does not lie with just the present, but with its freedom.

Shih T'ao[18]

The Chinese are known to their neighbors (the Vietnamese, for example) as a strongly practical and realistic people. Realism in this context requires that life be intimately understood both in its flow and its temporary pauses or specific instances. To face reality squarely and sensitively, without positive or negative escapism, is to see "the small in the large and the large in the small; the real in the illusory and the illusory in the real" (Shen-Fu). The idea of realism in art, and more particularly in realistically powerful media like photography and film, should be linked with the principle of life (and death) by which things, endowed with existential and spiritual force and never static, continue to grow, to change, to renew, and to move. The freedom implied in the internal and external projection of these "landscapes of life" on canvas, on celluloid or on screen, lies in the availability of mind—and heart—that declines to limit one's perception of things and events to their actual forms. Such freedom also allows for the fearless assumption of the hyphen—the fluid interplay of realistic and non-realistic modes of representation, or to quote a Chinese opera expert, of "bold omissions and minute depictions."[19]

TO THE READER The passages quoted are sometimes indented, other times included in the text. Also some are italicized (when not directly quoted) and others are in plain letters. These are all deliberate choices that do have different reading effects.

1. Wen Yi Hou. "Being in America," M.A. thesis, University of California, San Diego, 1990, 1; 14-15.
2. Ezekiel Mphahlele. *The African Image* (New York: Praeger, 1962, rpt., 1966), 15.
3. *Ibid.*, 54.
4. Wole Soyinka. *Myth, Literature and The African World* (New York: Cambridge University Press, 1976, rpt.,1978), 127.
5. Mai-mai Sze. *Echo of a Cry: A Story Which Began in China* (New York: Harcourt Brace, 1945), 202, quoted in Amy Ling, *Between Worlds. Women Writers of Chinese Ancestry* (Elmsford, New York: Pergamon Press, 1990), 108.

6. Nanying Stella Wong. "The Return," quoted in Russell Leong, "Poetry within Earshot: Notes on an Asian American Generation 1968-78" *Amerasia Journal* 15:1 (1989), 172.

7. Al Robles, "Tagatac on Ifugao Mountain," quoted in *Amerasia Journal* 15:1 (1989), 175.

8. "Being in America," 27.

9. Andrei Tarkovsky. *Sculpting in Time. Reflections on The Cinema*, trans. K. Hunter-Blair (New York: Alfred A. Knopf, 1987). The quote from T. Mann is on p. 104; the rest of the quote is on p. 109.

10. In Earle J. Coleman. *Philosophy of Painting* by Shih T'ao. A Translation and Exposition of his Hua-P'u (New York: Mouton Publishers, 1978).

11. Tarkovsky's italics, *Sculpting in Time*, 104; 110.

12. *Philosophy of Painting*, 15.

13. Homi Bhabha. "The Other Question: Difference, Discrimination and The Discourse of Colonialism," in *Literature, Politics and Theory*, ed. F. Baker, et al. (London: Methuen, 1986), 163.

14. bell hooks, *Talking Back. Thinking Feminist, Thinking Black* (Boston, Massachussetts: South End Press, 1989), 107.

15. Claire Johnston. "Women's Cinema As Counter-Cinema." In *Movies and Methods. An Anthology*, ed. Bill Nichols (Berkeley: University of California Press, 1976), 211, 214.

16. See James Cahill, *The Compelling Image* (Cambridge: Harvard University Press, 1982), 72, 74, 82, 96. The complexities of Cahill's discussion on the influences from Europe among Chinese artists cannot be conveyed in the few general lines I have drawn here.

17. Quoted in George Rowley, *Principles of Chinese Painting* (Princeton, New Jersey: Princeton University Press, 1947, rpt., 1959), 66.

18. *Philosophy of Painting*, 142-43.

19. Huang Shang, *Tales from Peking Opera* (Bejing: New World Press, 1985), 7.

RADIO AND THE

WORLD:

THE CASE OF THE

PHILIPPINES

MARICEL

PAGULAYAN

RADIO AND THE THIRD WORLD: THE CASE OF THE PHILIPPINES

Maricel Pagulayan

Ferdinand Marcos was first elected president in 1965 and then became the first Filipino to be reelected by a majority vote in 1969. During his second term Marcos began to guide the policies of mass media. Critical of oligarchy control of the media, Marcos built his own through governmental agencies and friends.

The list of governmental bodies formed by Marcos to oversee broadcasting is long and not important to this discussion except to note that bureaucratization is one important factor in the control of media. It was during Marcos' second term in 1969 that the Filipino people were increasingly dissatisfied with his policies. Marcos responded to his criticism by cutting them off from basic human needs and rights. With the backing of the U.S. military, Marcos gained control of the bureaucracy, the legal system, the media and much of the wealth of the country. Vocal critics in the media were censored, jailed, reported missing or simply turned up dead. On September 21, 1972, martial law was declared and Marcos took control of the nation's communication and information structure.

In 1986, Philippine broadcasting was dominated by three radio networks, all owned and operated by distinct entities. One of these was the government itself, which through the Ministry of Public Information's Office of Media Affairs controls the Maharlika Broadcasting System (MBS). MBS owned and operated twenty-two AM, two FM, and four short-wave stations. Marcos' personal stamp was placed on the network with the Maharlika name. The Philippine name for noble, it was the name given to the phantom 8300 guerilla resistance unit that Marcos falsely claimed to have led during the Japanese occupation.

Funded by religiously-motivated American private citizens and a foundation, the Far East Broadcasting Company (FEBC) began broadcasting with a 1000 watt medium-wave transmitter from Manila in 1948. The station's express purpose was "to proclaim to the world the Gospel message of Jesus Christ." Also staunchly anti-communist, FEBC served a second function as a monitor of the "Chinese Communist Party's assumption of control in Mainland China in 1949." Through the utilization of the airwaves, the founders of FEBC believed that they could bring the word of God to the Asian people and warn them of the dangers of Communism. By 1986, FEBC owned and operated seven AM, two FM, and two short-wave stations. The network broadcasts in twenty-one languages although a majority of the air time is in English (eleven hours daily). Financial backing continues to come from the Evangelical Christian Church, based in the United States.

The third station, Radio Veritas, refers to itself as "the Voice of Asian Christianity" and has as its Chairman Cardinal Jaime Sin. Founded in 1969, Radio Veritas is a non-commercial station and member of the Philippine Federation of Catholic Broadcasters. Radio Veritas, with 50kw, is one of the two most powerful transmitters in the Philippines. It can also be heard in most parts of Asia, broadcasting in twelve languages. Radio Veritas' domestic activities are funded in part by the Bishop's Conference and the Catholic Businessman's Council. It has also been reported by U.S. Undersecretary of State Michael Armacost in April of 1986 that "Radio Veritas enjoyed our financial support and that of the Asia Foundation among others."

During the 1986 change in government in the Philippines, the Philippine people learned what was occurring largely through radio broadcasts. It is important to note that the Philippines is a large rural country composed of over 7,000 islands scattered over five hundred thousand miles. The three radio services presented markedly divergent perspectives of the events that took place in February 1986. Editorial, news and commentary policies are determined by ownership and control of media outlets. Reflecting upon who owns and operates the networks suggests a basis for influencing what news stories are produced and how these stories are presented.

The MBS radio station network reported the February elections from a pro-Marcos perspective. MBS attacked Corazon Aquino's party, alluding to their responsibility for election fraud and violence and suggesting collusion with the Communist party. It is not unique to the Philippines that media serve the purpose of advancing the values, beliefs and culture of the ruling elite. But more to the point, MBS is an example of the authoritarian press.

Choices made by the FEBC evangelical organization are consistent with many other international religious broadcasters. Broadcasters on foreign soil are usually not allowed to broadcast programming that might be critical of the host government. FEBC supported the party in power by presenting news and information from the party's perspective and was rewarded with long leases, governmental support and the help of the U.S. military. In 1986, FEBC found itself in the awkward position of supporting Marcos' interpretation of the election. Once it became clear that Aquino was garnering international support, FEBC responded late in the crisis.

Radio Veritas was clearly the most willing to criticize the Marcos government and the only one to give air time to Corazon Aquino and members of the Catholic church's hierarchy. As tension began to mount, the people had taken to the streets especially as Marcos' troops were being deployed. Radio Veritas acted as a conduit for information. From all over the city of Manila, people called the station to report troop movement. Throughout the Philippines citizens listened to the station, playing their radios in their homes and on the streets. The station told the people where they were needed to swell the crowds at the resistance rallies and requested each night that they turn on their lights to show their support. When tear gas was fired into the crowds, Radio Veritas was notified and they told the people how they could help by taking water and linens to the areas where people were hurt. On February 22, Marcos' personnel destroyed the transmitter that powered Radio Veritas. But the spirit of the "people's radio station" had not died. Aquino's supporters took over and occupied MBS radio and television stations. The station became known as DZRB, Radio Bandito. Without Marcos' usual control of the media, his attempt to call a nationwide curfew was frustrated. He tried to broadcast on one of his radio stations by way of a phone patch but the connection was on a party line that was picked up and the nation heard instead a small child interrupting him.

Media, specifically radio, has been used as a tool to influence the internal affairs of many countries. The CIA's manipulation of broadcasting is a historical fact. Radio Liberty and Radio Free Europe were one-time CIA radio services. In the 1950s the CIA used clandestine radio stations to broadcast into Guatemala to destabilize the Arbenz government. The list continues.

Perhaps the activities of the CIA in Philippine broadcasting adds a new twist to how a country's media can be used for covert activities. In this instance support was given to an established popular movement that was well underway despite the Reagan administration's support for Marcos.

What does seem clear is the impact of Radio Veritas on the events of February 1986. Radio Veritas functioned during the time of crisis as a tool for national integration. Public events lend themselves to broadcast coverage, serving the cause of national integration by giving the widest possible currency to symbols that evoke national pride and the sense of community identity. The station became what Bertolt Brecht called "a machinery for communication."

PARIS IN TOKYO

PARIS IN TOKYO IN L.A.

IN L.A.

Bruce Yonemoto

BRUCE

YONEMOTO

If America elects to develop her art wholly out of herself, without reference to the accumulated experience of older civilizations, she will make a mistake, and protract her improvement. . . . We have not time to invent and study everything anew. . . . No one dreams of it in science, ethics, or physics. Why then propose it in art? We are a composite people. Our knowledge is eclectic. . . . To get artistic riches by virtue of assimilated examples, knowledge, and ideas, drawn from all sources, and made national and homogenous by a solidarity of our own, is our right pathway to consummate art.[1]

James Jackson Jarves, art collector and critic, 1864

Although James Jarves' advice may seem as if it were written for a contemporary art program promoting cultural diversity, further reading of Mr. Jarves' writings reveals his xenophobic opinion that "older civilizations" or cultures included only those of European extraction. Writing about Japanese art in 1876, Jarves espouses the United States' contradictory expectations of itself and non-European cultures:

Easel paintings are not found in Japan, unless we admit into this category recent attempts to imitate our(s), all (of) which are striking failures, as are also our experiments in their line innovations on either side, by the practice of the one is guided by the principles of the other, having a common result. Either system must be kept to itself, intact, or wholly abandoned. There can be no happy mixture of the antipodal elements of Oriental and European art, or subordination of one practice to the other, although we may largely gain by studying their fundamental principles and acquiring a knowledge of their materials and technical secrets.[2]

Jarves' conviction that eastern (Third World) and western aesthetic canons were "antipodal" is an obvious prejudice that persists in art to this day. Cultures outside of the "dominant" discourse constitute(d) a useful resource for American/European artists, who appropriate its stylistic solutions for their own artistic purposes. In this respect, the threat of westernization of a culture such as Japan implied the loss of welcome stimulation where previous generations of artists had drawn inspiration. Contemporary art history is a fusion of cultural exploration or "exploitation." The African masks of Picasso's Les Desmoiselles d'Avignon to the influence of the Japanese Gutal-group on contemporary performance art underscores western modern art's unmitigated appropriation of diverse cultures.

As Asian American artists working within the confines of western art history and theory, we are in a double bind. On one hand, we are expected to reflect a cultural diversity based upon our ethnic heritage, and on the other hand "our" art history references our European based education. In other words, is it possible for us to create an authentic art which differentiates a non-western art inspiration from the cultural exploitation model inherent to modernism.

My consciousness of cultural activism began at Berkeley during the late sixties. "Third World" Asian studies were a prerequisite for a responsible non-white undergraduate. Although the curriculum was not as defined as say Poly-Sci 2, the excitement surrounding the emergence of a new power base was intoxicating. As an artist, I wrote short one-act plays about the Japanese American relocation camps, and attempted to infuse racial prejudice as the content of my assigned art exercises. However, as any student of art in America, I desired to find my artistic "roots" in the art history of Europe. I learned French and planned an extended trip to the center of my cultural history. Although I was not disappointed by the art treasures that I found, everything seemed extremely familiar and most European cities resembled museums. As a third generation Californian who had never set foot in Japan, I can remember my initial consternation concerning my physical appearance. I was identified as an Asian rather than as an American. I realized that my education was far from complete.

Tokyo in the early 70s was a teeming megalopolis on the brink of sophistication. Its fashions, buildings and people still retained a charm which could be described as provincial. The Japanese still looked to the West for its popular cultural cues, and the dollar was still worth more than 300 yen. At graduate school in Kunitachi (a suburb of Tokyo), I found vestiges of the Master/Disciple traditions and art "leagues" that resembled a pre-World War I France. At the time, I thought that most of Japan's contemporary art was "reactionary," and I felt sorry for the artists my age who longed for independence and authenticity. I gravitated to those artists who desired to project the "self" into their work and who lived in contradiction to the status quo. Those artists, who like myself, had bought into the western "modernist" myths. It had not been until very recently that I have been able to reevaluate my negative opinions towards contemporary art structures in Japan. I now realize that my prejudices predated my experiences in Japan.

Academic training in beauty is a sham. We have been deceived, but so well deceived that we can scarcely get back even a shadow of the truth. Art is not the application of a canon of beauty but what the instinct and brain can conceive beyond any canon. When we love a woman we don't start measuring her limbs. We love with our desires . . . although everything has been done to try and apply a canon even to love. . . . It's not what the artist does that counts, but what he is. Cézanne would never have interested me a bit if he had lived and thought like Jacques Emile Blanche (a French academic painter), even if the apple he painted had been ten times as beautiful. What forces our interest is Cézanne's anxiety—that's Cézanne's lesson; torments of Van Gogh—that is the actual drama of the man. The rest is a sham.[3]

Pablo Picasso, 1935

It was as if I were a young Picasso wandering through the narrow, dimly lit alleys of Tokyo searching for tormented anxiety-ridden artists who smoked "Peace" cigarettes until their fingers turned yellow, and who lived in paper-walled rooms the size of a shoebox. Looking at the past through deconstructed yen, I can now see the power of the romantic modernist myth. The artist-as-Bohemian-hero filled my youthful fantasies as I "floated" in a drunken stupor through the Asian demi-monde in search of artistic inspiration. By categorically rejecting the academic traditions of Japan as being "inauthentic," I became an unwitting disciple of a system which had systematically denied non-white artists into the pantheon of western art history. In retrospect, when I reflect upon the art (particularly the oil paintings) that I saw in Japan twenty years ago, I can clearly remember paintings that could be compared favorably to Anseim Kiefer or Susan Rothenberg.

I know now that it is necessary to reexamine modern art history in order to find models with which we may reinvent ourselves. By revising history we can repopulate the past with artists that may have already faced a similar dilemma.

Returning to the birthplace of Modernism, Paris of the 1920s, I have recently focused on the plight of a group of young Japanese painters who, much like Picasso and Braque, were drawn to the city "where all commonality had seemingly disappeared to be replaced by a barrage of conflicting artistic styles and philosophical obligations, some as political as aesthetic (a trademark of the Modernist movement)."[4] The atmosphere in Paris was one of cynical abhorrence of historical authority born amid the ravages and horrors of World War I.

In the summer of 1924 a friend took Saeki Yuzo to meet the painter Maurice de Vlaminck. Saeki and his friend expected words of encouragement for the young promising painter. Instead Saeki was met with prescient criticism. Vlaminck called the work academic (an attack at this particular juncture of art history). He told Saeki that he must abandon all styles he had been taught in the Master/Disciple academic tradition and find his own personal and authentic voice. Shocked by this challenge which seemed to nullify all that he had learned, Saeki abandoned his teachers and began to paint alone. He had attempted to pull everything from within himself and exhausted himself in the process. Since his move to Europe had already severed his ties with mainland Asia (the Chinese cultural orbit), and consequently much of his Japanese past, Saeki became obsessed with the void he now faced. To locate the self and to cast it up on the canvas, without any cultural supports (unlike western painters such as Vlaminck who were consciously and unconsciously reacting to two thousand years of traditional western art history) proved an effort that would eventually consume him.

In forming a portrait of an artist such as Saeki Yuzo, who had ironically been canonized in Japan as the "suffering" artist doomed to exist outside of all convention and success, one must deconstruct perhaps the most durable myth of modernism; the artist-as-Bohemian-hero. This search for self based in psychoanalytical theory and reflected in painting is still considered by the popular media (and by many contemporary artists) as the essence of the artist and his work . . . the symbol for the avant garde.

Sometimes it tempted me downright irresistible to appear as a "horror of the bourgeois," to express in words or action something which I know must have a strange, even repulsive effect on others . . . my outward being does not agree with my inner needs.

attributed to Egon Schiele

With the emergence of this avant garde context the disciple was forbidden to copy his master's work. What the disciple could copy was his master's attitude, his stance vis-a-vis his art and society. It was at this moment when the European academic traditions were crumbling and the "authentic" artist-as-Bohemian-hero came into being that the Japanese artists were relegated to second class status. They were accused of being "copyists" or worse, not authentic. This notion that non-European based contemporary art, particularly painting, is of secondary value persists to this day. It is ironic that many of the problems faced by Japanese artists of this period still plague us while some of their liabilities would today (albeit in a very convoluted way) be considered attributes of "success." The fact that they "copied" the work of western artists now considered masters could hardly be considered a liability in the context of today's art market and theory. (In Japan they did the copying from the only references at hand, photographs!) And their very position as artists working from a cross-cultural perspective without a strict historical base, in effect creating an ahistorical art with free-flowing art references (at least in traditional Western terms) makes them sound very contemporary indeed.

The parallels between Saeki's ahistorical position and my dilemma as a contemporary American artist of non-European descent gives me inspiration to try and revise a chapter of modern art history. Now that Modernism has been devalued, I want to help revalue the work of these Japanese artists and their pioneering confrontation with the provincialism of western art and more to the point, the provincialism of the modernist sensibility and its myths. I believe that just as post modernism has revised the "content" of art from that of "attitude" to one of cultural representation or ownership, the "cultural activism" of the 1990s can revise contemporary art history to include diverse non-white artists who have been heretofore systematically excluded by a singular ethnocentric view of the past.

NOTES
1. James Jackson Jarves, *The Art Idea* (1864; Cambridge: Harvard University Press, 1960) 166-167.
2. James Jackson Jarves, *A Glimpse of the Art of Japan* (1876; reprinted Rutland, Vermont: Tuttle, 1984), 184.
3. Herschel B. Chipp, *Theories of Modern Art* (Berkeley: University of California Press, 1970), 172.
4. Shuji Takashina, J. Thomas Rimer, with Gerald D. Bolas, *Paris in Japanese Encounter with European Painting* (St. Louis; Washington University; Tokyo: Japan Foundation, 1987), 65.

THE MAKING OF HALMANI

Kyung-Ja Lee

When I submitted the half hour script of *Halmani* (1988) to the American Film Institute graduate thesis program, the story was convoluted because it tried to deal with too many issues; interracial marriage, coming of age, bicultural conflict and the struggle of new immigrants. It was important for me to realize, particularly as a first time filmmaker, that the simpler story would have more depth. The original inspiration came from the idea of looking at three generations of women in the new world: the mother, who is absolutely tradition bound; the daughter, who adapts to the new world; and the granddaughter, who is the new generation. For the main focus of the film, however, I decided to examine the two most conflicting characters. Subsequently, the story of the grandmother and the granddaughter emerged as the central theme of the film uniting the two characters through love and understanding despite their language barrier. It was a breakthrough when the idea of using the Korean vase was chosen for the key element to accomplish this premise. Although I was concerned about its obvious foreshadowing effect, the overall impact to the storyline seemed to fit naturally. I went with what felt right rather than pondering and worrying over logical reasonings. In fact, this trusting one's own judgement was earned as a result of numerous mistakes I made throughout the filming of *Halmani*.

The endless journey of compromise was evident every step of the way especially when I realized the fact that the film would not be the same way I had originally imagined and the script was just a mere guideline for the filmmaking. I had to continuously reshape the film as the location was found and the actors were chosen. I had to become willing to redefine the personality of the film through these changes. I remember standing in the middle of the desert facing the difficulty of setting up the shots under the harsh light conditions and the constant gusts of wind; the romance of the desert landscape quickly went out the window. It literally became a matter of survival as the crew held down the bouncing light canvas before it sailed off. Every night I struggled with insomnia, utter physical exhaustion, and the fear of losing a grip on the film. To add to my sleepless nights, childhood traumas like getting beaten up started to creep into my already troubled psyche. During production, however, I learned the importance of the script development process which guided me in keeping to the vision of the film.

It was a constant struggle to keep up the morale of the crew members and the actors when I felt like drowning in the middle of the ocean myself. During times like this it is natural to ask questions like, "Who am I?" or "Is this what I really want to do with my life?" Amazingly, however, you feel the answers to all those questions could only be found by doing it again. And this time you tell yourself that you would do it better. Whatever that means. . . .

INVESTING IN

INVESTING IN POSITIVE IMAGES

POSITIVE IMAGES

Peter Wang

PETER WANG

Any filmmaker attempting to make narrative movies for commercial release faces daily challenges and difficulties. On top of these regular problems, I find that as an Asian American filmmaker my greatest challenge is to convince my fellow Asian Americans that there is a serious need for positive images of us to reach the mass media. We have been misrepresented by the media for years, and based on my experience in the industry I feel it will be quite a while before we regularly see less derogatory portrayals of Asian Americans on T.V. or in films.

I have met with much difficulty in my attempts to raise money for my films from Asian American businessmen and other qualified investors. Most of them do not consider an investment in positive images to be worthwhile; they are far more concerned with financial gain. For instance, a few years ago I spoke to a group of doctors in California about how a film of mine would counterattack the negative stereotypes of Asian Americans found in the media. They chose instead to invest $250,000 in a hamburger joint. In another instance, a group of wealthy Asian Americans interested in investing in films considered giving me backing but chose instead to put their $600,000 towards the production of a bloody, non-Asian, made-for-video action picture produced by a dubious ex-Hollywood producer. I am sure both groups made a handsome return on their investments. Sadly, most Asian Americans either aren't aware of the way they are stereotyped by the media, or they do not care enough to change this situation. For this reason, I believe we'll continue to see less than favorable portrayals of Asian Americans for a long time to come. I can only hope that the next generation will realize what a problem this is and fight for change.

Routes of Passage

103

ASIAN AND ASIAN AMERICAN CINEMA: SEPARATED BY A COMMON LANGUAGE?

ASIAN CINEMA AND ASIAN AMERICAN CINEMA: SEPARATED BY A COMMON LANGUAGE?

Luis H. Francia

In film festivals, the exhibition of both Asian and Asian American works implies a commonality and inherent discourse between the two cinemas. This is not usually true; significant differences become readily apparent once the juxtaposition is examined. To begin with, it would be a mistake to talk of Asian cinema as a homogeneous entity—different national cinemas are involved after all—just as it would be a mistake to describe European cinema in undifferentiated terms. And so to discuss Asian American cinema in relation to Asian cinema (and vice versa) in the absence of the proper context can only be misleading. My brief comments here are meant to provide a tentative context for discussion.

Each cinema has its own distinctive characteristics, based on language, racial, and ethnic traditions. While most Asian American films utilize English, for example, a film from Asia will use one or more languages and dialects. There are also differences relating to history. Asian histories have been shaped by a variety of forces, such as colonialism (the Philippines and Hong Kong, for instance) and have overlapped (Pakistan and India, China, Korea and Japan). And such histories are of course reflected in their films. In terms of filmmaking by Asian Americans (or other people of color considered minorities in the United States), the dynamic of history has been crucial, determining their focus and format. This historical dynamic accounts for a major difference between Asian and Asian American cinemas.

Once Asian groups emigrated to the United States, wildly different as they were, they shared a common history once they shared a common land. Looked upon by a xenophobic white society as "barbarians at the gate," they settled here in the face of discrimination, bigotry and physical assaults. Especially after the Second World War, they faced—and continue to face— mounting pressures to assimilate and obliterate their own Asian identities and histories.

Not surprisingly, since the late 1960s, the abiding concern of Asian American filmmakers has been to reclaim their own history and humanity from racist depersonalization and isolation imposed by cultural, social and political chauvinism. Its origins fueled by the civil-rights movement and the Vietnam War, Asian American cinema over the past two decades has developed mainly as a Cinema of Opposition and Criticism, a way of sounding an effective counterpoint to the powerful drone of assimilation.

This oppositional and critical approach—reflecting an emphasis on self-definition and empowerment—has meant a preference for the documentary. The documentary thus becomes an alter ego to the filmmaker's "I," probing for the parameters of what it means to be Asian American. It also becomes a way of subverting official history, to include the points of view that have been allowed to slip through the cracks. As I once wrote for a program on Chinatown which I curated for the Whitney Museum of American Art, "In Asian American cinema the documentary has become the logical antithesis to the . . . mainstream view of Asian American culture and history."

Let me just cite three examples. In Loni Ding's *Nisei Soldier: Standard Bearer of an Exiled People* (1984), forgotten history is revived when we learn of the bravery of Japanese American soldiers during World War II, fighters whose families were interned in concentration camps by a paranoid, racist U.S. government. In Curtis Choy's *The Fall of the I Hotel* (1983), we witness the valiant but futile stand of a San Francisco community against the demolition of the legendary International Hotel, home to hundreds of Filipino old-timers. And the fatal consequences of mistaken identity (tied into the stereotypical notion that all Asians are alike) are brought home dramatically by Chris Choy and Renee Tajima's provocative *Who Killed Vincent Chin?* (1989).

These and other Asian American works question white officialdom's views. As a result, definitions blur. Kavery Dutta, a Calcutta-born documentary filmmaker who has lived in the United States since she was six years old, points out that "there's always a battle over boundaries, over who we are, and what exactly is the mainstream." Interestingly, Dutta's two documentaries, *First Look* (1983), about Cuban artists visiting the U.S., and *One Hand Don't Clap* (1989), on the calypso music of the Caribbean, have nothing to do with overtly Asian American concerns. Dutta is one of the few Asian American documentarists to explore other issues.

Even in Asian American feature films, questions of cultural and personal identity loom large. Bill Gee, writing in *CineVue*, notes that non-documentary Asian American films exhibit a "bias toward the sociological," and that "In Asian American fiction filmmaking today, the primary impulse appears still a pedagogical one, aiming to be instructive of Asian American life, rather than to be descriptive of it." Often the development of the theme is set against the conflicts that ensue when the traditions of two societies impinge upon an individual's life.

Such conflicts are evident in Wayne Wang's *Dim Sum* (1985), where the tradition-minded Chinese mother wants her American-born daughter to marry before the mother passes away, and in *Eat A Bowl of Tea* (1988), where the marriage of a young couple is looked upon as a symbol of regeneration by the aging, womanless bachelor society of New York's hermetic Chinatown. But it is in his 1989 film *Life Is Cheap*, in my view his strongest work to date, where Wang turns the whole premise of identity upside down. The film unfolds in Hong Kong (Wang's original home turf), a locale where nothing and no one is who he or she appears to be, and where, even as the cowboy-like Asian American protagonist ponders on his identity, the other characters seem to have multiple personas, and the identity of Hong Kong itself becomes an object of scrutiny in the light of 1997.

Wang's film comments indirectly on the dilemma of the Hong Kong-born artist—one roughly analogous to that of an Asian American counter-part who struggles with two loyalties. There will be those who will find this argument specious, pointing out that a Hong Kong-er is still Chinese. But this is true only if we consider the matter strictly from a *racial* perspective. But from the point of view of *culture* things shift radically. Hong Kong culture is different enough from that of the mainland for there to be both opposition and discourse. Several Hong Kong films have dealt with this ambivalent relationship with the mainland. Yim Ho's *Homecoming* (1984) and Ann Hui's *Boat People* (1982), for instance, deal with the complex question of reunification, albeit in very different ways.

In contrast, of course, Asian filmmakers by and large take questions of cultural identity for granted. Put another way, unlike Asian Americans who are a minority in the United States, Asian filmmakers belong to the majority culture. The absence of this particular burden gives Asian filmmakers greater latitude. This may explain why Asian filmmakers show much more interest in the feature format than in the documentary. And, unlike the usually independently-produced Asian American features, Asian features for the most part are studio produced. Fifth-generation filmmakers of the People's Republic of China—such as Chen Kaige and Zhang Yimou—or South Korea's Im Kwon Taek and the Philippines' Lino Brocka: all are auteurs who have worked mainly within the studio system. While shown at festivals throughout the world, these directors' films have also been commercially screened—something unknown for most Asian American features.

Because Asian directors work mainly with studios (though this is no longer true for Chen who, because of the Tiananmen massacre, has opted to stay in New York), funding and distribution aren't as difficult as they are for Asian American directors. Anyone involved in the funding game will tell you that it's much easier to raise money for a documentary than for feature films. On the other hand, the facts of studio sponsorship and commercial distribution exert more pressure on Asian filmmakers to turn a profit. Which in turn means more layers of control over the final product, and often unsubtle pressure to have some entertainment value in the final cut.

In contrast, the expectation that Asian American films, feature or otherwise, will generate profit is virtually nil, since they rely for the most part on grants from public and corporate agencies. One almost expects them to lose money—an irony given that they operate in the world's largest capitalist society. But a closer look reveals that the mechanisms for promotion, distribution, and dissemination of Asian American independent films and those by other peoples of color are extremely limited.

Two decades after Asian American filmmakers began making their presence felt, we see a more diverse artistic field, with experimental, narrative and animation films—and videotapes—competing for our attention. With a collective Asian Pacific American identity solidly established, the need to assert ethnicity is not as compelling as it once was.

Of course historical processes do not begin or end neatly. And so ethnicity will remain an essential element, even if only in the perception of the American public. Paradoxically, as Asian American filmmaking broadens its horizons and speaks in a confident voice, it may come to resemble Asian cinema in precisely those areas in which they now differ.

Yet in this age of *perestroika* and *glasnost*, with the rise of ethnic and nationalistic movements worldwide—in the Baltic states, Central America,

Routes of Passage

105

ASIAN AND ASIAN AMERICAN CINEMA: SEPARATED BY A COMMON LANGUAGE?

Armenia, Tibet, Southeast Asia, to name a few areas—and the dramatic changes in Eastern Europe; and with global revulsion felt for the Chinese leadership in the wake of Tiananmen Square, there seems to be a marked shift from a stress on the collective to that of individual rights. It's entirely probable that a parallel shift will occur—is no doubt already occurring—in many Asian cinemas, where film becomes instrumental in reasserting and redefining once-submerged ethnic identities.

Abridged and modified from an article originally published in *Cinemaya*, no. 8.

don't let them fool you
the story always
starts the same
we become the discovered
    people even though
we were already there
but there are no snake dancing
    igorots
casting coins reading ashes
in isabella
in isabella
where guns grow on trees
bullets the stillborn fruit
ating tao
harvest in the dark

E M I L Y A   C A C H A P E R O

"miss philippine islands at the miss universe contest"

Liwanag, 1975

THE REEL HAWAII
DIANE MEI LIN MARK

Fade in. Coconut trees in a moonlit grove sway gently in the balmy tropical breeze. The soothing melody of an Island love song rises off the strings of a steel guitar. Waves roll quietly to shore, crashing white upon the beach. The camera zooms in on a man and a woman in a passionate embrace. Cut! Print! (and print, and print, and print. . . .)

Sound familiar? Movies and television programs made in and about Hawaii and the Pacific Islands have recycled this and other familiar scenarios for the greater part of this century. The exotic scenery and romantic Island Paradise stories sell movies, gain sponsors, and boost the tourist dollars that many Island economies depend upon. Hollywood has been so successful in promoting certain images of the Pacific Islands, however, that it has been difficult for other stories, real Island stories, to find a place in the market.

Those who understand Asian American, Black, Hispanic, or other stereotyping know of the great power the media wields in the shaping of public attitudes toward people and places. Fu Manchu, the Dragon Lady, and Suzy Wong have nothing over the Hollywood portrayals of Polynesian chiefs, warriors, and hula maidens. Often the stock images overlap. The Charlie Chan character was a detective with the Honolulu Police Department, and several Charlie Chan films were set in Hawaii.

Hawaii Goes Hollywood

Historically, those who have had the tools of filmmaking in hand have naturally controlled the images created. In the Pacific, those people have until recent times been primarily outsiders looking in. In his book *Hawai'i in the Movies: 1898-1959* (Hawaiian Historical Society, 1988), Hawaii's state statistician Robert C. Schmitt reports that the first films about Hawaii, shot in May 1898 by two of Thomas Edison's photographers, were *Honolulu Street Scene*, *Kanakas Diving For Money*, and *Wharf Scene*.

In time Hawaii became a popular locale for Hollywood movies. The first were probably *Hawaiian Love* and *The Shark God*, shot in 1913. These first movies were replete with the exotic setting, nubile native maidens, *kahunas* (priests), *haole* (foreigner, Caucasian) interlopers, and white man–native woman love plots that were to be tapped as a successful formula in the decades to come. Schmitt's analysis of one hundred twenty movies made about Hawaii pre-1960 revealed several stock themes repeating themselves:

MABALOT FAMILY PORTRAIT
Mabalot Family collection

the South Sea romances, travelogues, crime thrillers, undersea adventures, and military hero tales. Emerging from the *hoi polloi* (of average to below-average movies) were but a few films of critical acclaim. They included *From Here to Eternity* (1953), *Mister Roberts* (1955), *South Pacific* (1958), and *The Caine Mutiny* (1954).

With the Westward Ho movement played out across the nation to the shores of California, Americans seemed fascinated with the possibilities for adventure in the vast Pacific. Hawaii, annexed to the United States in 1898 after foreign overthrow of the Hawaiian monarchy, was the most accessible to American filmmakers. In addition to being an American territory (and a state by 1959), it had great weather, beautiful stretches of beaches and palm trees, dramatic waterfalls, lush green valleys, fiery volcanoes, and a handsome, English-speaking local community. The tropical setting so fired the imagination of Hollywood moviemakers that when they couldn't shoot in Hawaii, they shot many Hawaii movies on California sets made up to look like the real thing.

Just as the locales were interchangeable, so were the actors. Although Hawaiians such as Duke Kahanamoku (the Olympic swimmer) and Hilo Hattie played supporting roles in numerous films, native Hawaiians usually served as background musicians, dancers, beach boys, and hotel help. Native Polynesian characters in starring roles were usually played by non-Polynesians. Actors and actresses who have donned "Hawaiian face" have included Sessue Hayakawa (Japanese), Dolores Del Rio (Mexican), Rita Moreno (Puerto Rican), Esther Williams (*haole* American), Agostino Borgato (Italian), Ray Mala (half-Eskimo), and even Maurice Schwartz (a Russian from the Yiddish Art Theatre!).

In the 1940s and 1950s Hollywood produced a host of war adventure and romance movies with Hawaiian settings—*Sands of Iwo Jima* (1949), *The Big Lift* (1950), *Operation Pacific* (1951), *The High and The Mighty* (1954), and others. In the postwar years, Hawaii continued as a popular setting for movies starring Elvis Presley, et al., surfing films, and an occasional historical saga like James Michener's *The Hawaiians* (1970). When *The Hawaiians* was released, I asked my then eighty-year-old Chinese grandmother, who had lived through that history, what she thought of the film. "That's Hollywood," she laughed.

Since the 1960s numerous episodic television shows have based themselves in Hawaii and have been translated for broadcast throughout the world. They have included "Hawaiian Eye," "Hawaii 5-0," "Magnum P.I.," "Jake and the Fatman," "Tour of Duty," and "Island Son." Their principal casts are invariably *haole* actors and actresses imported from Hollywood, though a few Asian American actors have also been cast in supporting roles. Storylines are often unrelated to the reality of the Islands. Characterizations of local people in most television programs follow the lines of Steve McGarrett's Hawaiian sidekick Kono ("Hawaii 5-0"), who seemed rarely scripted beyond "Okay, boss."

Every so often a glimmer of hope flickers on the horizon. Richard Chamberlain and the producers of the T.V. series "Island Son" expressed the desire to expose more of the Island culture through stories and characters. But how tenuous the flickering flame; cancellation of the "Island Son" series was announced after the show's initial season.

WAKE OF THE RED WITCH (1949)
Diane Mark collection

Elsewhere in the Pacific

Although space does not permit a detailed account of Western filmmaking in other parts of the vast Pacific, suffice to say that patterns have been similar when cameras have been aimed at other indigenous Pacific peoples. The reference here is primarily to dramatic work rather than documentaries. Our understanding of the lifestyles and cultures of the Pacific has been aided by early ethnographic film documentation accomplished by Alfred Haddon among the Torres Strait Islanders, Baldwin Spencer among the Australian aborigines, James McDonald among the Maoris of New Zealand, Frank Hurley among the Papua New Guineans, and others.

Robert Flaherty's *Moana of the South Seas* (1926; with sound, 1980) was unique in its attempt to weave accurate documentation of village life and custom into the storyline. In preparation for the film, Flaherty and his wife Francis lived in Samoa for twenty-one months in order to more realistically portray the Samoan experience.

But in most feature filmmaking, superficial knowledge of Pacific life as well as the success of such early hits as *The Hurricane* (U.S./Tahiti, 1937) led to repeated use of romantic South Sea Island images. To this day, mainstream moviemakers have continued to use these images out of laziness, timidity, lack of imagination, an unquestioning business acceptance of the tried-and-true "South Seas movie formula," and often all of the above.

Since Asian American activists began decrying stereotypes in the 1960s, Asian and Asian American characterizations have improved slightly, albeit in a one-step-forward, two-steps-back fashion. Although little in the way of organized reaction to Pacific Island stereotyping has been mounted, Pacific filmmakers are beginning to respond in another way—with their work. Because of the limited exposure to media technology and the lack of learning opportunities, local film and videomakers are few and far between. Exceptional countries in the Pacific region are Australia and the Philippines, where viable bodies of film work developed within recent decades. As filmmaking becomes a more familiar technology to other Pacific peoples, and as the video format makes production more affordable, works by and about the various Pacific Island communities will continue to increase.

Some contemporary Pacific Island films pointedly tell the unheard side of history. Contrary to popular belief, not all native peoples naively and peaceably handed their land over to the European settlers/traders. In Geoff Murphy's *Utu* (1983), the Maori warrior spirit is boldly personified in protagonist Te Wheke, guerrilla leader in the New Zealand Land Wars of the 1860s. *Ngati* (1987) is a 1940s story of a young Australian's visit to a Maori town that becomes embroiled in an economic crisis. The community's response leads to a turning point in the Australian's life. *Ngati* was the first feature film written and directed by Maoris, Tama Poata and Barry Barclay, respectively. Barclay was also director of the ground-breaking documentary series "*Tangata Whenua*," or "the people of this place." Merata Mita has directed political documentaries such as *Bastion Point* and *Patu!*, which hold the magnifying glass to race relations in New Zealand, and *Mauri*, a poignant drama that illustrates the complexities of contemporary Maori life. Leon Narbey's 1988 drama *Dreams of Home* (formerly titled *Illustrious Energy*) tells the story of a Chinese miner and his son-in-law as they search for gold in turn-of-the-century New Zealand.

The 1970s and 80s also brought more sensitive documentary portrayals

VAITAFE (1981)
Visual Communications

of Pacific Island experiences. The Australian film *Angels of War* (1982) by Andrew Pike, Hank Nelson, and Gavin Daws, used interviews, archival footage, art work, songs, and poetry to tell the story of the World War II campaign in which one million Americans, three hundred thousand Japanese, and five hundred thousand Australians turned Papua New Guinea into a mass battleground. Films such as *Land Divers of Melanesia* (1973), *Mary Pritchard* (1971), and *Bark Belt* (1988), are valuable recordings of aesthetic and religious traditions.

Nothing to Do, Nowhere to Go (1977) examines youth problems in Moen, Truk. A *Nuclear Free and Independent Pacific* (1983) juxtaposes the beauty of Vanuatu with scenes from a conference on nuclear disarmament and a demonstration at the island's French consulate. *South Pacific: The End of Eden?* (1978) records James Michener's return to the South Pacific of his writings and examines the impact of Western industrialization on the native cultures of such places as Tahiti, Easter Island, Pitcairn, New Guinea, Bora Bora, New Hebrides, Guadalcanal, and Eniwetok. In her 1984 documentary, *Liberation 40*, Annette Donner portrays the hard changes in Chamorro life brought about by the World War II Japanese occupation of Guam.

Other films have explored foreign impact on traditional lifestyles. *Trobriand Cricket: An Ingenious Response to Colonialism* by Jerry W. Leach and Gary Kildea (1973) looks at the unique transformation of the missionary-introduced British cricket game into a Trobriand sport laden with political, sexual, and ritualistic connotations. Directed by Australian Dennis O'Rourke, *Cannibal Tours* (1987) records the wide-ranging reactions that tourists have to villagers, and vice versa, in the Sepik River region of Papua New Guinea. An earlier, important work by O'Rourke, *Half Life: A Parable for the Nuclear Age* (1985), told the story of survivors of the March 1, 1954, hydrogen bomb experiment in the Marshall Islands, and concluded that the Americans used the 236 residents and twenty-eight U.S. servicemen as "guinea pigs."

In addition to reflecting upon the various degrees of Westernization within a given Pacific Island community, some films draw further impact from the drama of internal class struggle, or the tug between old and new ways. Filmmakers Robin Anderson and Bob Connolly spent eighteen months documenting the conflict between Joe Leahy, a wealthy coffee grower who has swung a good deal on Ganiga land in the Highlands of Papua New Guinea, and members of the impoverished Ganiga tribe, who want it back. The resulting film was *Joe Leahy's Neighbors*, which won the Grand Prix Cinema Du Reel at Paris in 1989. Several of these films were screened at "Moving Images of the Pacific," theme of the 14th Annual Pacific Island Studies Conference, held in November 1989 at the Honolulu Academy of Arts.

Contemporary Film and Video—Hawaii

Film and video expression of the Hawaii experience is on the increase, though those trained in the field are still few in number. Historically, few local people have had the opportunity to work in media production. Pioneering in the field was George Tahara, who dramatized Hawaiian and Pacific Island legends in films that were viewed by decades of school children in Hawaii.

With the Americanization of Hawaii in the twentieth century came the gradual erosion of traditional culture among various ethnic groups. This included the native Hawaiians, who had diminished in number due to foreign

LI'A: THE LEGACY OF A HAWAIIAN MAN (1988)
Boone Morrison

disease and other factors. There seemed to be little hope for perpetuation of the native culture—young people had little interest in learning the Hawaiian language, or dancing the hula, or playing the *meles* (songs). But by the 1960s, as the civil rights movement and other events led to renewed ethnic pride among people of color, an exciting Hawaiian cultural renaissance blossomed.

One of the leaders of that cultural renaissance, musician/composer Eddie Kamae of the Sons of Hawaii, in 1988 completed *Li'a: The Legacy of a Hawaiian Man*, a film tribute to mentor Sam Li'a (1881-1975). Known as the "songwriter of Waipio Valley," Li'a was a fiddler who composed music that celebrated the ethereal beauty and chronicled the life and times of the lush Big Island valley that was his home. Kamae collected material for the film over the course of eighteen years, and spent two years shooting, with wife Myrna Kamae as producer. The film imparts a deep sense of the traditional Hawaiian balance between the people, their music, and the land. It has the important (and unfortunately rare) touch of a filmmaker who has taken the time to truly understand his subject.

In the 1980s a substantial body of video work on Hawaiian life was produced locally. Educational Television (ETV), production arm of the State Department of Education, produced numerous Hawaiian Studies television programs for school children. The *"Na Ki'i Hana No'eau Hawai'i"* and *"'Olelo"* series teach cultural tradition, values, and language through dramatization, puppetry, animation, and Hawaiian titling. Joan Lander and Puhipau of the independent production team Na Maka o ka 'Aina ("The Eyes of the Land") have focused their lenses on current political and cultural movements in the Hawaiian Islands. Their numerous productions on developer—resident land struggles, Hawaiian nationalism, and preservation of native culture and the arts have included *The Sand Island Story*, *The Kaho'olawe Experience: RIMPAC '82*, and *Faces of the Nation*, a multi-pronged argument for Hawaiian nationhood.

Network-affiliated television stations have produced weekly magazine format shows and occasional features on local subjects such as the thirtieth anniversary of Hawaii's statehood. "Island Music, Island Hearts," a KGMB summer series (1987), was a rare spotlight on the contemporary creators of Hawaiian music and comedy. The multi-cultural nature of Hawaii is reflected in production as well. Several television features were produced, for example, in commemoration of Hawaii's Chinese Bicentennial in 1989. They included "Sojourners and Settlers," produced by Joe Moore of KHON and "Sandalwood Mountains" and "Beyond the Great Wall," produced by Bob Jones of KGMB.

KHET, the local PBS affiliate, presents local slices of life in its weekly "Spectrum" program (executive producer, Holly Richards). The station also periodically premieres original dramatic features such as *Brothers Under the Skin* (1989), based on the 1938 Hilo Massacre, a jarring incident off the pages of Hawaii's union history. The program was written by Tremaine Tamayose and directed by Tamayose and Joy Chong, with Chris Conybeare as executive producer. Chong and Conybeare have teamed up on numerous other KHET productions, including the 1987 "Voyage of Rediscovery," documenting the journey of the *Hokule'a*, a reconstructed double-hulled canoe that retraced the sea journey of ancient Polynesians en route to Hawaii.

Other recent productions on the Hawaiian experience include *Enduring Pride* by Heather Guigni and Esther Figueroa; *Reflections of Lana'i* by Esther

Figueroa; *Hawaiian* by Lynne Waters and Roland Yamamoto; *Hawaiian Soul* by Victoria Keith and Naomi Sodetani; *Hawaiian Rainbow* and "*Kumu Hula*: Keepers of the Culture" by Robert Mugge.

Putting the Tools in Place

Though corporate Hawaii is still a hard sell for filmmakers seeking funding, the state government has been supportive. With cheaper labor sources in other parts of the Pacific and Asia, Hawaii's sugar and pineapple companies are moving shops elsewhere. In its search for diversified and non-polluting new industries, Governor John Waihee continues to push development of a film industry.

The Robert Mugge and Eddie Kamae productions received monies from the Hawaii state legislature, which continues each session to hear legislation detailing funding for upcoming films. The Legislature also allocated $242,000 over a two-year period (1986-87) for film preservation, initiating a statewide film and video archive project. In 1989 the legislature approved major funding of $250,000 for the Hawaii International Film Festival, which has served as a premier showcase for new Pacific Island film work. In 1990, the legislature funded Stephanie Castillo's *Father Damien of Molokai: Simple Courage for the Age of AIDS*, a documentary in which Father Damien's historic, courageous work among the Kalaupapa lepers is paralleled with the efforts of those who work with AIDs patients today.

Georgette Deemer, manager of the film industry branch of the State Department of Business and Economic Development, reported in January 1990 that revenues from Hawaii's film industry in 1989 were on an upswing, totalling more than $60 million. This represented a 150 percent increase over 1988, a year plagued by writers' and teamsters' strikes and the loss of "Magnum P.I." and "Tour of Duty." By mid-1990, however, the high cost of shooting in Hawaii had discouraged other episodic television producers from basing themselves in Hawaii, and attracting the industry remained a challenge for the state.

Development of the film industry in Hawaii has not been without controversy. There are those who feel that government should be less involved in subsidizing the industry. There are others who oppose the state's plans to enlarge the Diamond Head film studio, claiming that it would cater to Hollywood producers at the expense of neighborhood considerations.

What effect does the state's courting of production dollars from Hollywood, Japan, and elsewhere have on local producers, directors, cinematographers, writers, and technical personnel? Most out-of-town producers bring key personnel with them, so local hires have generally been restricted to support personnel (union drivers, production assistants, etc.). Occasionally professional connections are made, leading to work for local filmmakers and videomakers, but this is not a common occurrence. The overall build-up of the Hawaii film industry has some beneficial effect, however, for more technical support services are available and support groups like the Hawaii Film and Video Association have been formed. Education and training programs are gradually being put into place as well. The University of Hawaii offers continuing education courses in filmmaking and an annual Film and Video Summer Institute. It will hopefully be only a matter of time before the university initiates a year-round program curriculum in film and television so that local students can gain the background necessary for work in the field. Pre-

KUMU HULA: KEEPERS OF A CULTURE (1989)
Robert Mugge

viously, young people interested in studying film have had to enroll at colleges on the U.S. mainland.

Futurists have predicted that the next century will bring the locus of world history to the Pacific Basin. Films by and about Pacific Island peoples will document stories from their perspectives and preserve the soul of tradition and history in the midst of rapid regional changes. *IMUA* (go forward), filmmakers of the Pacific! For there is much about Pacific living—whether it be in Hawaii, Guam, Truk, Ponape, Bikini, Samoa, Tahiti, New Zealand, Australia, the Philippines, or on the hundreds of islands beyond—that the rest of the world can learn from.

REFERENCES

"Moving Images of the Pacific," 14th Annual Pacific Islands Studies Conference, Nov. 1-4, 1989, Honolulu, program notes. "Guide to Films About the Pacific," Pacific Island Studies Program, University of Hawaii, 1985. Hawaii International Film Festival program guides, 1986-1989. Author's interviews.

118

Though talented, how can we
put on wings and fly past the
barbarians?

CANTONESE POET, ANONYMOUS

Songs of Gold Mountain: Cantonese Rhymes from

San Francisco Chinatown 1911-1915

P671·133

FOR THE ASIAN

FOR THE ASIAN AMERICAN, AFRO-AMERICAN, NATIVE AMERICAN AND MEXICAN AMERICAN FILMMAKERS AND THEIR FRIENDS

Carlton Moss

A story is impelled by the necessity to reveal; the aim of the story is revelation, which means that a story can have nothing—at least not deliberately—to hide. This also means that a story resolves nothing. The resolution of a story must occur in us, with what we make of the questions, with which the story leaves us.

James Baldwin, Afro-American novelist and essayist

Most people will tell you that motion pictures are make-believe. Further, they will explain that films break the rules of drama and create productions to provide you with escape, beautiful people in fine clothes, riding in fancy automobiles, and sleeping in first-class houses and condominiums. This is the style of the popular film, although occasionally a movie appears that for the most part reflects life the way it is.

However, in portraying the Asian American, Native American, Afro-American, and Mexican American, it seems there is always something missing. Or, to borrow from the novelist James Baldwin, "something is deliberately hidden." Each of these ethnic groups have the same width, height and depth as all other humans. Yet, the normal dimensions are missing in their film portrayals. This may be explained by looking at the early history of motion picture making. The first producers formed a code which said, among other things, the picture makers would not make a story that encourages whites to marry into any of the colored ethnic groups. However, the rule was broken when D.W. Griffith opened his film *The Birth of a Nation* (1915) with (over a film shot of black people) "The Bringing of These People to America Sowed the Seeds of Disunity."

This title was followed with a series of incidents to show that the emancipated ex-slaves had one fundamental drive, and that was to possess a white woman. D.W. Griffith was so skilled in the presentation of his characters, and his technique was so new and startling, that the dominant audience was frightened into responding to the film's thesis that the Africans should be put back into slavery. The picture became the industry's first blockbuster. To understand the significance of D.W. Griffith's message, it

ANNA MAY WONG
Yoshio Kishi Collection

is necessary to go back to the time period referred to in the opening title of *The Birth of a Nation*.

The Africans were brought to the New World by the English invaders, who were fast making this their land. Unable to bring working people from their homeland, they made an attempt to enlist the indigenous people to do their work. When the natives objected, for inspirational and cultural reasons, the English invaders used force against the reluctant, uncontrollable workers.

Before long, a body of language evolved that described the natives as savages. The common slogan throughout the community was "The only good Indian is a dead Indian." As the native population was pushed aside, captured Africans were shipped in to replace them. The Africans, stripped of their language and immediate family ties, were subdued by ball and chain and forced into a tightly organized system of slave labor and slave breeding. This system, in time, propelled the rise of the cotton kingdom.

Now there were those who saw a contradiction between what the New World was saying about liberty and the treatment of the Africans. To this group should be added the white working man who saw a threat to his wages as long as men were working for nothing. Neither were the Africans passive. Their acts of sabotage, attempts at running away, and logistically laid out insurrections were a problem to the plantation owners, not only in military output but frightening to the plantation lifestyle.

Meanwhile, not all colonists were supporters of slavery, but the power of authority was in the hands of the slave owners, the shipping merchants, and their manufacturing friends. These "gentlemen" provided the educational and cultural information for the total population. They believed that God had divided His children into colors: to the whites he gave superior intelligence, and to the coloreds He gave inferior intelligence. It was their responsibility to lead the non-whites into civilization. It might be noted that long after the Chinese had demonstrated their advanced civilization, George Washington was shocked to learn that the Chinese were not white.

As the cotton kingdom continued its rise, the cotton planters and their allies extended their influence in the direction of the country. At the Constitutional Convention, they designed an apparatus to solve the African/Native American question; the Africans were to be counted as three-fifths of a man—thus, no vote. They (the Africans) won their citizenship two hundred fifty years after they arrived. The Native Americans were awarded their citizenship in 1924.

The colored people in America were not the only targets of the profit seekers. As the cotton kingdom pushed the nation into the trade world, the American businessmen looked toward the remaining part of the undeveloped world. With their rough warning, the Westerners also brought their home-grown attitude toward colored people and applied it to the Japanese. In semi-official language, word was spread throughout the world—the Pacific Coast is our own racial frontier; we are of European heritage with a bloodline to the Anglo-Saxon stock responsible for the progress of modern civilization.

For a short time, Asians were admitted to the U.S. without government obstacles. However, when the planters and railroad builders saw a source of cheap labor in Asia, this immediately put the Asians in the same despised work category held by the Afro-Americans. The hostility against the Asians was compounded by the size of their work population. The Anglo-Saxons soon spread stories which said an invasion of yellow people was imminent; they were on their way to take over white America. As their fear became everyday thought and permeated the language in the country, laws were passed that excluded Asians. The Chinese, beginning in 1882, were not normally admitted until 1943. The Japanese were restricted by alien land laws and very special procedures for the admission of Japanese women. With this legislation, the Asians found themselves second-class citizens. In school, they were discriminated against. In housing, they were restricted. In social life, they were outcasts.

In 1850, William Walker, the gray-eyed man of destiny, struck several times in Latin America. For a time, he took Nicaragua and proposed to extend slavery there. During the same time period, John Quitman, governor of Mississippi, was indicted for encouraging a pro-slavery invasion in Cuba.

Meanwhile, the neighbors bordering the U.S. became the prize of the slaveholders who dreamed of obtaining that land for the expansion of slavery. Although they did not gain full control, they did receive an enormous piece of that state. The peace agreement put the victors in a position wherein it was possible to assign the losers the second-class status held by the Blacks and the yellows in the melting pot.

As the motion picture business moved into nationwide distribution, the place of the Blacks, browns, and yellows in what was called a "free, white and twenty-one" country was visibly defined. D.W. Griffith (himself the son of a defeated Confederate army officer), a pioneer master of filmmaking, created in *Birth of a Nation* not only the first full feature-length film in the U.S., but in it also drew attention to film as a medium with great technical potential, photographic possibilities, and storytelling devices. It particularly demonstrated the special informational potential of the motion picture. Griffith was so skilled in projecting the slaveowners' position in the U.S. Civil War that when President Woodrow Wilson viewed the film, his enthusiastic reaction was, "It was like writing history with lightning." Griffith's message and selection of images made his film a model on the subject of interracial relations to the present.

On one hand, he presented the ethnic characters as docile, irresponsible and stupid; on the other, they had one obsession, and that was the desire to socialize—with emphasis on romance with white women. This, at the expense of all other human desires and ambitions. A few years later, D.W. Griffith applied this worship-of-white-skin obsession to a Chinese in *Broken Blossoms* (1919). Here, the Chinese man's infatuation was with a teenage Anglo child. The man, a Chinese scholar, went beyond surrogate father protection and involved himself in what was staged to indicate the colored man's obsession with the prize, i.e., the white female. Later, in Cecil B. DeMille's *The Cheat* (1915), an Asian man extends his obsession for the prized white lady in such a way that he places a branding iron on her bare back to illustrate his possession. On present-day television, there is a film dealing with the relationship between a white man and an Indian woman. Here the woman bypasses all of the men within her own culture and seeks out the man who is representative of her people's sworn enemy. The fact that they are in love is not the issue. What is troublesome is that the attraction is based on color and not on normal human identification. Consistent with the motion picture producers' conduct code, these lovers are not permitted to live; one of them must be eliminated. The great John Ford, reminiscing about *Stage Coach* (1939), said that in the film he moved the Indians in masses so that the audience couldn't get to like them. Chief George, in speaking about *Little Big Man* (1970), which featured Dustin Hoffman, said "The Anglos make pictures which show that they think *we* can't think." In *Sayonara* (1959), one couple married but ended up committing suicide to end the legitimacy of their marriage in order to uphold the motion picture code.

D.W. Griffith did not start the practice of using white performers with their faces painted to create an illusion of "race." This practice began with the American theater. In the early days of the American stage when the drama called for action by a black person, the director, in an attempt to avoid physical contact between white and black actors, removed the non-white player from the pool of white actors. Then the face of the white actor or actress was painted to create what was demanded by the script.

The first organized challenge to this human distortion and denial of opportunity to the non-white artist did not take place until 1970. In that year, Asian Americans picketed before a Los Angeles theater to protest the play, *Teahouse of the August Moon*, for not employing Asians in key roles. The unsuccessful finale of this demonstration set in motion a protest movement that only recently (1970-1990) made a positive impact on the national intellectual community.

The film also had its individual filmmakers who had the energy and commitment to see the film in the humanistic tradition that has pushed America towards a democracy to be enjoyed by all peoples. These values have appeared in such films as *Los Olvidados* (1950) Luis Bunuel/Mexican; *Man and Boy* (1972) Bill Cosby/Afro-American; *Blood and Sand* (1941) Rouben Mamoulian/Hispanic; *Who Killed Vincent Chin?* (1988) Christine Choy and Renee Tajima/Asian. To these may be added rare positive revelations of Native Americans in small parts in major films.

Since the initial shouts of praise for *Birth of a Nation*, the social and political power it influenced has been challenged by the world's movement of non-white people and their supporters. Now the times need the scholarship and community identification of the black, brown, and yellow people of the present generation. They must accept the responsibility of portraying the aspirations and conflicts in life as they are.

Perhaps a final word from James Baldwin is fitting:

The role of the artist is somewhat like a lover. If I love you, I have to make you conscious of things you don't see. No one wants to see more than he sees. You have to be driven to see what you see.

MANDARINS
IN HOLLYWOOD
CHARLES L. LEONG

My mother has always pointed to my crop of stubborn, black hair as being something permanent as the Great Wall of China. All together—mother, a $1.59 drug store hairbrush, and even myself had settled long ago, with fine Chinese courtesy and amenity, the fact that I had a crop of stubborn, black hair. I was quite proud of it.

Even as dynasties and Great Walls crumble, so I found one day, with mingled joy and sorrow, that the luxurious matting of crowning glory of which I had been so proud had to be shaven. Shaven bare as a locust-plagued rice field.

Speaking of locust-plagued rice fields—but then, that's another part of this tale of my loss of equilibrium, loss of my jet-black hair, my discovery that Hollywood is NOT Hollywood without its Chinamen who are laundrymen disguised as movie actors. And also the fact, ironically enough to me as a Chinese, that the first movie studio built in Southern California was next door to a Chinese laundry.

Zzzzzzzz—the buzz of the studio barber's cutter shaved my hair cleanly and completely. I sat gingerly in the chair, like a bridegroom brooding over the fatal step. Suddenly the old bait-tune joined the ZZZZzzzzzzzzzzzzzzzzzzzzz buzz . . . "ching-chong-chinaman, sitting on a rail . . . along came a white man and chop off his tail. . . ." The tune struck me as being very funny. Because this time the Chinaman had to be paid for having his tail fastened on. And very handsomely too, at the exchequeur of seven-fifty a day. Couple of more fast ZZzz's and I was initiated as another movie actor, a young farmer in Metro-Goldwyn-Mayer's production of *The Good Earth* (1937).

This was my bare-headed entry within the sacred portals of Movieland, the so-called sacred portals for which thousands would pay anything to pass. I paid with a crop of fine black hair.

What did I get in return? Strange truths more incredible than some newsreel stuff that is shot; confirmation that the Hollywood Chinese is a paradox, an oriental mosaic in the cinematic pattern created through no effort of its own, and yet a most vital part of the whole design; that in this land of movies and madness, cuties and quixotism, your chop-suey waiter of today may perform tomorrow on the screen as your favorite warlord; that an Irishman controls the Chinese actor's market; that the only Chinese temple I ran

CHARLES L. LEONG, (circa 1936)
Leong Family collection

across in Hollywood was Shirley Temple, when she spoke Mandarin in the picture *Stowaway* (1936); that where else and how else would I have a chance to play billiards with Gary Cooper?

This was Hollywood, I found out, the land where the best known Chinese happens to be a Swedish gentleman by the name of Mr. Warner Oland. This was Hollywood, the land of the 100% pure, unadulterated bona fide, *Homo Sapiens* of Mongolian stock who had to be taught how to tie a Chinese queue by an American makeup man. Do you blame me, then, for even expecting to see Harpo Marx play the immortal part of O-lan in *The Good Earth*? And so, as I trudged along to M-G-M's wardrobe department, I expected to get some Robert Ripley one-twos on the chin—believe some things whether I wanted to or not—and high adventure in Hollywood. I even secretly hoped that Ted Healy would get some Chinese stooges.

Mental left jab number one crossed me up as soon as I reached the wardrobe department. Hundreds of ragged, peasant-blue Chinese coolie and farmer robes hung on the wardrobe walls. Torn, worn coats and trousers with cavernous holes and mud. Filthy-looking rags. After being brought up on a bath-a-day regime, I couldn't quite stomach the idea of having to wear all this next to my skin.

The wardrobe girl asked my coat size.

"Thirty-six, please," I answered absently, as my eye checked off the varying blackness of dirt and mud on each costume on the racks. She evidently noticed my meticulous reluctance, as I looked at the terribly ragged coat and trousers given me.

"It's all right, bright boy," she smiled, "all this stuff is sterilized . . . a'matter, new at the game?"

Sterilized. So this was stark movie realism, with health certification on dirty farmer's clothing guaranteed by Hollywood's death-to-germs brigades. These hundreds of costumes after a hot, sweaty, dirty day at the studios— sterilized, and ready the next day. One almost expects them to be wrapped in cellophane.

New at the game? I was, and bewildered, in jumping fresh from a sedate college atmosphere to the crazy, whirling satellite called Hollywood. I certainly didn't learn in any "industrial trends" classes that dirt and filth-ridden costumes are sterilized every night. College geography didn't mention that Movieland is the ONLY place in the whole wide world where the Chinese population, men, women, and children, know what it means when the assistant director yells, "Quiet!" College geography gave no indication that the best replica of a Shanghai Bund is the result of skilled carpentry right inside the studio; that the best Tibetan scenes, outside of Tibet, such as in *Lost Horizon* (1937), are at the edge of the Mojave desert; that the most fertile Yangtze valley farm is located in a Los Angeles valley called Chatsworth.

After getting my wardrobe number punched on the "work check," I proceeded to the makeup department. We get a different "work check" from Central Casting every time. For you see, it's not EVERY day that your children of the glamour world work, or shall we say act? And so it's not every day either that they eat.

The check is one's open sesame. I get it at the casting office. It has my name; the costume I am to get—whether for the day I am to be a coolie, farmer, mandarin, vendor, or soldier. And most important, to me and to everybody else, the stipulation of the day's work—five dollars, seven-fifty, or ten dollars. It seems the cleaner the role the higher the paycheck.

Of course, for the farmer's roles in the *The Good Earth* for which I had to sacrifice my well-admired crop of hair, there were special agreements and reimbursements. I was guaranteed three months' work. Every morning to me was as exciting as an Irish Sweepstakes drawing. As soon as I get the precious work ticket, I know whether or not it affords that new book, tie, or flowers to the girl.

Even in the makeup department, my ticket is checked. All wigs are accounted for. And here, for the first, but not the last time in my life, I wore a queue. Artificial one, fastened and kept secure with an adhesive, but a queue nevertheless. The year was 1936, the scene a Hollywood studio, twenty-five years after the banishment of the old Manchu regime in China, and with it, the banishment of queue—and a bunch of young American Chinese, all of whom have never been to China, learning how to braid pigtails, just like their fathers did years and years ago.

Of course, we have our banal chatter as the makeup men adjust our pigtails. Just like a bunch of mannequins with nervous tongues. Well, Hollywood's higher-ups may have its Jack Oakies, vitriolic Dorothy Parkers, et cetera, who are noted for their bons mots. Hollywood's Chinese movie colony also have their ideas of what is called a "snappy comeback."

On that very first day, when the makeup men were dawdling over the pigtails, out of the clear I heard some Oriental Jack Benny cut with:

"Aw, go mind your own P's and Queues."

But then, maybe he didn't mean it that way at all. Just like some extras weren't meant to be sturdy Chinese farmers, after hard nights of bar life—and had to be tanned with studio make-up and grease paint to look like the real McCoy.

Check, costume, wig, makeup—this was the regular routine, when on the lucky days we worked. I say lucky, because once, for instance, we waited eight (eight, count them) days on an outdoor shot to be taken. Got up every morning at 5:30, dashed to the studio, and then coldly informed by the weatherman that "Sorry, that *particular* cloud effect for background did not appear." At least, we got breakfast and carfare money.

And so, on to the set assigned for the day—with heads high for art and hearts light for the seven and a half shekels.

Again, on the eventful and equilibrium-upsetting first day, another dose of irony. Old Tom Gubbins, the Irishman who controls the Chinese actors' market, and who speaks Cantonese as well, if not better, than the most hardened Grant Avenue chop-suey cook, is the Chinese headman on the movie sets. He is sometimes technical director, and all the time the Chinese "straw boss."

He is already a living legend. Born in China, and adventured to the States when a young man. Like many other Hollywood figures, he rose meteorically with the industry. From studio prop boy, he is now the "unofficial mayor of Chinatown." Gubbins owns a curio shop, supplies most of the Oriental props to movie sets, and is the contact man for Chinese players to all the major film factories. He thinks Chinese, talks Chinese, eats Chinese food all the time, and possesses one of the most effective and picturesque string of Celestial phrases which I have ever run across.

Gubbins' too-picturesque and lashing command of the Chinese tongue comes in good use throughout the regular routine of the studio play. We Chinese extras are no different than the American player. It's a routine of sitting around most of the time—and hoping the stars, directors, cameramen, and technical workers don't coordinate. Because the longer they stall the longer we work. And in sitting around, we have plenty of time to talk; to queen the prettiest girls on the set; to play skadunk, which is a short and expensive studio version of poker; and to wonder what it is all about.

In the midst of wondering what it is all about, we would be awakened by Gubbins' staccato Chinese commands. Or that of his assistants. It always makes me laugh. Imagine, hiring a bunch of Chinese interpreters to relay the director's English instructions. And every son of old Mother China speaks English. That's Hollywood.

But a studio lunch is not Hollywood. No sir, it's old China come alive. We jostle and push in line for the studio lunch when on location. I missed my first midday meal by being too polite in line. It never happened again.

Anyway, eating lunch, whether in the studio restaurant or on location, is just a prelude to the big show. After that is when the real eating comes. The more women working that day, the bigger the feast. We always make a rough count in the morning, and could figure on noonday Chinese delicacies of all sort.

Probably years ago some Mrs. Wong brought slices of rare Chinese roast duck to eat at the studio during the lunch hour. Many Chinese still eat nothing but Chinese food, you know. And a Mrs. Lee or Mrs. Sing, as women of all nationalities, would bring something better than Mrs. Wong's to eat and offer. And so this fine old Chinese custom is firmly established in the studios. We young extras love it.

It's a regular riot, like a colossal festive day in a Chinese village. To the ladies, studio work is pin money, and a fine social occasion to outdo the other in culinary skill and magnanimity. And relaxed, sitting around the sets, which are real enough, one actually lives and breathes China, thousands of miles across the ocean. We are all in costumes, of course. Fine ladies, stiff in rich brocades; pretty young girls, some in peasants' costumes, some in peacock-hued gowns, all passing around banana-flavored sweets, preserved gingers, spiced olives and prunes, cured duck's liver, and other delicacies to their favorite young swains.

My favorite was a sweet old matriarch, who had several daughters and grandchildren acting on the set. She was a Mrs. Leong, whom I discovered, through some connivance of genealogy, to be a distant cousin of mine. Here I was, a nice young man away from home—and you know the strong family ties of the Chinese. The good lady plied us, for the duration of *Good Earth*, when she worked, with roast duck, pork, chicken, and nice sweetmeats every noon. It was a gastronomical holiday for me.

Every noon hour was a holiday for everybody. Actually, mothers find this a chance, with the whole Los Angeles Chinatown colony moved to the sets on a big scene, to point out subtly the culinary and personable qualities of their daughters. Three or four Cantonese dialects fluidly fill the air with banal, joyful, and happy Chinese talk and laughter. The cackling old men, smoking on willow pipes, would secretly glow at the generous spreads of good food, and openly grumble "Huh, what food WE had when we were young men in the old country."

It was natural that the old folks reminisce, speaking of old times, friends, and things in faraway China. Somehow, these synthetic, plaster and frame

Luise Rainer, Paul Muni & Chingwah Lee in M-G-M's "The GOOD EARTH"

movie sets did something to them. Hollywood created a nostalgic mood for them.

I, and all the other young ones listen eagerly, absorbing of the China which we have not yet seen. Everyone is transplanted, through the animated magic carpet of "back home" food and talk, to the land of his love. Soundly and smack with realism, I was transplanted one day to a China of which I had never dreamed. It happened the first day on location.

The scene was a carefully copied version of a Chinese rice field. The replica of the now-famous farm for *The Good Earth* at Chatsworth had cost M-G-M thousands of dollars. It was authentic. Too authentic. Long, dark rows of fertile, hand-tilled soil; straw-thatched huts of the peasant farmers in the background. It was a most incongruous scene—there were sound apparatus, movie cameras on cranes, to follow the "shots." We had on coarse peasants' wear, with artificial queues coiled on our heads. The directors, sound and technical men, all wore the sartorial flash of Hollywood. The old, the new.

I was barefooted and hoeing a thin row of rice shoots. I felt the warmth of the soil. I was in China. And back of me, a camera followed my every action.

Twenty other young brown bodies gleamed in the California sun, tilling the rice fields. Glistening, actually working and covered with more sweat then clothing. Here we were, twenty young American-born Chinese, trying to simulate, to reenact, for the movies, a scene which was part of the national fiber of our forefathers. My mind was far from the usual prosaic things. Was this a dream, a fantasy, realism? Was this China or Hollywood?

"This, but for the grace of God," I thought, "I might actually be doing." Confucius made the classic allusion when he said that a picture is worth a thousand words. One picture was certainly worth more than that to me—fun, money, and a first-class, personally-guided Cook's tour of Movieland, with all the side shows thrown in for good measure. My routine in *The Good Earth*, with slight variations, was the same in all the other Chinese pictures.

I was lucky to crack the celluloid fortress in 1936, the biggest, and to borrow a Hollywoodian phrase, most "colossal" year for Chinese pictures in the history of the industry. Even a big silent opus, like Richard Barthelmess in *Broken Blossoms* (1919) was in comparison to a super such as *The Good Earth*, a subway ride against a cruise in a Dusenberg. I worked into supers, *The Good Earth* and *Lost Horizon*, and several class-mounted productions, like Shirley Temple's *Stowaway* and Gary Cooper's *The General Died at Dawn* (1936). Had a chance to play billiards with the elongated Mr. Cooper between sets in this film. And Mr. Cooper was a very good billiard player.

Half a dozen other film factory products also utilized my slight histrionic abilities. In one year, I worked in ten pictures. And every other permanent Chinese resident of Los Angeles and Hollywood has appeared before the camera.

During the past ten years, there have been about thirty-five productions, major and minor, utilizing Chinese players. Practically the same bit players and extras, at one time or another, have appeared in them all. No wonder the American gag claims that "All Chinese look alike." They are alike, and the same persons—in the movies, anyway.

All the year in Movieland, in and out of sets in a half dozen studios, I rubbed elbows, well, at least elbow distance, with all the big names and stars that furnish magazine and news material. From Mr. Robert Taylor at M-G-M to Kay Francis at Warner's. And never once did I run across the two biggest and most successful Sino stars of Hollywood—Anna May Wong, the actress, and James Wong Howe, the cameraman.

My Hollywood enthusiasm even ran to a little theatre movement. Years of sitting on gallery seats watching legitimates had developed in me a yen for little theatres. I figured that here, in the hotbed of acting, was the natural, the ideal spot. But my idea that a Chinaman will make a more authentic-looking Chinese actor than an Irishman was a flop, in spite of an affirmation from the old Irish trouper, Dudley Diggs.

"Me . . . trying to look like a Chinaman," grimaced Mr. Diggs. "Hmp."

He was playing an important part, "Mr. Wu" in *The General Died at Dawn*. It was a fat role, but like most fat roles, Occidentals take the Chinese parts, because the average Hollywoodian Chinese would dawdle over scotch-and-sodas, rather than sweat over lines. This was, I imagine, no more of a paradox than the Hollywood Chinese colony itself.

During my whole year in the flicker world, I felt like a Chinese Gulliver, who had accidently landed in a strange land, one whose inhabitants are so alike and yet so remotely different than myself. They are a people apart, molded of Asiatic clay to resemble the features of the fantastic molder, The Film Industry.

MODERNIZING WHITE PATRIARCHY: RE-VIEWING D.W. GRIFFITH'S *BROKEN BLOSSOMS*

JOHN KUO WEI TCHEN

All industries are brought under the control of [businessmen] by Capitalism. If the capitalists let themselves be seduced from their pursuit of profits to the enchantments of art, they would be bankrupt before they knew where they were. You cannot combine the pursuit of money with the pursuit of art.[1]

George Bernard Shaw, 1924

Don't you see that you produce communities by creating common feeling? What really counts in our action is feeling.[2]

Governor Woodrow Wilson, 1911

Broken Blossoms made its world premiere in New York City's George M. Cohan Theatre in 1919. Based on Thomas Burke's short story, "The Chink and the Child," the film depicts the tragic story of a sensitive "Yellow man," Richard Barthelmess, a tender wisp of a "Girl" played by Lillian Gish, and the Girl's depraved father, the boxer "Battlin' Burrows." All is set against the backdrop of London's exoticized Chinese settlement, known as the Limehouse district of the working class East End. The film influenced generations of international filmmakers, including Sergei Eisenstein, and it made a respectable profit for United Artists. Yet despite the superlatives associated with the film, it has received little scholarly comment.

Blossoms is indeed puzzling to read; inscrutable. First, it was produced during an era of anti-Chinese/Asian xenophobia. The "yellow peril" threat of dime novels, melodrama, pamphlets, and newspaper headlines was now enacted on film. Early portrayals of Chinese were either as dastardly villains as in *The Yellow Menace* (1916) or a childlike comic relief, such as the slapstick *Chinese Rubbernecks* (1903). *Blossoms* was neither. Critics to this day cite the film as "a sympathetic portrait of an alienated Chinese man in London, [and] contrasts a sensitive Chinese hero with a brutal, depraved Cockney antagonist."[3] Did Griffith present us with an anti-stereotypical film? Griffith himself is enigmatic. Had the staunch advocate of the Ku Klux Klan in *The Birth of a Nation* (1915) become anti-racist? These knotty paradoxes open fresh

BROKEN BLOSSOMS (1919)
Museum of Modern Art

speculation on the emerging mass culture of twentieth-century American society. This essay is an attempt to review *Broken Blossoms* both in the context of its release in 1919, and in terms of the era in which it was fashioned.

The Film

Thomas Burke was a popular chronicler of what was considered the seamy side of London life. In his prose, working-class folks and slum dwellers were "sinister intriguers" given to brutish "vendettas" and "murder schemes."[4] He followed in the Mayhew/Dickens narrative tradition of exploring the lives of street characters, but with none of their humanistic convictions. Burke was a professional tourist or "slummer" who made a comfortable living writing about sections of London his genteel, bourgeois readers would dain to visit. In 1916, he published *Limehouse Nights*, a volume of short stories sensationalizing London's small Chinese quarter.

Nights is more journalistic and more concerned with interpersonal dynamics than the tales of the sadistic megalomaniac, Dr. Fu Manchu, created by fellow Britisher Sax Rohmer in 1911. Together, Burke and Rohmer created the popular fiction of a mysterious, exotic, evil Limehouse Chinatown. Both authors were "orientalists" in the sense Edward Said has developed the word. The "oriental" for both authors was the occidental's "other."[5] Rohmer's Fu Manchu embodied pure evil and all values opposite virtuous white, Anglo-Saxon, Protestant civilization. Burke's "Chink" embodied a lethargic, antiquated, and de-sexualized lover, a "worthless drifter of an Oriental."[6]

Burke's "orientalism" must have titillated Victorian sensibilities. "Each corner, half-lit by a timid gas light, seems to harbor unholy creatures." Here "life is in the raw, stripped of its silken wrappings." This perceived rawness of violent and sexual passions titillated Burke. To him "the East is eternally fresh because it is alive. The West, like all things of fashion, is but a corpse electrified."[7]

The Chink and the Child tells of an unconsummated miscegenous love between an alienated, love-starved Cheng Huan and a poor, abused twelve-year-old white orphan girl. Lucy, the "Child," is regularly whipped and beaten by her drinking and philandering foster father, "Battling Burrows," the "lightning welterweight of Shadwell." After meeting in an opium den, the "Chink" leads her to his drab room, treats her with a kindliness, albeit with ulterior motives, that she has never known. For several blissful days and nights, he showers her with exotic clothes, scents, and food. The shabby apartment is turned into a wondrously lavish suite and the couple enjoy a chaste, but tender, love affair. Suddenly, this idyllic world is shattered. While Cheng is out to buy more flowers, she is removed and the apartment/shrine to her is torn asunder. She has been nabbed by her outraged father who believes that "of all creeping things that creep upon the earth the most insidious is the Oriental of the West." Heading directly for Burrows' house, the "Chink" discovers Lucy's limp body. She has been beaten to death by her drunken father. He brings her back to his flat. The next morning, they are discovered—the "Chink" is kneeling beside Lucy "with a sharp knife gripped in a vice-like hand, its blade far between his ribs."[8] For Cheng Huan, life was no longer worth living. But the tale does not end here. Battlin' was also found with the surprise gift Cheng Huan left him. It was a snake that had managed to coil itself around his neck. Ah, the cool, calculating vengeance of an Oriental!

What might have given *The Chink and the Child* real power, magic, and popularity was that it delivered more than the sensationalistic headlines of the daily tabloids. As Chinese sailors began to gather in temporary lodging houses by the docks of the British West India Company, London newspapers began to tell of strange goings-on. Headlines read: "East London Opium Dens" (1909), "Limehouse Chinese v. Police" (1912), "Riot at Limehouse China Town" (1916), "The Lure of the Yellow Man, English Girls' 'Moral Suicide' " (1920), "Yellow Peril in London" (1920), and "White Girls 'Hypnotised' by Yellow Men" (1920).[9] Burke's story both reflected and elaborated the cultural perceptions of Chinese in London. His desirous, yet still chaste *Chink* in 1916 had become a highly sexual and menacing Fu Manchu by 1920.

Across the Atlantic, Griffith retold *Chink and the Child* and made some subtle but significant changes without Burke's consultation and apparently not all to Burke's liking.[10] First, the title was changed to *Broken Blossoms*, tilting it towards a poetic tragedy and away from the implications of miscegenation. Even the derisive word "Chink" was changed in the subtitle to "The Yellow Man and the Girl." Cheng Huan is recast from a lethargic schemer to a noble but frustrated idealist with proto-"Christian" values. Even the revenge upon Burrows is more manly (by western standards). Instead of the devious, indirect use of a snake, Cheng shoots the killer with a gun, almost in self-defense (a much more acceptable American method).

Griffith's recasting was masterful. He had transformed a second-rate, pulpy tale into a memorable tragedy. The modified story line, the effective acting, the authentic sets, the pioneering use of close-ups to capture subtle facial expressions, the lighting, the use of tints all combined to work extremely well. Together they articulated Griffith's use of the story to make a sentimental universal plea against abusive cruelty. The film's initial intertitles state his position simply: "We may believe there are no Battlin' Burrows striking the helpless with a cruel whip but do we not ourselves use the whips of unkind words and deeds?" In sharp contrast to Burke, the Orient is used as a symbol of rationality and morality, not raw passions. And the West is presented as "barbarous Anglo-Saxons, sons of strife and turmoil," not an artificially sustained "electrified corpse."[11] Here Cheng Huan represents misunderstood noble and civilized values and Burrows represents unenlightened, animal brutishness. Although Burke and Griffith used the East to symbolize very different qualities, both used it as a means to complain about the West. Perhaps Griffith was still getting back at those who wanted to censor *Birth of a Nation*? Was *Blossoms* a way for Griffith to prove he was not a racist? If this is the case, is *Broken Blossoms* a plea for racial tolerance?

At first glance, Griffith appears enigmatic regarding his racial attitudes. In 1915, he created the racist epic *Birth of a Nation*, then responded to his critics and boycotters with *Intolerance* (1916) and the pamphlet "The Rise and Fall of Free Speech in America" a year later. Then came *Broken Blossoms* and two years later a yellow peril-genre *Dream Street*. If anything he appears contradictory. At one moment he's a racist, the next he pleads for racial understanding, and then he creates another bigoted, stereotyped film. But a more fruitful understanding of Griffith can be arrived at if we analyze racial stereotyping.

Griffith's Huan appears to be a favorable portrayal of a Chinese or Asian. Indeed, when measured against Rohmer's Dr. Fu Manchu who is described as "evil incarnate," or caricatures of Chinese laundry men appearing as comic relief in the early stage and film melodrama, or Sessue Hayakawa as a sadistic and enslaving Japanese antique dealer in Cecil B. Demille's *The Cheat* (1915), or even Griffith's own "Evil Eye" that he invents in *Blossoms*, Huan is a positive figure. This was the era of the Chinese Exclusion Acts where violent attacks against Chinese were still commonplace. Samuel Gompers, the founder of the American Federation of Labor, for example, penned a pamphlet entitled: "Meat vs. Rice? Asiatic Coolieism or American Manhood Which Shall Survive?" in 1905. Burke and Rohmer were part of the mainstream "orientalist" view and Griffith was not.

This fact, however, does not qualify Griffith as one promoting the cause of racial tolerance. If anything, he eschews the standard stereotype of the "heathen Chinee" already well established in the previous century, and adapts the alternative image of the good-for-the-West "John Chinaman." "John" was the image of the tame, aristocratic, clean, honest, and often Christianized Chinese man promoted by traders, missionaries, and the wealthy who had direct personal interests in promoting good relations with China.[12] This "good Chinaman" image is more tolerable but equally removed from reality as the pure evil of Dr. Fu Manchu. Griffith, to my understanding, was a racist. He did not break already established stereotypes to reveal the experience of an overseas Chinese as they actually may have been. But he was no more a Sinophobe than others of his position and perhaps less than many.

To focus simply on Griffith's racial attitudes probably distorts our understanding of *Blossoms*. Indeed, race, class, gender, family issues are interwoven. Like Thomas Nast's cartoons depicting favorable images of Chinese immigrants in order to dump on thuggish Irish immigrants, Griffith used the Yellow Man as a symbolic foil to complain about the abusive, immature authority of lower-class white men.[13] Lucy was so love starved, even the affections of a "Chink" were better. As a twelve-year-old virgin, she needed a father more than a lover. A gentlemanly patriarch is what Lucy needed. If anything, this may have been the key moral message of *Broken Blossoms*.

But a detailed frame-by-frame textual analysis is needed to argue this point. Besides the filmic text, what does the cinematic text reveal? Such questions as: who was the targeted audience, and how was the film received, may shed light on the role *Blossoms* could have played in 1919 America.

The Cinematic Context

The visualization of this bitter-sweet story is, I have no hesitation in saying, the very finest expression on the screen so far.

Julian Johnson, *Photoplay Magazine*, 1919[14]

Broken Blossoms came to the screen, a masterpiece in moving pictures. . . .

New York Times, 1919[15]

Commercially speaking, Lillian Gish cites Griffith as realizing in advance that he could not make much money from the film. She says that "Its strange poetic beauty won Griffith instantly, although he declared that it would never make a penny as a film. It cost about $90,000 and made over $2,000,000—in the motion picture industry then such a small profit was considered a failure."[16] If the film was such a critical success, why did it make such a modest net income?

Vance Keply has written a revealing essay on how *Blossoms* was packaged for the public. Griffith, he argues, wanted to distance his artistic endeavor from the standard fare of "anti-Oriental harangues." In order to maximize the chances of the film's successful public and critical reception he devised a distribution schedule targeted for an elite and cultured audience. Billed as "the Art Sensation," the film's actual story line was played down; instead the film was emphasized as a "poetic, delicate work of art, a tragedy of the first order," by Griffith.[17] Seeking to appeal to "a class of patrons that [sic] do not care for the regulation program," Griffith charged three dollars, the price of theater tickets and prohibitive to most working folk. During this exclusive run all seats were reserved. The film, Griffith and his colleagues felt, warranted an audience which would value its high artistic intent. An indiscriminate release to the working class public would be like "casting pearls before swine."[18] These special showings of *Blossoms* were further dressed up with a live prologue, a one-act ballet authored by Griffith himself. Titled "The Dance of Life and Death," an allegorical tale of a young girl who breaks the "chains of everyday existence" and dares to reach for the "flower of love." Punished by a whip-wielding Fate, she dies. But the story ends when "she rises with movements as though of a bird uplifting itself into the blue sky. At the end is glowing white light into which she ascends."[19] Love transcends all. Then *Broken Blossoms* was shown.

The elitist contention is that proletarian audiences were insensitive to the delicate genius of the film.[20] The notion of individual genius is at the core of the "auteur" theory of a film's greatness and deserves serious consideration with respect to Griffith. [21]

Griffith's strivings to make films that would attain the status of high art certainly earned him his reputation as creative genius; however, he was not unique to his time. Arnold Genthe (1869-1945), for example, was an accomplished photographer who did portraits of such elite luminaries as John D. Rockefeller, President Theodore Roosevelt, Isadora Duncan, and the like. He first established his reputation by photographing San Francisco's Chinatown, the subsequent earthquake that destroyed the city, and the local gentry. Their creative approaches are parallel in many respects. Genthe was a frustrated painter who took up the camera with hopes of achieving artistic greatness equal to painting. And Griffith was an aspiring writer who never made it, but had a second chance in films. Genthe's view of Chinatown was influenced by such stories as Frank Norris' "The Third Circle" about the imagined seamy goings-on in San Francisco Chinatown, just as Griffith borrowed from Burke. Yet both sought a sort of authenticity of subject matter. Genthe's Chinatown shots are often mistakenly identified in photography history books as those of a documentary photographer. And Griffith staged reenactments of historical scenes in *Birth of a Nation* and hired a Chinese consultant to advise him on accuracy of costumes and character mannerisms for *Blossoms*. But Genthe was not a social documentary photographer in the manner of Lewis Hine; he freely retouched his negatives and prints by consistently ridding his scenes of white folks, signs in English, telephone poles, etc. His image of Chinatown was not what it was in reality, a mix of Chinese and American people and culture, but a "pure" and exoticized "Canton of the west." He was a pictoralist guided by his own romanticized artistic vision of what he saw. Griffith created magnificent, epic statements of opinion. He used actual historical events to promote his own personal universal statements. Perhaps both can be described as romantic realists.[22] Whatever labels we give them now, both were quite successful in their art.

BROKEN BLOSSOMS (1919)
Museum of Modern Art

San Francisco clients lined up to have their likeness flattered by Genthe's soft focus and dramatic lighting. Griffith's *Blossoms* was both art film and hailed by bourgeois critics. Both men have been described as creative geniuses, but such an auteur approach is not sufficiently critical. Genthe's similarities cannot simply be ascribed to happenstance. They were both individuals creating within a specific temporal and cultural continuum. Just as *Blossoms* cannot be viewed simply as a film abstracted from its target audience, Griffith cannot be pulled away from his social milieu.

Film and Ideology

Griffith viewed film as the great educator and predicted the medium would have a preeminent role in the shaping of modern technological life. In 1915, he asserted:

It is the ever-present, realistic, actual now that "gets" the great American public, and nothing ever devised by the mind of man can show it like moving pictures. . . . The time will come, and in less than ten years . . . where the children in the public schools will be taught practically everything by moving pictures. *Certainly they will never be obliged to read history again.* (Italics added.)[23]

Although his public school prediction was off, Griffith clearly understood how film could be used to portray reality and shape our moral view of the world.

By demonstrating the emotional appeal of well-crafted filmic moments, such as an agonizing close-up of Gish's screams of terror while locked in a closet, hiding from her father's violent wrath, audiences accustomed to the fixed distance to stage actors in live theatre were being convinced of the strength of this new technology. Film could increasingly be understood as a modern industry with heightened persuasive or educational powers, parallel to Taylorized assembly line factories that greatly multiplied profits and control over production.

Hence, Griffith's strivings to push film to levels of high culture began to explicate an upper-class world view. This view was encoded with a moral ideology of what was good and evil, how dominant class, race, gender and family values could be imparted to the lower levels of society. *Blossoms* must have stirred many real concerns among its elite audience. For example, we view Lillian Gish entering an authentic-looking slum and entering a shambles of an abode. We also witness an evil opium den full of "Chinamen" and their female victims. What upstanding Christian would not squirm at such a scene?

Lillian Gish, and even the "Chink," are but helpless victims of the cruel dictates of Fate. But even in such wretchedness, hope glimmers. Although they all die, they have experienced a chaste and caring love. She will, after all, rise above Limehouse to a better life in heavenly peace. But this hope, depending on the audience's own convictions, also leads to a plea for social reform. Tragedies such as this need not happen. What if the Girl had a proper home? What if we learned a bit of compassion from the orient? What should we do when young innocents are stuck with such parental abuse? Shouldn't we rid the urban environment of evils as liquor and prostitutes?

Broken Blossoms easily lent itself to an upper-middle-class progressivism during the early twentieth century. Such was the social milieu of reformers as

Jacob Riis pushing to improve the slums of the lower East Side and Mulberry bend, or Jane Adams and Hull House in Chicago, or immigrant social service agencies as the Henry Street Settlement. Historian Michael Rogin has argued that Griffith was very much a part of the perspective reform movement. "Reform was sweeping the country," Griffith wrote, "Newspapers were laying down a barrage against gambling, rum, light ladies, particularly light ladies. There were complaints against everything. So I decided to reform the motion picture industry."[24] These were paternalistic efforts from the top down that gave birth to the current human services sector. Immigrants, the working classes, the poor needed help from above. *Blossoms* not only conveyed a vicarious pathos, but gave some of its elite audience a sense of mission.

The film's artistic and moral perspective resonated among this nation's cultural elite. Griffith played a role in elaborating a coherent ruling cultural ideology. More than any other filmmaker, he was responsible for pushing the film industry beyond its Edison years as a means to sell motion picture machinery and past the New York-based, immigrant-orientated cinema of Mack Sennett. Film was becoming a means to articulate the moralism of society's upper crust onto the new-orientated mass public.

In this regard, *Blossoms* was a further development of *Birth of a Nation*. Both films helped to reforge a national identification between northern and southern elites who had not resolved deep animosities stemming from the Civil War and Reconstruction. Griffith's genius can be attributed in part to his persuasive reinterpretation of the national conflagration, "The opposition between white and black."[25] Rogin locates the actual birth of the nation referred to in the title as with the creation of Griffith's film itself. The film and the KKK represent the ideological birth of a renewed, and now nationally articulated, anti-black racism.[26] President Woodrow Wilson, who like Griffith was a Southerner, lauded the film. "It is like writing history with lightning and my only regret is that it is all so terribly true."[27] The KKK had redeemed white manhood for the United States. As *Birth* shattered middle-class attendance records across the nation, Woodrow Wilson segregated the Federal Government. "Jim Crow" triumphed.[28]

Blossoms was an elaboration of *Nation*'s ideological thrust. Having explicated the white racism of the formative national culture, Griffith moved on to the theme of the City. The growing urban metropolises of London and New York were the backdrops of Burke's *Chink* and Griffith's *Blossoms*. The segregated working classes of the East End of London and the immigrant ghettoes of New York's Lower East Side confused, frustrated, and shocked Victorian moral sensibilities. By the twentieth century, the cultural romanticism of rural pastoralism was not sufficient. The growing urban elite needed new ways to understand and order their cities. Moving away from a city's problems, as with the ever uptown movement of nineteenth-century New York gentry, was no longer practical. The city had become everywhere. But what to do about the filth, the crowds, the rudeness of the uneducated? Burke described it, romanticized it. Griffith joined reformers in advocating outside, paternalistic authority. The chaos could be managed. The uncouth could be assimilated. And that was the role of the upper crust, to meld immigrant and lower-class whites into a properly moralistic bourgeois culture.[29]

Ironically, Griffith himself succumbed to the "evil Bottle." Like his father, he died a broken, alcoholic man. Like the Civil War eclipsing his

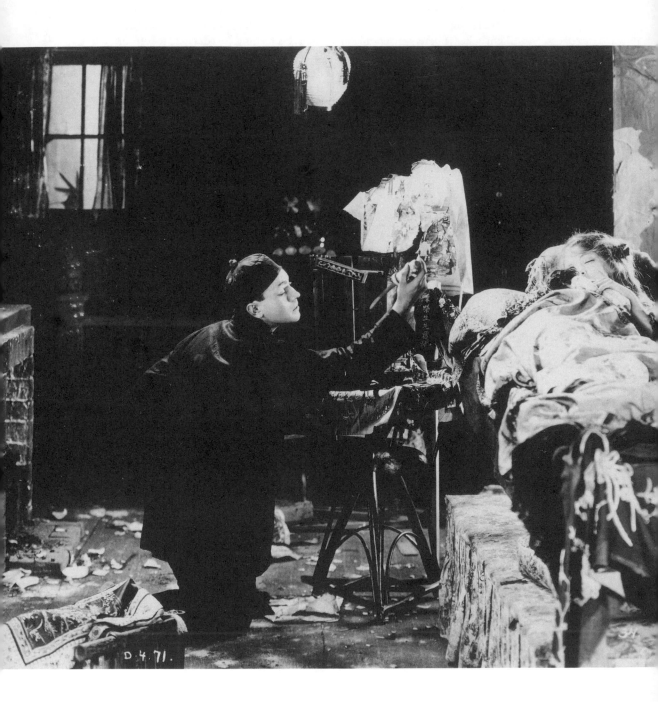

BROKEN BLOSSOMS (1919)
Museum of Modern Art

father's glory days, World War I had irretrievably changed his filmmaking universe. Cecil B. DeMille's dazzling portrayals of a new America, a new consumer society, pulled in the masses that did not go to *Blossoms*. Griffith's films, key in the creation of modern cinema, were elevated to the pedestal of art films. The film industry moved to Hollywood, the 1924 Immigration Act curtailed further immigrant hordes, and new cultural institutions to manage urban society were in place.

Griffith embodied both the past and the future. The romantic rural pastoralism portrayed in *Birth* and the almost expressionist urban existentialism of *Blossoms* redefined and modernized American cultural patriarchy. The idealized family patriarchs of yesteryear were dead, but the new authorities were very much alive.[30] Proper society should be managed so Blacks would be segregated and kept in their place, and poor whites, immigrants and native alike, would be acculturated into bourgeois society. But if Griffith was a cultural midwife, he was also a cultural victim.

NOTES The author thanks Thomas Bender, Russell Leong, Judy Susman, and Marilyn Young for helpful comments and suggestions on this essay.

1. Quoted in Robert Sklar, *Movie Made America* (New York: Vintage Books, 1975), 49. .
2. Quoted in Paul Boyer, *Urban Masses and Moral Order in America 1820-1920* (Cambridge: Harvard University Press, 1978), 261.
3. Vance Kepley, Jr., "Griffith's *Broken Blossoms* and the Problems of Historical Specificity," *Quarterly Review of Film Studies* 3:1 (1978), 38.
4. Kepley, 41.
5. Edward Said, *Orientalism* (New York: Vintage Books, 1978).
6. All "Chink" quotes from Thomas Burke, "The Chink and the Child," *Limehouse Lights* (New York: Robert M. McBride & Co., 1922), 30.
7. Kepley, 41.
8. Burke, 36.
9. Pennyfield's Chinatown Newsclippings File, Local History and Genealogy Room, Tower Hamlets Public Library, London, England.
10. Kepley, 46, ftn. 25.
11. From *Broken Blossoms* intertitles, 1919 MoMa Film Library Collection
12. See Stuart Creighton Miller, *The Unwelcome Immigrant: The American Image of the Chinese, 1785-1882* (Berkeley: University of California Press, 1969); and John Kuo Wei Tchen, *Genthe's Photographs of San Francisco's Old Chinatown* (New York: Dover Publications, 1980), 150.
13. Nast's pro-Chinese/anti-Irish cartoons were part of his campaign against the corruptions of Tammany Hall. For discussion of this, see Albert B. Paine, *Thomas Nast* (New York: B. Blom),150.
14. Griffith File, Media Study Center, Museum of Modern Art.
15. *Ibid.*
16. Lillian Gish, "D.W. Griffith—A Great American," *Harpers Bazaar*, October 1940.
17. Quoted in Kepley, 43.
18. Quoted in Kepley, 42.
19. Quoted in Kepley, 45.
20. A.G.E. Film Society notes, Series VII-Program VI, Kent Theatre, February 1, 1962. Griffith File, Media Center, Museum of Modern Art.
21. The "auteur theory," in film emphasizes how great films come from great directors and underplays socio-historical contextual analysis. For such an example, see Iris Barry, *D.W. Griffith: American Film Master* (New York: Museum of Modern Art, 1965).
22. All Genthe information from Tchen, 3-18.
23. Harry M. Geduld, ed., *Focus on D.W. Griffith* (New Jersey: Prentice-Hall, 1971), 34.
24. Michel Rogin, "The Sword Became a Flashing Vision": D.W. Griffith's *The Birth of A Nation*," Representations (9), 156.
25. Rogin, *ibid*. Lary May, *Screening Out the Past: The Birth of Mass Culture and the Motion Picture Industry* (Chicago: University of Chicago Press, 1983).
26. Rogin, 152.
27. *Ibid.*, 172.
28. Benjamin B. Ringer, *'We the People' and Others* (New York: Tavistock Publications, 1983), 341.
29. Boyer, and Raymond Williams, *The Country and the City* (New York: Oxford University Press, 1973).
30. Antonio Gramsci, *Selections from the Prison Notebooks* (New York: International Publishers, 1971); and Carl Boggs *Gramsci's Marxism* (London: Pluto Press, 1976).

JAMES WONG HOWE: THE CHINAMAN EYE

FRANK CHIN

Once James Wong Howe sees you, there's nothing left of you to see. Jimmie wouldn't hit you if you called him a "Chinaman." Maybe. Call him "Chink" and he'd hit you. Ask Richard Dix. If you meant it, Jimmie meant it.

The Christian Chinese Americans of the first generation of Hollywood yellows gave visual legitimacy to the Christian stereotype and looked to James Wong Howe, the reigning rebel, innovator and genius of the movie camera since the birth of the movies in the era of silents, as an example of assimilation. As a cinematographer, director of photography, and director, Wong Howe made his reputation shooting movies that had no Asian characters, or subject matter—*Body and Soul* (1947); *Viva Villa!* (1934); *The Rose Tattoo* (1956); *Hud* (1963); *The Old Man and the Sea* (1958); *The Molly McGuires* (1969). The Hollywood yellows led me to believe Wong Howe shared their dream of losing their stigmatizing culture and being absorbed and assimilated by the "host society."

How wrong they were is obvious in the interview. From greeting us in the oldest homeliest Sze Yup Cantonese I'd heard since Chinatown and the old passport photo Wong Howe showed me and photographer Nathan Lee, old James Wong Howe was a Chinaman. He took us out for Chinese food and ordered for everyone like a Chinaman. He got along with whites, was the genius of the most American art—Hollywood movies, married the white woman whose beauty and wit struck him speechless, was regularly nominated for Academy Awards for cinematography and had two Oscars without losing any of his Chinese language, culture, or taste.

We first interviewed Wong Howe in his home in the Hollywood hills, a few blocks up from the Sunset Strip. He was seventy-two years old. We interviewed him over a period of days on two trips to Los Angeles in 1970. For a little less than an hour, Wong Howe's wife, Sonora Babb, the writer known for her stories set in the Southwest, joins the interview. Wong Howe dropped his jaw, went dreamy eyed at the sight of her. He was in love with her and wanted us to hear her tell the story of their marrying at a time when marriages between whites and Chinese were illegal. They then told the story of playing go-between in the marriage of their friend and the writer C.Y. Lee, author of *Flower Drum Song*, the best-selling novel that inspired the Rodgers and Hammerstein musical. One night Nathan Lee and I arranged for Wong Howe to

meet the Japanese American actor Mako for dinner at the Full House Cafe on Hill Street in Chinatown.

Mako was the founding artistic director of the East West Players, at that time the only Asian American theatre action in existence. Mako was nominated for an Academy Award for Best Supporting Actor, for his portrayal of Steve McQueen's buddy in *The Sand Pebbles* (1966).

Wong Howe was anxious to meet Mako and involve him in his dream project: Romeo and Juliet set in the story of the evacuation and internment of the Japanese Americans. Not a white Romeo and a Nisei Juliet, but a Nisei Romeo and Juliet. Wong Howe and Mako played tug-of-war with the bill, argued about it and Jimmie picked it up. I cut the interview with James Wong Howe published in *Yardbird Reader,* Vol. III (1974) into a narrative form, from transcripts I'd made of all the tapes from all the visits. This excerpt is from "The Early Years, 1899-1936."

If I had to do it over again, I would have explored his childhood in China. He said he had gone to school in China. I would have used my store of Chinese children's stories and heroic adventures to sniff out the stories he heard, the stories he learned. His childhood in Pasco, with Indians on his porch and white kids playing baseball, seems an extension of the heroic tradition, and he proves himself making his way as a boxer, a prize fighter in clubs, without feeling in any way he is contradicting Chinese traditional behavior. I think we were too quick to believe his boxing was, in his eyes, taking on white behavior, this quickness being the result of ignorance combined with a journalist's, if not the social scientist's, arrogance of the mike.

Tapes and transcripts of the interview with James Wong Howe can be found in the CARP collection of oral history in the Bancroft Library, at the University of California at Berkeley. James Wong Howe (Wong Tung Jim) took his name from the Anglicization of his father's name, Wong How.

The Early Years 1899-1936

I came over from China in nineteen-four. I was five then. And that would make it . . . my father was in China then. And nineteen-four, that would make it. 1899 he was in China. So he would be in over this country around eighteen eighty sometime.

That would have been before he went back. He could have been over here in 1870 something. 1880 something. Maybe 1885 or maybe 'fore that. See? I have to go backward, and make a guess at it.

He came over himself. Alone. As a young man, to work. And after he made his stake, he went back and got married. You know how it is in the Chinese. In those early days. They couldn't bring their wives over. So when they all came over they thought they could save "ten thousand dollar" Chinese call *"yit mon gnum"* then go back to China.

When my father went back to China, he married my mother. And when she gave birth to me, they thought she had died in childbirth.

They had her already laid out in a casket! And they were ready to nail the top on. Goin'ta bury her. And as they put the top on, she moved! She wasn't dead. See? But between the meantime, when she was that way, my father had to get married again to somebody to take care of me! She was supposed to take care of me, ya see? But she was my stepmother. And now the conflict came. Two women, see? So when my father came over to America, my stepmother being the youngest one, and the prettiest I guess, he brought my stepmother over. She had, by that time had two children. A boy and a girl. So I came over, see as the oldest son. And she was the stepmother. And she didn't like me so much. Because of her son. And my father liked me very much. He took me to wherever he went. So she was probably jealous. And afraid that I was goin to inherit everything, but I never thought about these things. I was busy playing ball! 'n' playing games, you know.

My father stayed in China, raised the family, and then brought us over.

I remember a few things. I remember I went to school in China all right. I remember that we had a big orchard. And he had a house there. But I think it was the kind of a place where the caretakers lived. And he used to smoke. So he would leave stubs there and I would pick 'em up you know. And I remember, I was smokin behind under a staircase someplace, and he saw a lot of smoke, he thought 'The place is on fire!' He saw me smoking. Well, I, naturally what do you do? You get a licking!

I remember that I had a jade bracelet. And I remember. Raining in China 'n' running so I fell 'n' I cut my wrist. You know? And my thumb, then it was adhesion formed. And since then I could not straighten this thumb out.

Only by pulling it, can I move it. When I, when I was a kid, I loved the piano. I wanted to play a piano when I came over to this country. But because of this thumb, I couldn't hit, hit the notes, you see? So I gave it up. Now in 1957, I'm making a picture, with David Selznick, called *The Prisoner of Zenda* (1937, United Artists, D. John Cromwell). You ever see that? With Ronald Coleman?

And he had a lot of horses comin' toward the camera. And there was a big rock out there and I thought, "Jesus, they might hit those rocks and they might stumble." So I ran out and grabbed the rock and threw it. And I heard a noise!

And my hand! I couldn't move a finger. And it started to turn blue. All along my arm. I thought I broke my wrist.

They sent me to the first aid, at the hospital. Took X-ray and everything was all right.

You know what had happened? From the time I was four years old that adhesion stuck there, and when I dug the thumb into the ground it tore the adhesion loose. So my thumb now is all right. But for about two weeks, I couldn't pick up a paper between my thumb and this finger. Can you imagine that? But now it's too late for me to go ahead and start that piano thing again. But, I probably would have been very good at the piano because I think anything I start out to do, I work at it very hard.

And we lived in a place called Pasco. And the Northern Pacific called it a "Division Point." That's where the trains would stop. And they would change the engines. And there used to be a bridge. Oh, it must've been a half a mile long. Across this Columbia River. It was a wide place. At least it looked wide to me, when I was a kid. You know, everything looks bigger when you're little. We used to walk across the bridge. And the train would come and we'd sneak over on the edge and hang down, and drop down onto the big cement pylons. And I used to go durin the summer and set there and look at the river runnin by you know and imagine lotta things, you see.

I spent most of my childhood days in Pasco.

My father had a grocery store there. He sold hardware and clothing. General merchandise. My father built a little house uh, in the backyard. We built a house out of adobe.

> *"The Indians used to wear hats that were dark, black hats.... And the Chinese wore the same kind."*

There were a few Chinese that worked on the railroad. My father worked on the railroad when he first came over. Now they had to have a place where they come and buy provisions. There's all American customers excepting the Chinese that worked on the railroad. We had all herbs there for them and we carry Chinese groceries. When I got old enough I used to deliver groceries. Small packages and things. We had a horse and buggy. And I remember I used to drive down the street 'n' the horse be going. And if you saw it from the back, the back of the seat was so high, when I set down you couldn't see me. I used to scoot down there. They thought the horse was running away. Why I had people used to chase after it. When they catch it they see me there driving see? From the back you couldn't see me. Because of the back of the wagon seat. The help in the store, my father used to eat with them. Once in awhile I would be invited to eat there. Otherwise I ate at home with the kids. My brothers 'n' sisters. See? with my stepmother, in the little house built in the back. And Indians used to come and uh buy their groceries from my father. Lotta Indians there. They lived down by the Columbia River. Now, did you ever hear of the term called "Squawman"? That's a white man who marries an Indian. Well I saw a squawman. And I don't know what. But I knew that he was drunk. And he got in an argument with the Indian. The Indian got on the horse and started riding off. And this squawman grabbed this horse by the tail. And the last I saw of 'em was this horse draggin 'em both off, you see? When I was a kid I played with the Indian kids. They showed me how their folks made arrows. For the bow. We seem to get along much better than I did with white kids.

There weren't any banks in this town. Where they could put their savings. So they would leave it with my father. He would keep their account. Put it in the safe for them. You see? And then on Sundays when they didn't work. They would sit in the back, in the yard. That one day, they would relax. Talk about days, or whatever it is.

Now, my uncle. Underneath the store there's a big basement. Now my uncle. He ran a gambling house. And sold opium. In those days the law didn't bother them much. They sold opium to the Chinese that smoked it. And then they'd gamble.

There was a dirt floor. And they threw sawdust there. And my job. I used to pick up the sawdust. And sprinkle it. And clean it. And there was no paper money much in those days. They were always gambling silver or gold. And I would sift the sawdust out, and I would find money too, you see? I used to do that. Made a little money.

I had a little pigtail until 1912. That's when the revolution that China became a republic took place. And they all cut 'em off then. Kids used to pull it. They used to pull it. And tease me with it. We were the only Chinese family there. All the rest was Caucasian kids. The Italians! There was one Negro family. I used to play with them. But I got along with certain white kids around there that were friendly.

I hadda bribe them! This is a funny thing. Now when I wanta play ball they wouldn't let me play. So I used to go out with a sack of jellybeans. Candy! I'd get it from the store, you know? And I would stand there watchin. I'd be eatin. They'd say, "Whatcha eating, Chinkie?" You know, they call me "Chinkie." You see, they never call me Jimmy.

And I says, "Candy." See.

He says, "Gimme some!"

I say, "No."

He says, "Well, we'll let you play ball, if you give us some." So I, Hell! I used to have to go home and steal candy to give 'em so I could play baseball, you see? But in those days, I wasn't aware of discrimination, but you're too young.

I never was much of a Chinese, because we were the only family there, and I was raised amongst the white kids. And I caught all their ways, you see? Because I thought you had to be that way in order to be! I wanted be American! You see. And I knew that I look different than them. I had my flat nose. I used to even, at night pinch it up. I put clothes pin on it, hoping to make it like them. You see? I want to get away from the Chinese thing. Other than my looks I was all purely American. In the ways of my mind, and everything, you know?

I remember I was invited to a party. I was maybe about ten years old. Some kind of party. And I was quite surprised I was invited. I was very happy to go. There was a game that they played, set around in chairs. The boys and girls set. And you go behind the chairs . . . I forgot what they call it.

But I remember that one of the girls says, "Oh, I don't wanta sit by him. He's a Chinaman."

See. I was quite hurt. But then I didn't still realize that it was any discrimination. You know what I mean? Cuz you're too young. I didn't become really aware of discrimination til when I was about fifteen or sixteen.

Anytime there was trouble, cuz of my stepmother, I got blamed for it. And I was always the one that got the licking. And the more my father licked me the more I resented it. I didn't like it. And that was when more or less then I wanted to leave home, you see? Then when he passed away, she took over the store. And then try to run it. Things was kinda unhappy and I left! 'n' I went down with my uncle in Astoria, you see?

I went down to work for my uncle. In Astoria, Oregon. In a fish cannery. And I went into a restaurant run by a Greek.

And I sat there and sat there at the counter. And they wouldn't serve me. And finally the woman came around and says uh, "We don't serve Oriental people here." And I was only a kid! Then I was aware! See? Then, from then on, I remember I came here in California. Used to go over some place wanta get a room. They said, uh, "I'm sorry, we don't rent to Orientals." See?

No, my father never did explain it to me, no. You know how most Chinese fathers are. That they always want the kids to behave. Not to get into trouble. I remember I got in a fight one time. See, when we came there, there wasn't any water service. Everybody had to have their own well. In the back. We had a well.

Then when the uh water system came through we were the last to get it.

Now, there was a family call' the Heeter family. They had a boarding house, where these railroad engineers lived. They had three kids. And they had a hose, with a nozzle you know. Sprinkle. And, gee that was fun.

I wanted to sprinkle. And one of the kids and I got into a fight. I went home cryin all wet. My father wanted to know what. An' I tol' him that you know, I got into a fight with a kid. He took me over there in front of this kid and beat the hell out of me, you see?

The Indians accepted us because, you know. The whites treat them just the same way they treat the Chinese. You see? And so it threw them together, and they had a certain thing in the common thing. And that threw them

"I use' take pictures of my brothers and sisters and most of 'em had their heads cut off because I didn't have a view finder."

together. And so my father's relations with the Indians were very good. He got along very fine. I remember the chief like him very much. The chief had a young daughter, and they thought they could make a marriage, between me and the chief's daughter.

I remember hearing them talking about it. Ya see? But nothing was ever happen. That just . . . you know. But, you know how the Chinese—and I guess the Indians too they make these matches, when the kids were young.

And the Indians used to wear hats that were dark, black hats. And their, the brim a wide flat brim. Then they had the crown. And they never did squeeze it in, you see? They just left it. And the Chinese wore the same kind that worked on the railroad. See. And so, naturally you're being out in the sun all the time, they got pretty dark too. See? So they would see these uh Chinese with the queue 'n' so they maybe wanta know what tribe they were belong to. But they knew that there was some uh close relationship between them. Because of the way they braided their hair. Only the Indians had two, and the Chinese had one. You see?

My father didn't live long enough to see my work. That, that's the thing I've always felt very sad about. He passed away in 1914. That's before I even left home. I left right after he passed away.

Ever since I was a little kid, I was always interested in photography. I bought a little dollar box Brownie. And it didn't have a finder. So, I use' take pictures of my brothers and sisters and most of 'em had their heads cut off because I didn't have a view finder. And my father you know, being old timer, he was superstitious about having his pictures taken. Bad enough to have picture of him taken. But to take 'em without their head! That was terrible! So I had to explain to him why. And he gave me another five dollars to go and buy another camera. But I always was interest' in photography.

What interested me was to develop the film. And then print. And take a piece of white paper and print it and see if the image come through. It fascinated me. I always had a camera.

Ever since I was ten years old up. You see? Always had some kind of a Kodak. And I remember I had one uh . . . a Kodak that at the back you could flip it open there was a uh a little uh steel or metal pencil! . . . like. And then you could wrote on there, you know. And then fold it up and then when the film developed you identify it, you see? Now that's goin back. You don't see pupi camera like that anymore. The camera itself turned then somehow. It went a circuit. I remember they used to take pictures of us in school with a circuit camera. So the kids what we used to do then, we would stand on one end, where they first started it, then as it was goin, we would run around 'n' hide behind, get on the other end, 'n' be in two places in one picture.

When I first went to school I was the only Chinese. My brother Howard didn't go yet. He had a private tutor.

Now my third grade teacher . . . I forgot my first grade teacher. But I remember my third grade teacher. She married a man named Horrigan, an Irishman. My father gave him his first job as his American secretary to take care of the business.

My father couldn't read or write English. He couldn't even sign his name. He used to make an "X." And uh Horrigan later on became mayor of the town. He became judge. He became a big man. He's still alive but he's pretty sick now. And Mrs. Horrigan's still alive. And she was my third grade teacher. A wonderful woman.

I remember I had rubber boots. And went to school. And the town. The rain. And the streets. Got flooded. And that was about maybe a foot or two of water and it froze in the winter. And we used to play in the ice. But this one particular place. Where the wagons ran through it didn't freeze very much. And I went into the broke through the ice. Got my feet all wet. And I remember goin to school and Mrs. Horrigan took my boots off 'n' dried it in front of the stove 'n' sent me home. You see. Cuz she was afraid I'd catch cold. That was great because, you know, no school.

Ever since I was a kid, I was always interested in photography. I never knew I was gonna go into the movies. But when I came to California, I got interested in. Because I saw 'em making movies down around Chinatown there. And one of the cameramen was Len Powers, an American cameraman, who I knew up in Oregon. He came down earlier.

He was a prize fighter. And in those days, the movie stars used to get stables of fighters. But today they get stables of race horses. They had fighters in those days. So Len Powers one of the fights and became the movie actors'. They were interested in him, and so when he quit they gave him a job. And he learned to crank a camera. You know, everything was cranked by hand. Not motorized then. So I look up and there I see him! and knew him! You see, cuz I used to box a little bit. I fool around up there in Oregon. That's how I knew Len Powers. When you're kids, you always fought, you know? They would tease me 'n' I'd resent it. And I had to fight to learn how to participate, otherwise I wouldn't belong! You had to! You see? And I became quite good at it. And even when I was a young kid. The Elks, they would put on smokers. And they would match me, have kids come up and box, you know. And they matched me with a little Irish kid, who was a good friend of mine, Willie Hogan! And I beat him, you know? Hit him somehow in the throat somehow and he went out! And scared the life outa me. And there was a fight manager there and he thought, "Well, gee. There's a good chance to take him teach him more." You know and EXPLOITATION. You see?

So. When I left Astoria, it was around nineteen fifteen. I went to Portland. Cuz it's only a hundred miles. And there this manager then matched me with the Pacific Northwest Champion! Flyweight. Abie Gordon. I lost to 'im, but I gave him a good account of myself. I boxed a few more times and I won them and that's when I came down here, I thought I would box down there. But I didn't. I saw Len Powers.

I was a flyweight. He was a lightweight. So I said, "Hey, Len, what?" He said, "God! What're you doin' down here.?"

I said, "Well, nothin'. I just got fired from a job. I been a busboy out here in Beverly Hills Hotel, 'n' got in an argument with some fellow there, and the cook or something, and I left 'n' I got fired. See?" But before that I was a delivery boy for a commercial photographer. He used to deliver pictures, and I would help out. In the darkroom. With hypo and ferrotype prints! 'n' you know, you put 'em on tins and you rip 'em off it becomes very shiny. Glossy.

Nowadays, they don't do that very much now. They got glossy paper now. So I had it, that. I had that job for three or four months. Then a . . . a friend of mine in Chinatown said he was going to China. And he said he needed some passport pictures.

I said, "Well, come on up to the studio at night."

I had the key. And I had all the lights! 'n' I got the lenses. And I put it on there and taking pictures. And the boss came in. He needed the lens. He had to go out and do a job. And y'know I had fingermarks all over it! And he asked for it, and uh out I went.

That's when I left that job, 'n' I went out to Beverly Hills Hotel and got a job as a busboy. That was when I was around nineteen uh ohhh sixteen! See? Seventeen, and then I saw this Len Powers! Workin' down there. He says, "You know, I get seventy-five dollars a week just turnin' this thing around."

I say, "How do I do it?" And he told me, he said, "Well, go to the studio 'n' and uh try to get a job as an assistant. You carry the equipment around, you keep it clean, you make out reports, and you learn to load it, you know. 'n' all that. And then you, learn that way." You know. In those days there weren't any courses in universities.

They wanted somebody to pick up all the wrappings and the short end pieces of film and throw it around, you know? And . . . and at that time the film is . . . is almost like gunpowder. It's very explosive. Nitrate film. You know. And so, nobody'll take care of it. And so uh. The man said, "Well, look. We don't have a job for the assistant. I just put a fellow to work, about an hour ago."

And I said, "Oh, Christ! I been waiting for two hours!"

And he said, "But I can give you a job." He said, "If you wanta work!"

I said, "Sure!"

He says, "Okay."

Oh, I says, "Well, what doing?"

He said, "Well, I need somebody down that camera room. To take care of it. Clean it up." 'n' he says, "And then when we need somebody else, later on, well, I'll give you a chance." He said, "Doesn't pay much money. Ten bucks. Ten dollars a week." I said, "When do I start?" He said, "Well, you're gettin' paid right now. You're on salary."

You had to go and learn it from the bottom up! So I went here to the old Lasky Studios here, on Vine and Argyle. It was all orange groves around there then. You see, it was a farming country there. They made Westerns there. And they had the livery stable there. And they had some horses to plow the fields. That's where C.B. DeMille stop by and he saw this field 'n' there . . . where the horses 'n' he needed horses to make a picture called *The Squaw Man*. And they got the horses there. And they got the place. He came here to the San Fernando Valley over Cahuenga Pass. . . . Well, you come over now, you know it's all freeway!

In those days they had one road! And it took an hour to go over this hill, the mountain, to the other side. That's where the Lasky Studios started. Vine Street wasn't paved. It was full of pepper trees. And that's why it started. And Doug Fairbanks was workin' there, and Mary Pickford, and Mary Miles Minter . . . Oh! uh Gloria Swanson, and Bebe Daniels, big stars! See, in those days, every studio had to make one big picture a week. Cuz they owned their own theatres. And they had to keep those theatres going. And they didn't have double bills in those days.

Y'see they had one feature. Cuz in those days you used to go to a movie the whole night program. They have an orchestra. They'd have a newsreel. They'd have a special short. Then it comes, the feature. See today, you don't have the orchestra, you don't have the newsreel, you don't have the special short, you don't even have the cartoon now. You just go in and they give you an ad. What's gonna happen next week. What picture's coming on, and you know. In those . . . earlier days there was great showmanship. The days of

George of Grauman, you know, and those people. See, you folks probably don't recall ever hearing of a man like Grauman, there's a theatre, Grauman's Chinese. Named after him. Great showman! See, the showmanship today is gone. Everything gettin more or less automation. You know. That's what they're goin for now. See, the whole movie industry goin that way. All the entertainment, you know?

That was my first job. I worked for about six months down there. And DeMille was making a picture and they needed an extra assistant. They had three or four cameras. So I was sent up to hold the slate. It's a little piece of board and you wrote on it with chalk to identify the scenes.

I think it was called *Male and Female* (1919) with uh Gloria Swanson, Bebe Daniels, Lila Lee and Thomas Meighan.

DeMille took a liking to me, because I used to look over the slate to see what was going on. And I was smoking a cigar in those days. And I musta amused him. He said uh, to Wycoff, he said, "Well. Look. Keep him with us," you see, "So that we can use him." So I was the third or fourth assistant. Then they had a Japanese cameraman. His name was Henry Kotani. He used to take pictures for Sessue Hayakawa.

Sessue Hayakawa in those days was a big star. He was gettin three four thousand dollars a week then, you see. Big star! And Kotani was the cameraman. See? Now they had a hard time getting white kids, assistants to work with Kotani. Cuz they didn't want to work for an Oriental. Or a Japanese. They didn't want to take orders from 'em. You see what I mean?

The kids you know had a hard time. They resented working for an Oriental. They couldn't go out and take orders from 'im you know? So. They put me with him. You see? Well, by God! He and I fought more than anything! Cuz the Chinese and the Japanese didn't get along in those days too. I did one or two pictures with him. Then finally, they saw that we didn't get along very well and they put me with somebody else. I went in 1917. And by 1922, I was a chief cameraman.

When I was there, at Lasky making ten dollars a week, I bought myself a little five by seven view camera. To practice take pictures, you know?

I used to take pictures of these actors. Extras. They used to have their costumes on. I took it to 'em after work or durin lunch hour, and I would enlarge 'em to eight by ten 'n' they would order, you know, sometimes two or three dozen. Cuz they had to leave these pictures with their phone number and all that on the back at different studios. So when the studio wants to hire them they look at these different pictures and call 'em up.

I made good money. I made more money doin' that than I was getting as an assistant, you see. I almost gave up the movie thing and went into stills. Well. Finally, three, four years later, I had my camera. I was taking some pictures around one of the big stars who came by. Her name was Mary Miles Minter (Juliet Shelby).

Big star! Beautiful. Blonde. Curls. Pale blue eyes. So, I said, "Miss Minter, can I take two, three pictures of you?"

She said, "Well, yes!" So I made exposures. And made some enlargements. I gave 'em to her. And she looked at 'em. Half a dozen of 'em.

She says, "Oh, these are wonderful pictures!" Says; "Could you make me look like this in the movies?" I said, "Yes."

Well, two, three months later, I was called into the office. They said, "Jimmy congratulations."

I said, "Why?"

They said, "Miss Minter wants you to be her chief cameraman."

I was scared to death! "She's waiting to see you down 'n' her dressing room. Go down, She wantsa talk to you."

I went down 'n' knocked. And she says, "Who is it?"

And I says, "Jimmy. Jimmy Howe."

She says, "Come in." She had the pictures out on her dressing room table. She said, "Jimmy, I keep looking at these pictures." She said, "I never look as beautiful . . . as this." She says, "If you could make me look like this in the movies, you'll be my cameraman. I want you to be my cameraman." She says, "You know why I like 'em? Because you made my eyes go dark."

Well, in those days we had Orthochromatic film. Blue went white. You see? That's why it was difficult to find a white cloud in a blue sky. The sky would go white and so would the cloud. I didn't know how I made her eyes go dark! I walked outa there 'n' I scratch my head. I said, "How did I make her eyes go dark?"

You know, it was an accident! So I went back to where I took the pictures. And I stood and looked around. And lo and behold. Lo and behold there was a big piece of black velvet!

And I looked into that black velvet. I said, in my mind, I said, "Why the eye is like a mirror. It's reflected. So I got a little mirror and I held it up. And then I could see black! And I would raise it up to the skylight and it would be white. So that must be it. So I made a big frame, 'bout four by five feet. I could raise it up and down. I cut a hole in it and stuck my lens through. And I made all her closeups with the black velvet.

The news got around Hollywood. All these stars had their own groups you know. And they give parties. And they would talk, you know, "What's new?" they said. "You know what? Mary Miles Minter has imported herself an Oriental cameraman! And he hides behind black velvet. And he makes her blue eyes go dark!" Why I became a "genius"! Everybody that was a movie star who had blue eyes wanted me to be their cameraman. So I went back and told the boss about the different offers I was getting. I think I was getting seventy-five dollars a week. And I got offers to a hundred and fifty dollars a week. That's good money!

So they said, "Well, Jimmy," he says, "Look, you're not gonna leave us!" He says, "You know, we gave you the opportunity here," and all that, "Tell you what we'll do. We'll give you a hundred dollars a week to start out with. And in three years you'll be making a hundred and fifty dollars a week." The man said, "That's wonderful! Because if you're under a contract, if you don't work you get paid! You see? Fifty-two weeks a year. Just think."

By golly, they talked me into it. When they get me in there I was green. I thought, "Well," so I signed.

Boy, oh, boy! They worked me. They always find some kind of work. I never had a day off. You see? But I stuck it out. And I'd stayed with 'em from 1917 to 1926. There was one picture I was working on. Called *Call Of the Canyon* (1923) with Richard Dix. I had a grip. Oh, he was a big tall, six footer! And uh. We were sittin down at a table. And there's one chair left. They said, "Well, there's a chair." And he says, "No, I don't wanta sit by a Chinaman!" You see.

I finished dinner and when we came out I faced him see? I says, "Whadaya call" you know, "Call me?" 'n' all this dirty names 'n' all that. 'n' I punched him. Knocked him down. You see?

Nobody was fired. But the director said, "Now look, you two guys gotta get along, now, or I'll send ya both home," you see? Then he got along well with me. Cuz I didn't take anything. And I was satisfied that he knew. So we got along. And when you do that a couple of times. I get around. They says, "Don't fool around with that guy, because you know, he won't take it! See?" And I mean I punched a truck driver. You know? On location! Same thing. Shooting a dice game. They were always shooting dice or playing cards. And we packed up ready to go. And we waited for this driver to bring the car over to load up the equipment.

He was there busy gambling so I got in the car and drove it over. He says, "Get your fuckin Chinese hands off. Get your Chinaman hands off of this thing!" See? "You Chink!" 'n' all that.

So I got out of the car. Boy! He got it. Slugged him 'n' he was big! He finally got me down. They separated us. Then he wouldn't take me home. So I got a ride home by a truck! Then the boss did hear about that. And they did can him. See?

All these people, now. They. The more artistically involved they were, the less discriminatory they were. But the common everyday that I had to give orders to, electricians 'n' property men and stuff like that, because I had to tell 'm what to do. And that's what they didn't like! To have someone to be the boss. You see. Of being a chief cameraman you have electricians, carpenters, grips, painters. Property men. Nursery men. I found some of them resented it. Others and I got along fine. They weren't all that way. They was certain elements. On the set, yeah! On location. And I would punch 'em in the nose. Or they would punch me. And that was it.

FINAL MIX:
UNSCHEDULED

Yoshio Kishi

YOSHIO KISHI

The history of Asian Americans in the film industry either as performers or in production falls conveniently into four periods: the first, from 1893 to 1927, was the age of the silent screen. Owing to the primacy of the visual over the oral, where the mute image was international and language no barrier, many Asians gained entry into the industry, mostly as extras or in bit roles but also in production[1] and occasionally as independents.[2] At no other time would it have been possible for an Asian like Sessue Hayakawa to achieve such a phenomenal success in a field dominated by white producers and white audiences. His popularity cut across racial lines in a way that has never been repeated.[3]

The indisputable presence of a large Asian population in California was also a contributing factor—as local color or exotic background and as a story source. It was an influence that promoted taking advantage of an available labor force and ready-made settings. Producers' exploitation of a "Japanese village" near Santa Monica and of Chinatowns in Los Angeles and San Francisco were examples of this relationship.[4]

But the prospects of Asian participation in the new art and industry were eroded by an increasing racism here and abroad; the coup de grace was the passage of the Immigration Act of 1924 that barred all Japanese from coming to the United States. Earlier, the Chinese Exclusion Law of 1882 and subsequent legislation had blocked all Chinese immigration, and of course neither the Chinese nor the Japanese were eligible for citizenship. Hayakawa himself, responding to racist hostility, closed down his production company and abandoned Hollywood.[5] The introduction of sound a few years later destabilized the industry and further retarded the advancement, already precarious, of Asian Americans.

The second period, from 1928 to 1947, coincided with the development of sound film, the international crises of the depression and World War II, and the beginnings of the Cold War. This phase was conspicuous for its ambivalent (evil Fu Manchu, benign Charlie Chan, Christian Chiang Kai-shek) pro-Chinese perspective and a virulent, sociopathic anti-Japanese one. Those Japanese Americans who had not left the industry (for different employment or for opportunities in Japan)[6] were rounded up and transported to concentration camps in 1942; by default, Chinese Americans regained a foothold, mainly by impersonating Japanese soldiers or spies, and Chinese peasants; major Asian roles were still filled by whites.[7]

The third period, from 1948 to 1968, was marked by the geopolitics of the Cold War, the abolition of large studio monopolies on distribution, the rapid rise of television, and the explosive flowering of the civil rights movement. Overall, it was a time when Chinese Americans were again cast as Chinese, albeit as communists; Japanese Americans were slowly re-entering the industry; and both able to find minor positions in production.

The fourth period, from 1969 to 1990, to a large degree resembled the first: the rapidly modernizing, economically expanding, industrious and energetic Japan; an authoritarian, volatile, problematic and feckless China; and an individualistic, divided, short-term oriented and materialistic United States. By the late 70s due to the performance and accomplishments of the Japanese (not Japanese Americans) and the favorable climate generated by civil rights activism and legislation, many Asian Americans found jobs in production, particularly in crafts requiring technical skills, but fewer made it in front of the camera as performers, the demand for whom is always unpredictable and haphazardly determined by story cycles.

Since my experience spans the third period to the present—indeed I suspect that I am a disappearing species—and an account of a filmmaker living in the backwaters of Asian American history (the East Coast) may be an oddity, these notes will now take a personal turn:

A Japanese American raised in New York, I escaped the destructive effects of the concentration camps during World War II. A child of the depression, I grew up in Manhattan in an Italian/Irish neighborhood, just north of Hell's Kitchen, an area notorious for its poverty and crime. The few blocks that separated my family's tenement from comparable railroad flats were the difference between being criminal and being poor. Although it is crippling to be of Japanese descent in a racist society, it was worse for me, as a child and as an adolescent, being poor in a money-driven culture.

I learned decades later that there had been a kind of Little Tokyo nearby but I wasn't aware of it then and at most was acquainted with only one or two Japanese families, more my parents' friends than mine. I tended to be solitary in my ways, probably in response to the anti-Japanese fervor of the war, and spent most of my time reading books and going to movies. By the time I was fifteen, I had discovered Eisenstein's *Film Sense* and wanted to make films, a dubious ambition since filmmaking was not considered a respectable career and in the United States film schools hardly existed (one in California and another in New York). Despite a state scholarship, I couldn't afford an out-of-town college, so I landed up as a major in English with a minor in Films at the City College of New York which had recently established a film department under the chairmanship of Hans Richter, Dadaist artist and surrealist film director of *Dreams That Money Can Buy* (1944).

By today's standards, the film program was indeed primitive and inadequately funded, strong on theory (lectures and screenings) and weak on practice (little hands-on experience). The department woefully lacked equipment, facilities and supplies. For individual class projects, each student was allotted a single 100 ft. roll of 16mm reversal, use of an antiquated Filmo with a one-inch lens, and whatever lights that could be scrounged. All I learned about set-ups, camera work, and production was to come many years later. Nevertheless, I was able to study films—at a time when the convenience and accessibility of videotapes were unknown—up to four hours a day at school and often, on my own, two double features on Saturdays.

In the 50s, the boom of the war years was over and the film business was slow, or perhaps it felt that way when you're looking for a job. Luckily, a former classmate, now employed at a film company, asked me to fill in for him—as floorsweeper and film checker—while he went on vacation. After his return, I was kept on. I hadn't realized it then but I was at one of the last important documentary production companies in the country. Had I begun anywhere else, I would have gone in a totally different direction in films and certainly would not have come under the influence of men I still hold in respect.

Although a novice in my first paying job, I managed to be assistant to Jean Oser, the precocious and temperamental editor of Pabst's first sound feature *Kameradshaft* (1931); to Sidney Meyers, the sensitive and humane director-editor of the classic *The Quiet One* (1949); and to Peter Gluchanok, a director-cameraman, who revealed to me the magic of light and movement. Peter, indirectly, also taught me another lesson: when he and the producer had a falling out, I was offered a promotion and asked to replace him as editor. It struck me, had I accepted, as such a blatant act of opportunism that I refused. Somehow, even then, I was aware that there are situations when one must unequivocally say no. It delayed my reclassification to editor for at least a year.

I assisted Sidney Meyers on *American Farmer* (1954) which he had also directed. I had very little practical experience other than splicing and rewinding. I was, however, a voracious and omniverous reader and had probably studied everything of value in the literature (there wasn't as much then as now); furthermore, I'd seen more films than are healthy for a young man (my taste in certain things are irretrievably ruined). So I was good at analysis and on theory. Sidney, at that phase of my life, represented to me the whole filmmaker, just as Harry Alan Potamkin the whole film critic.

After *Farmer* was cut, I was asked to do the sound. I had never done any sound editing and my experience was limited to blooping (optical sound tracks in those days) and cleaning (a soft cloth dampened with carbon tetrachloride). But I was zealous and blessed or cursed with a youth's self-assurance that he knew precisely how sound should be handled.

The tracks were 35mm optical push-pull, which meant that you couldn't afford mistakes: if you screwed up a cut, you had to reprint. The picture was 16mm color which was also spliced with cement so you couldn't play around with it either: since you always lost a frame on each cut, you could always identify the inept editors by the number of slugs in the workprint. Today, when splices are joined with mylar tape, you can play around and make changes, play around some more, and keep going until doomsday.

I finished the sound score on schedule, made cue sheets, and got the reels over to Reeves Sound Studios where Dick Vorisek, the best mixer in the east, was to record. The session was probably booked for four hours since the film was a three-reeler. The hours passed—it was a complicated sound score; and passed—I believe I had eight tracks running; and passed: I think we ran four hours over. I was a bit worried; Sidney, meanwhile, did not complain or criticize or make changes.

The next day Sidney and I were on the carpet. The producer was upset about the overtime at the studio and the number of tracks I had prepared. I was nervous naturally. It's curious now that I did what I thought was essential for a good sound score and never compromised or aimed for less. I haven't changed but I've learned how to achieve results with limited means. Back then, however, there were consequences. An angry boss chewed me out despite Sidney's defense. After the answer print, the storm blew over.

The last significant influence was Leo Hurwitz, director of *Native Land* (1942), *Strange Victory* (1949), and other major American documentaries, in which the most advanced applications of ideological analysis and of film theory may be seen. I've never worked for Leo but I've screened his films and attended his seminars. Each of these people has taught me about the art of film; even more important, each in his own way has taught me the value of integrity and social responsibility.

I had been on staff for two-and-a-half years in a non-union shop, impatient to edit and champing at the bit to break out and move on. I didn't have a union card and couldn't apply for one since the International Alliance of Theatrical and Stage Employees had a closed roster. Nepotism, racism, fear of competition and corruption were major factors in blocking an open membership. As the IA was the only union recognized by the industry, having an IA card was essential. I couldn't quit (the family needed the income) or search elsewhere.

Those of us who were kept out of the IA (more old-timers with years of experience than youngsters like me) started up a rival union, the Association of Documentary Technicians and Film Cameramen, and undertook an aggressive campaign to organize and sign up shops in New York. Some twenty-five years of IA policy had excluded newcomers and Blacks and other non-white minorities, who needed little persuasion to join us. The IA waiting list was a built-in membership for the ADTFC. Our recruiting drive very quickly forced the National Board of the IA to accept en bloc our dissident union, so I became one of the first Asians in the New York film editors' local, if not in fact the first. Sometime later I met an older Chinese American, Hsin Chien, who may have preceded me. I've lost track of him and I believe he either left New York or took up a different trade.

My relief at finally getting into the union was, however, shortlived. After my initiation and the signing of a contract with an unhappy producer, I was fired.

I was out of work for the first time since college. I was young (callow), inexperienced (naive), and desperate (broke). Each day was punishment for not picking a respectable and secure occupation.

I don't recall the circumstances but I found an opening at an animation house operated by a former Disney artist. No matter how grateful I was for the income, that I was still an assistant galled me. I vowed to be patient until I learned the myriad technical procedures in animation. I told myself that I could line up another job in a few months.

Winter thawed out to spring and summer was approaching. I was despondent. Five months elapsed before I got a call for another job.

Because I was a hard worker—perhaps a bit opinionated and outspoken but nonetheless considered talented—acquaintances rarely had qualms about recommending me to others. One of the latter had recently established a film unit at WNYC and had shot a documentary on a home for the elderly. The footage was all in the can. Would I, he inquired, be willing to

YOSHIO KISHI (circa 1954)

edit it? At this point, lights flashed and gongs went off. I gave notice and set out to cut my first film.

In the mid-50s, films were shot in 35mm, 16mm being reserved for low-budget documentaries and industrials; optical sound was the norm although magnetic tracks were soon to supersede it. Steenbecks and Kems were in the future. At WNYC, there weren't even Movieolas, instead there was a primitive, cast-iron monstrosity called, I believe, an Acmeola, which projected a dim image on a dull, metallic screen. It was bulky and unwieldly, had no pedal controls, and was designed so that I could not reach the switches. I may have wept that first day.

I was totally baffled, naturally. There was no script, just raw footage. I screened roll after roll, stashed scenes on hooks, and filled barrel after barrel, hoping that something would strike me (lightning, a fire, an idea?).

Fortunately I was left alone. Strips of film multiplied and tumbled out of the barrels; a curtain of images encircled and isolated me. Editing is lonely and solitary work even with an assistant or two; alone it's worse and the illusions captured by the camera seem more real than reality, a state one strives for in theory while the urge to bring order to chaos exists. So I don't find it peculiar that I'm distant, remote, living in another world.

One day the director dropped in unexpectedly to see whether I was comfortable. When his pale face suddenly materialized between the flowing strips of film, like a baboon's in a vine-entangled jungle, I was startled. My silent stare of stupefaction must have been misinterpreted, for he was visibly embarrassed and apologized for disturbing me and hastily departed. To my relief, he never visited the cutting room again.

Eventually, a structure emerged and I was able to shape a script and bring the film together. At the conclusion of the first and only approval screening, the director remarked, "I knew you were the right man the instant I saw the barrels stuffed to the brim—only a good editor would handle film that way." Sure.

I was twenty-three and had edited an entire film (*Our Senior Citizens*). It was a beginning. Three more jobs and six months later, I landed up on staff again. I wasn't doing too badly and for one brief heady period, I was in the awkward position of editing more or less simultaneously five half-hour films while three envious editors were assigned less exciting labors. My private life, meanwhile, was in a grievous state: I had married too young to an even younger Hawaiian nisei who had developed, while attending a mainland college, a deep aversion to everything American. She knew even less about Japan than I, but she insisted on relocating and starting a new life as expatriates.

Despite misgivings, I quit my job, discarded or sold everything I owned (very little, except books), and flew off into the unknown. I never doubted that it was a mistake—the Korean War had given the Japanese economy a boost but the competition for jobs was as bad as ever; the structure of Japanese business, moreover, was such that a Japanese American, especially one who could not read, write or speak Japanese, had no chance at all of competing; and ultimately the kind of work I did best was intimately connected to the culture in which I was born and which could not be transplanted. Had I been an artisan in a different craft or a professional in the sciences, I might have been able to make the transition.

I was gone for six months. I couldn't find work, I was treated like the village idiot when I spoke, and I was often mistaken for an Eskimo. I had deepened my understanding of a country, people and culture I had always held in the highest regard, but re-confirmed that I belonged here. I returned a shade wiser, numb emotionally, and wary about beginning all over again.

By the end of the third period, I had written and directed my first film, "Lombardi" (1968), a CBS special that pre-empted the "Ed Sullivan Show" one Sunday evening, and had edited many more films than I care to re-member. Documentary, already in decline in the 50s, had succumbed to television's mediocrity and commercialism, and was no longer a serious, ideological instrument. Good or acceptable jobs were disappearing and it was becoming increasingly difficult to think only of earning a living.

Even before the Civil Rights March on Washington in 1963, which I joined with 200,000 Americans to hear Martin Luther King, I had been polit-ically active, noticeably a solitary Asian among whites or Blacks (I accepted this as inevitable since, other than family, I knew no other Asians). What had been to me a general discontent with the ills of society soon magnified into unavoidable issues. The assassination of JFK, the civil rights clashes, the escalation of the Vietnam War, the murder of Martin Luther King followed soon by that of Robert Kennedy, and the election of Richard Nixon: the real world was making career goals (had I any) an abstraction.

For the first time, I was drawn by a need to understand what it meant to be an Asian American. I began to investigate our history, initially as one must with the experience of the Chinese, and to seek connections with other Asian activists. Because there were so few Asian Americans in the film and T.V. industry here (unlike the West Coast), my life was on a double track and compartmentalized: working in films to pay the rent, and involve-ment with Asian Americans in order to understand the past and the future. Even today, I haven't been able to bring the two concerns together.

Reviewing the past four decades, I see many changes. The activism of the 70s has receded, overwhelmed by the destructive Reagan-Bush/ Republican 80s. The nation is divided and everyone except the rich is worse off. Anomie and self-interest have infected the beliefs and passions of the 80s and 90s—a comic-book generation in whom prevails a suffocating materialism that leaves little room for aspirations beyond the self, and a miserly narrowness of spirit that feeds on sexual obsessions, religious fun-damentalism, and racist hate.

Nor are Asian Americans immune to the driving forces that dominate our culture today and have not eluded their effects. The pressures to con-form or to make it in the white world lead all too often to self-deceiving pretensions and evasions. For us, as filmmakers, creating illusions is a real-ity but there is a danger of succumbing to the illusion and losing track of the reasons for the creative act itself—the basic, antecedent decisions that define the ethical, moral, and political grounds for composing a poem, painting a picture, or making a film.

Unfortunately most film people, from producer to go-fer, rarely ques-tion their motives for making a film or harbor doubts so long as the check doesn't bounce. If a filmmaker's aim is to comprehend the world and to reveal and communicate this understanding to an audience, a failure to examine the consequences of his labors is irresponsible, malevolent, and despicable. Ethical and moral concerns may strike those hustling for a job as frivolous and remote, but it is at the core and is the source of whatever we do as a craftsman or artist. A simple test—yet not simple in its de-mands—is to ask for what purpose a film is being made, who benefits? Whether what you do is actuated by greed, avarice, ego? Whether it is de-humanizing or life enhancing? Such a self-examination of motives and inten-tions is a necessary condition imposed on the filmmaker, perhaps more stringently on Asian Americans who, so often excluded, are tempted to enter the mainstream at any cost.

Life without art may hardly be life at all but art without life is absolutely nothing. There are many fields of employment that do not require such rigorous attention to what's right and what's wrong; art does, and if you can-not see the problem and frame the question, you belong somewhere else. Ultimately, choices must be made.

For Asian Americans in that small arena of the film and television industry where options are already limited, this may seem a double burden. But as we approach the last decade of the twentieth century, we have little to lose. Compared to the rest of the nation as a whole, the achievements are superficial and disappointingly low.

Asian Americans in the industry are more numerous, some more vis-ible and earning more, and certainly making more films. They are now in executive positions, in glamour jobs (on-camera T.V.), and more frequently in craft occupations. Not faring as well are actors and actresses who are forced to play musical chairs, opportunities fluctuating with shifting story lines. For any given interval, the total number of jobs for actors and actresses is fairly static and normally less than what it ought to be.[8] The reasons for this are a casting policy that dictates hiring (except during war-time) strictly along ethnic lines (Chinese always cast as Chinese, etc.), and discriminatory practices that promote and perpetuate the selection of whites over Asians and other ethnic groups.

In sum, there appears to be an improvement but the numbers fall short overall. A single Spike Lee production employs more Blacks in all categories than any film in recent memory involving Asian Americans. It is an observa-tion worth contemplating.

A large proportion of Asian Americans in films, moreover, is outside the mainstream and works in and for the community, a proprietary support group that encourages but does not necessarily stimulate the need for the best work capable of an artist or craftsman. While involvement of the artist in the community is important and obligatory, he often loses out on the training and experiences needed to compete beyond the ethnic enclave or audience.

In the film and T.V. industry at large, how many active (working steadily, if spottily) Asian American executives, directors, writers, cameramen, edi-tors, composers, actors, and so on, are there? A half dozen, a dozen in each category at any given time?

The primary obstacle, as we all know, is the ingrained racism of Ameri-can society, a condition that will not improve for at least another fifty years (and at whose expense anyone can guess). I have been luckier than most, but luck is fickle, indiscriminate and unjust. Hans Richter once said to me, "There are lots of opportunities but no jobs." To Asian Americans, I would say, "There are lots of jobs, but fewer opportunities."

NOTES

1. For the purposes of this essay, Asian Americans refer only to those of Chinese or Japanese extraction. Newsreel and documentary-type material were excluded but fictional films or scenes in which Asians *appear*, without any regard to themes, Asian or non-Asian, contained herein, are included in my analysis. In 1971 more than half of the films made in the U.S. were reported lost or destroyed; 4,500 of those extant are now preserved at the American Film Institute archives. From the Library of Congress copyright registration records, the AFI catalogs, trade papers, and reviews of diverse origin, I have identified 438 films for the period 1900-1928. Prior to 1900, only two kinetoscopes are recorded, and about thirty more are of a newsreel or factual nature. 1928 is the terminal date for this survey in order to allow for silent films released after 1927. An extrapolation of 438 films minimum and 800 or greater maximum is a feasible and acceptable count. Although the practice was to cast whites in Asian roles, it is not too far afield to suggest that a good number of Asians, albeit in minor roles, were employed. As early as 1908, William M. Selig, who was the first to establish a studio in California, rented the rear lot of the Sing Loo Laundry, between 7th and 8th on Olive Street in Los Angeles, and hired local Japanese as "roustabouts, scene-shifters, carpenters and extras." Bob Okazaki, *Pacific Citizen*, March 2, 1956; "Scoop" Conlon, "First Movie Studio in California Starts in Old Chinese Laundry," *San Francisco Chronicle*, January 15, 1922.

2. The Japanese-American Film Company, "the first company in America to be owned, controlled and operated by Japanese," released its dramatic film, *The Oath of the Sword*, on November 12, 1914. Based in Los Angeles, the company planned to make films in Japan and in Hawaii; the president of the corporation was K. Numamoto and the secretary, J. Takata. Among the forty Japanese players were Hisa Numa, Tomi Morri, Kohano Akashi, and Jack Y. Abbe. *Moving Picture World* 22:3 October 17, 1914:314. In 1913, the Yamatograph Company of Portland, Oregon produced "a number of films, amounting to 12,000 feet altogether" (approximately three hours and twenty minutes) on the Japanese in Oregon, Washington and California. Apparently they were intended to inform the Japanese back home "what the Japanese [were] doing in America and under what conditions" and to counter the vitriolic anti-Japanese campaigns of the period that sought to bar Asians from owning and leasing land. "California 'Movies':, and "Immigrants in 'Movies':, *The Japan Weekly Mail* (Tokyo), December 6 and 13, 1913.

3. Between 1914 and 1922, Hayakawa appeared in 53 films; 25 were produced by his own company, which he founded in 1918. He once boasted, "I made two million in the four years. No taxes." *Sessue Hayakawa* (Oral History Research Office, Columbia University New York, April, 1959): 29.

4. A Japanese fishing village between Santa Monica and Inceville was utilized for scenes. Thomas H. Ince, in Richard Koszarski's *Hollywood Directors, 1914-1940* (New York: Oxford University Press, 1979), 66. "Here was a fragment of the Orient," writes George C. Pratt. "Had the Santa Ynez range suddenly gone mad?" In 1914, Ince scheduled "Civil War, Puritan, Irish and Japanese stories." *The Wrath of the Gods* with Tsuru Aoki and Sessue Hayakawa was the first "Japanese spectacle film" made under this program. George C. Pratt, "See Mr. Ince," in Marshall Deutelbaum's, ed., *"Image" on the Art and Evolution of the Film* (New York: Dover; Rochester: International Museum of Photography, 1979), 85, 90. Later M.G.M. as well had a "Chinese Village" set which was used, for example, on *Too Hot to Handle* (1938).

5. Hayakawa in an interview explained that he was "goaded and humiliated" by one of his financial partners. He was insulted and advised, "People in this country have no use for Chinks." "Every man in that room looked uncomfortable," he added. "Then I bow with politeness to all and I leave that room. . . . Next day this is how I answer. I attach every piece of property of that company permitted by law. That same day, I dismiss all my servants—I close up my house and put caretaker in charge. I cancel all my engagements. I said to myself, 'Now I am through.' I take many *little* insults and humiliation—but no—nothing so big as this." "What Happened to Hayakawa," *Motion Picture*, 36: January, 1929.

6. For instance, Masajiro Kaihatsu started an antique and Oriental costume rental business in Los Angeles. Among those who went to Japan are Yutake Jack Abe, actor-director-writer, later producer at Nikkatsu; Henry Kotani, acclaimed for his photography on DeMille's *Joan the Woman* (1917), who joined Shochiku; Thomas Kurihara, who became a film distributor; Henry Heihachiro Okawa, actor and stunt flyer; and Kamiyama Sojin, who had made his debut in Fairbanks's *The Thief of Bagdad* (1924).

7. Among many: Lon Chaney, Helen Hayes, Katharine Hepburn, Johnny Hines, Boris Karloff, Peter Lorre, Myrna Loy, Ramon Novarro, Warner Oland, Anthony Quinn, Constance Talmadge, Lupe Velez.

8. A rough tally of feature and T.V. films which employ Asian actors and actresses is as follows:

1900-1927 (28 years) = 412	1948-1968 (21 years) = 252
1928-1947 (20 years) = 368	1969-1990 (22 years) = "300"

(Since my notes end with 1968, I've projected an average figure.)
Even without allowances for films lost in the 1900-1927 period (and losses are greater the earlier the date because of the deterioration of nitrate stock and of indifference to the economic and aesthetic value of film), it's evident that the most active span was the silent age. As expected, the second period (1928-1947) during which interest in both China and Japan was fanned by news headlines, the figure remains high. The numbers are deceptive in that they include films in which only a single Asian appears, usually in the butler-cook-gardener category. In sum, the chances for roles lessen with each passing year, or if you prefer to be optimistic, remain the same. *Motion Picture 1894-1969* (Washington: Copyright Office, Library of Congress, 1951-1971); *Kleine Collection of Early Motion Pictures in the Library of Congress* (Washington: Copyright Office/Library of Congress, 1980); *Moving Picture World* (1907-1928); *Variety Film Reviews* (1907-1925); *American Film Institute Catalog* (1921-1930 & 1961-1970); various periodicals and newspaper articles and reviews (*Photoplay, Moving Picture, New York Times, Billboard, Exhibitor's Trade Reviews*, etc.).

THE SECRET GAME (1917)
Yoshio Kishi collection

PIONEERS AND GROUNDBREAKERS

YOSHIO KISHI

Even if accurate records were kept by studios, locating and identifying Asian American actors and production personnel of the silent period after more than six decades, or nearly a century if you count from the birth of the movies, is well-nigh impossible.

Those fortunate enough to be cited in the credits, press books, or reviews are recallable from the past; countless others are lost forever. Some may yet survive in the memories of relatives and friends or in scrapbooks, photo albums and papers forgotten in attics and basements; perhaps someday they will surface. It is with this hope that this brief and incomplete list of names is compiled. Any information about the people they represent will be appreciated. To remember the past is one way of honoring those who have preceded us and hewed a path for us to follow.

The main sources: *Moving Picture World* (1907-1928); *Exhibitor's Trade Review* (1916-1928); *Variety Film Reviews* (1907-1925); period fan magazines like *Photoplay, Moving Picture Story*, etc.; *American Film Institute Catalog* (1921-1930); and various newspaper reviews and articles like Bob Okazaki's columns in *Pacific Citizen*.

Names are given as found: misspelled or incorrect names, pseudonyms, and inaccurate transliterations. Correct names, when known, are in parentheses. Doubtful names—figures perhaps not falling within the silent period or not Asian at all—are indicated with a question mark.

Abbe, Jack Y. (Yutake Jack Abe)
Ahn, Pock Pock
Ahn, Ralph
Akiyama, Yukio
Aleong, Aki
Aoki, Tsuru
Aoyama, Yukio (Kaihatsu, Masajiro)
Chan, Lee
Chan, Ole
Cheung, Louie
Chew, Frank (?)
Ching, Bo
Choy, Sook

THE WRATH OF THE GODS (1914)
Yoshio Kishi collection

Chung, Lee
Chung, Walter
Fang, Charles
Fong, Charlie
Frejiti, Tayo
Fujita, Toyo
Fung, Paul
Fung, Willie

Hayakawa, Sessue
Ho, Andy
Ho, Chew
Ho, F. K.
Ho, Peter Chen
Ho, T.S.
Hoo, Hayward Soo
(Soo Hoo, Hayward)
Howe, James Wong
Hoy, Danny (?)
Hsieh, Warren
Ichioka, Media
Ichioka, Toshyie
Imazu, Eddie
Inokuchi, Makoto
Iribe, Paul (?)
Jung, Allen
Jung, Shia
Kaito, Maui
Kim, Helen
Kim, Jay
Kim, Sam
Kino, Goro
Kishii, Fujii
Komai, Tetsu
Konishi, Michi
Kotani, Henry
Kuma, Profulla
Kumagai, Frank
Kung, Shang Jen (?)

Kurihara, Thomas
Kuwa, George
Lani, Prince Lei
Lani, Pua
Lau, Wesley
Lee, Eddie
Lee, Etta
Lee, Tung-foo

Lefong, Won
Ling, Bo
Leong, Jimmy (James B.)
Ling, Nien Son
Liu, Yu-ching
Long, Lotus (Suyetomi, Pearl)
Louie, May
Lung, Charles
Lung, Clarence
Mei, Lady Tsen
Mita, Ura
Mori
Mori, Tashia (Mori, Toshia)
Morita, Miki
Nakahara, Yumiko
Nambu, K.
Okawa, Henry (Okawa, Henry Hiehachiro)
Okubo, Benji
Saito, Tatsuo
Satow, Kiyoshi
Seki, Frank M.
Seki, Misao
Sojin, Kamiyama
Sui-Te-Wan, Madame
Sung, Willie (?)
Takemi, H.
Tamamoto, T.
Tokunaga, Frank
Tong, Kam
Wang, James (Jim)

(Photos from left to right)
THE TALE OF THE SEA (1922)
THE FIRST BORN (1920)
THE FIRST BORN (1920)
WHERE LIGHTS ARE LOW (1917)
HOUSE WITHOUT A KEY (1926)
GEISHA HOUSE STREET SCENE
Yoshio Kishi collection

Wata, Sussie
Wing, Ah
Wong, Bessie
Wong, Bruce (?)
Wong, Foo
Wong, George W.,
Wong, Iris (?)
Wong, Jean (?)

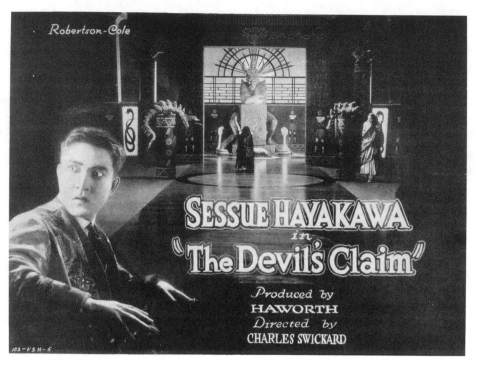

Wong Jim (?)
Wong Joe (?)
Wong, Lulu
Wong, Mary
Wong, Olive (?)
Wong, Ti Set
Wong, Mrs. Wing
Yamamoto, Togo
Yamata, Mr.
Young, Chow
Young, Ming

THE DEVIL'S CLAIM (1920)
Yoshio Kishi collection

Many of us "below the line" film workers who do all the schlepping and dirty work do not seek the spotlight, but instead accumulate the experience that translates into production value in someone else's intellectual property.

CURTIS CHOY

DON'T LET

THEM KNOW

GERALDINE

KUDAKA

DON'T LET THEM KNOW

Geraldine Kudaka

This week, I am flying to Cincinnati to online my "epic" video series. As crazy as it sounds, my "epic" is being onlined by a mobile news unit between broadcasts. Truly guerrilla filmmaking at its best. What started out as a simple weekend project has taken me over three years to finish. Three years, a bank loan, and thousands of hours of agony. And the irony is that this series is a simple how-to video. The only thing "epic" about this show is how long and how hard I've had to work to finish the tape.

It would be easy to lay the blame on a flaw in my character, but the real reason is insufficient cash flow. Producing means I work and, instead of buying a car, I buy a week's worth of time on an editing system.

Everything I do is determined by money. I write because paper and pen are cheaper than film. I made a how-to tape because it seemed like it would be cheaper than doing a dramatic feature. Little did I know it all would come down to the same hard reality—cash. There are only so many favors one can pull in from friends. It still comes down to money. Love, loyalty, and honor are easily bought. It's just a question of the number of digits behind the dollar sign.

Don't get me wrong—I still believe in love, loyalty and honor. I make choices based on my intrinsic value system. But a lot of the choices I've made have been based on an unrealistic understanding of money. I haven't plotted out my career based on what would take me to the next step. I've had a poverty-stricken attitude of just getting the next meal. Typical ghetto syndrome. You don't deserve any better, so you're willing to make do with what your hands can touch. Deep down inside, you think you can do better, but nowhere in your lower-class upbringing were you ever taught the tools of achieving your dreams. You weren't even allowed to dream. It was enough you got by.

In my family, money was an alien entity. A hostile force constantly threatening brutalization. There are those who romanticize poverty, but anyone who comes from an economically deprived childhood will tell you there is nothing romantic about poverty. There is a terrible brutalization of spirit. Of mind. Of confidence. Even of love.

Once, I asked my mother, "Did you ever love us?" and my mother said, "What do you mean? We fed you, didn't we?" (I wonder if Steven Spielberg

MICHAEL CHIN,
CINEMATOGRAPHER

ever asked his mother that question. If he did, I doubt his mother said, "What do you mean? We fed you.")

Class structure. The effects of class have more to do with our fates than we care to recognize.

Example: I worked on a "radical leftwing" Iranian film. The director had been involved with a group of filmmakers who plotted to kidnap the Shah's son at an international film festival. The plot was discovered. Most of the filmmakers were executed. This man was lucky. He was imprisoned. Years later, after the fall of the Shah, he was freed. He, like a lot of Iranian liberals, left Iran. They had now come together to make a film about the plight of Iranian refugees.

Paradox: The dividing line on this film between above the line and below the line was clearly demarcated by one's class background. The key Iranian talent were all from the upper middle classes. The lower technical staff were working class.

The sound mixer explained it to me—after the fall of the Shah, most of the upper-middle-class intelligensia fled. The electricians and grips stayed behind. Ironically, because of the void left by the fleeing producers, directors and upper-level management, these lowly grips and electricians were moved into producing and directing.

Paradox: At Beverly Hills High School, the most commonly spoken language is Farsi (Iranian).

Paradox: While we were paid slave wages, the producer used production funds to remodel his house (which doubled as the principle location). His carpenters were paid more than the set electrician.

So much for "radical leftwing" filmmaking.

The owner of a lab once said to me—"Filmmakers. There's no lower breed. They'd sell their mothers if they could."

Cash—the omnipotent force behind filmmaking. So little of what we do has to do with creativity. We need an army to make a film—a feature film, that is—and that army needs its supplies.

I look at myself and realize I lack the gentility of an officer, much less a general. If anything, I embody the rough brutalization of a private. Cannon fodder. Yet I refuse to accept this pigeonholing. I refuse to be cannon fodder. I thumb my nose at the limitations of my class, of myself, and trod on.

Bam. Smack into a wall. The wall I hit most often is myself. My secret fears. Coming from a background of deprivation, the only thing I can imagine is lack.

Yet without imagination, without dreams, it's impossible to go out there and do better. Have more. If you cannot imagine it, you cannot have it.

It's impossible to make films if what is buried in your subconscious is a fear of hunger. You can't stand in a roomful of people pitching projects if your inner voice is singing a litany of hunger and failure. You have to lose that fear, and do it with grace. You can't sugar-coat it and expect it to disappear. It will always be there, sabotaging you. It has a way of surfacing when you least expect it. If you secretly believe you will fail, you will fail.

Why is this important? Investors want projects which smack of success. People who have money are afraid of hungry people. Even bankers who hold your savings hostage. The next time you walk down skid row, think about how you feel. Repulsed? Envious? Afraid?

Cardinal rule of filmmaking. Don't let them know you're hungry.

MAKING THE CUT
IRVIN PAIK

I am a second generation Korean American raised in Los Angeles. I am making an above-average living in motion picture editing. If I had more than one child and my wife did not work, that would not be the case. I feel that being Asian has held me back because those doing the hiring will not assume that I am as capable as a white person. While they readily accept me as an assistant (which is basically a glorified filing job), I have to prove that I think and create like an American. The old bromide that "You've got to be twice as good as the white boys to get ahead" still applies.

The ways of getting into the Hollywood establishment labor pool all have a common thread, knowing somebody. Whether your father is head of the studio or you start in the shipping room of an obscure film lab, eventually somebody has to recommend you. If you can't deliver packages properly you will be ignored until you learn how, unless your father is head of the studio.

I always wanted to be in show business. I was in the drama club at Manual Arts High School and majored in theater arts at UCLA. After two years of theater, I realized that my chances of making it as an actor were severely limited and as an Asian actor almost impossible. George Takei, Mr. Sulu of "Star Trek" fame, was in the class ahead of me. I played a "Puppy Salamander" in children's shows, a rabbit in a one-act play and even appeared in blackface. I commuted two hundred miles a day for two weeks to appear in *Flower Drum Song*, one of my few human roles. I switched to motion pictures because I'd heard that defense industries had documentary film units in which I could always find a job in case I failed to break into Hollywood films. This was in 1960 when the theater department met in wood bungalows and motion picture majors were "technicians" not talented enough to participate in theater. Steven Spielberg and George Lucas had not inspired future filmmakers to "Go to film school—direct *Jaws* and *Star Wars*." Students were focused on civil rights and "freedom rides" to help southern Blacks.

Four years later, I had a masters degree but lost my student deferment and was about to be drafted into the army, so I joined. I signed up for a new program which took forty college graduates from recruits to second lieutenants in ten months. It worked for me. I did what I was told, most of the time, and was promoted in a timely manner. Throughout my artillery training I wrote letters to everyone I could think of explaining that my masters degree in motion pictures could be put to better use than firing cannons.

Everyone was up the day our permanent assignments were announced. Everybody wanted Europe because there was no war and you could take your family. Married lieutenants did not want Korea because it meant another year's separation from loved ones. Being Korean and single and having never set foot in "the land of the morning calm," I would have welcomed the assignment. I was pretty good at shooting cannons and was actually looking forward to lobbing a thousand pounds of explosives a few miles down the road, on practice targets only. No one wanted Vietnam, because a second lieutenant's life expectancy in a battle is something like five seconds. It was May 1965, and President Johnson had just bombed the Gulf of Tonkin in North Vietnam which signaled large scale commitment by the United States. The immediate affect on us was to relax all unnecessary harassment and graduate as many lieutenants as possible. I was saddened to see some of the career married men assigned to a year's separation from families. Others were looking forward to airborne school to learn to jump out of airplanes and probably be assigned to Vietnam. And then my name was read. I was the shortest person in the class, one of two Asians, a Californian and got called before the commandant for criticizing some of the training as "show and tell." There was great interest in my assignment so when the sergeant read "New York City," there was much hooting and hollering. I was called "New York City" for the next month. On stage at graduation, the Commandant said, as he shook my hand, "Oh, you're the one."

I was assigned to the Public Information Office in New York City. While on leave, my assignment was changed to the Defense Information School in New Rochelle. Upon arrival, I was told I would be teaching television techniques to officers above me in rank. I explained my schooling was in motion pictures and the commandant seemed relieved that he had an excuse to transfer me immediately to the Army Pictorial Center in Long Island City, the assignment I had been trying for since my enlistment!

So hard work paid off with the promotion to First Lieutenant and a reserve assignment in the Signal Corps as Captain. I bought a new car, travelled in the eastern and southern United States, Hawaii, Japan, Europe and even survived six months in Vietnam. The gods were with me; surely directing features was just around the corner.

My first job upon discharge in 1967 was with UCLA friends making Disney films in Utah, Alaska, and Florida about owls and peregrine falcons. I was camera assistant, set builder, transportation captain, still photographer and cat trainer. I did this for about two years and advanced to production manager. The crew and cast varied from four to eight. It was non-union to be sure.

Back home in Hollywood, I started making the rounds of small commercial companies and college friends who were on the fringes of the Hollywood establishment. No one cared how hard I had worked getting great photographs of animals. Unless I had experience in their little niche, I didn't know anything. I camera-assisted and did editing jobs for friends from UCLA or was recommended by them. That should have been a clue to me but I still believed that hard work alone would yield promotion.

On an episode of the T.V. show "All in the Family," Archie Bunker bellyaches about protest demonstrations saying "No one marched in the street to get me my job," to which his wife, Edith replies, "No, your Uncle Louie got it for you." My "uncle" got me a job too, my Uncle Sam, that is.

While on a one-day shoot for a television special, the familiar question of how to break into the Hollywood establishment came up and another camera assistant told me about the U.S. Justice Department ordering the producers to hire minorities. This was five years after the Watts riots. He told me whom to contact and I applied and was rejected for the training program because I had too much experience. I said I didn't care, I just wanted a foot in the door. I was told to put my name on a minority job roster and to apply directly to individual companies. I did so, not realizing that one contact was not enough. Resentment was high among skilled workers because now the position being saved for a niece or nephew would be used by a minority.

Hard work got me into the training program after all. One trainee was so efficient that the editor hired him and the last few months of his training was now available to someone else. Headline: "Minority succeeds and lives!" Although I heard much bellyaching about the minority who got hired and fired the same day because he wasn't qualified, I never heard about the ones that succeeded. I was called to replace him because I would not become overwhelmed in an accelerated program. I trained at Paramount, Universal Studios and Warner Brothers learning picture editing, sound effects, dialogue replacement and laboratory procedures. I was placed with people who were understanding and helpful and I was paid $100.00 a week! I was getting paid to go to film school.

At the end of the program, I was hired by Warner Brothers to "make leader." This is an apprentice job of taking thousand-foot rolls of film and removing the soundtracks so the film without sound can be reused. I sat at a rewind machine all day and spliced and rewound. Boring, boring, boring, but I was officially in the "Hollywood" labor force.

Not everyone in the movie business has a glamorous job. Rarely do you read about behind the scenes workers who process film, build sets, haul cameras, record sound, edit picture and sound effects, and do all the jobs that when done correctly never draw attention to themselves. Producers bemoan the "high" costs of union labor, but these costs pale when compared to the twenty million given to Dustin Hoffman and Warren Beatty before a single frame of the film was exposed for *Ishtar* (1987). The four highest paid executives in California for the 1989 year were from Walt Disney, receiving combined compensation of over 119 million dollars (*Los Angeles Times*, May 27, 1990). "Ego" expenses are paid because most films are "packages" of director, writer, star put together by independent producers. Each participant wants to feel that his importance is acknowledged. The highest paid star has to have the largest dressing room or the longest mobile home.

After three months of working as an "apprentice," I was promoted to "assistant" in the dialogue replacement department. Normally, I would have had to stay an apprentice for three years but the minority program exempted me from this rule. Two years later, I was promoted to dialogue editor. It was 1975, and normally, I couldn't have had this job until 1977. I received a few complaints from non-minorities who had to serve out their time and resented my rapid advancement above them. So far, I found that most people related to me as a person, once we got to know each other.

Warner Brothers suffered cancellations of several television shows and my department was cut back. I was out of a job. May through August is a very slow period and the majority of the industry is out of work. Through people I had worked with at Warner Brothers, I got a job at Paramount and then at Universal where I worked steadily for almost ten years except for the slow

"With no one to promote me, I found I had to promote myself and had not developed those skills."

months. I went back to assisting but for picture editors because I wanted to edit television and then move on up to features and then onto directing and producing.

I worked on film television such as "Kung Fu," "Airwolf," "Knightrider," or "Miami Vice" as opposed to videotape half-hour situation comedies like "Family Ties" or the "Cosby Show." The editing techniques and staff are very different.

Universal was producing thirteen television shows when I started in 1976. Each show had three, maybe four, picture editors. When air dates got closer and closer to the end of shooting, there might be six editors on an episode. Assistants were being moved up to editors on a regular basis, if the editor you worked for put in a good word for you. I learned to edit, by cutting scenes in my spare time after finishing my assisting duties. I did not socialize after work and did not notice that those assistants who got moved up were all in the same social circle. My spare time was consumed in taking care of a recently purchased home. Some assistants advanced themselves by showing producers film they had cut while tricking other assistants into doing their work. Depending upon the person, he could be labeled a go-getter, brown-noser or cut-throat. By 1982, I got my chance at editing but television production slowed down. The number of jobs were cut in half and continued to decline. Management changed. Independent and non-union companies were draining product away from major studios. The networks were turning away from expensive action filmed shows to half-hour videotape comedies. The editor I worked with left Universal. He had worked there for nineteen years.

With no one to promote me, I found I had to promote myself and had not developed those skills. People who advance quickly have a sense of other people's feelings and know how to take advantage of them. They can gain the producers' confidence with small talk and common interests like golf, drinking, going to sports events, and partying. I thought that work was work and play was play and the two shouldn't mix. I wanted to be promoted for my work ability separate from relying on friends. Wrong! Friends were the only people who hired me since leaving the army. My first job came only after the supervisor got to know me personally. A slick resume and a masters degree never earned me a job.

Twenty years ago, I sat with thirty Asian Americans who demanded to know from Edwin Lester, Director of the Los Angeles Civic Light Opera, why he had cast a Caucasian to play an Asian in the musical version of *Teahouse of the August Moon*. He defended himself by explaining why he wasn't prejudiced. He cast solely on talent and correctness for the role. Race had nothing to do with his decision. We were wrong for accusing him of being a bigot. Last year, I was part of a committee to study discrimination within the Motion Picture and Videotape Editors Guild. The Board of Directors was very understanding and in agreement that discrimination existed and it should be looked into. Twenty years ago last year, the results were the same: ignore the problem and maybe it will go away.

Racism is extremely subtle and is intermixed with personality. You are hired more by who you are than what you know. There is no examination or rating system for entry or advancement. Competition for jobs is intense so relatives and friends are first to hear about opportunities. Affirmative action from within the union is impossible because no one is willing to give someone else an advantage.

The union committee on discrimination was in response to a member threatening to sue the union for alleged racist comments by its business manager (the person paid to run the union on a day-to-day basis). Two people on the committee were convinced that there was no racism. After listening to comments from various minorities, they conceded that minorities might have a more difficult time, but it could be overcome. The committee drafted a questionnaire to be sent to the membership to statistically measure racism. It drafted a letter to be sent to department heads encouraging awareness of racism in hiring. Various members wrote articles on racism for the newsletter. The union board of directors killed all of these efforts. The board has to represent all two thousand members. It cannot give one group an advantage over another. Any affirmative action would have to include women, the disabled and older workers. After a few months of weekly meetings, new board members were elected and the committee was never reinstated.

Three years ago, I started working in feature films (films made to be shown first in theaters instead of television). I liked working for quality and storytelling as opposed to television where the most important goal is finishing by the air date. Perhaps, if I had started in features, I would have enjoyed the swiftness of television. An episode can be finished in a month, while a feature can last a year or two.

I had to go back to assisting as no one wants a television editor to cut his feature. A producer wants the hottest actors, the most-wanted director, the editor with the best track record, etc. I know several television editors with impressive credits who have tried to get feature jobs and they're always asked, "What features have you cut?" There's an elitist attitude in Hollywood in which everyone thinks his particular job is special and no one else can do it. I've heard male editors arrogantly pontificate that women can't cut action scenes. No one ever suggested that men can't cut romantic scenes. Editors get labeled by their last job as television editors, action editors, comedy editors, romance editors, etc., which has more to do with image than reality.

Personal contact overcomes most obstacles. I know a television editor who was recommended by a mutual acquaintance to be a second editor on a feature. Sometimes television producers take along one of their editors when they do a feature. It's more likely that the producers will "upgrade" to a well-known feature editor. The first assistant on a feature often is a second editor. If the editor becomes ill or gets a better job, then the first assistant may be given a chance to be the editor. If your father is the editor, there's a good chance you will eventually be a co-editor.

The major studios are becoming more and more like independents. Universal eliminated all sound effects, music and dialogue editors. These editors form independent companies and compete against each other in bidding for work. Union members are in competition with each other instead of being united when management tries to take away benefits in contract talks. Last year, all unions lost the right to have Saturday and Sunday as overtime paydays. Management can make them work any five consecutive days at straight time.

Employment is from movie to movie. The producer hires a director who hires the editor who hires the assistants and second and third editors. Rarely does an administrator hire any of these people. They start a few days before the cameras roll and are laid off when the film is finished. Hiring is rarely done from union rosters. The first persons called are friends and relatives and they

> *"I've heard male editors arrogantly pontificate that women can't cut action scenes. No one ever suggested that men can't cut romantic scenes."*

recommend other friends if they're busy. When an additional person is needed in the editing room, it's usually for the next day. The producer has to see the work piled up to justify increasing his labor cost. Getting a job often depends upon being at home when the phone rings, because the first person contacted is often hired on the spot.

Career planning is impossible as film projects appear and disappear at the whim of the public, stars, directors, schedules, current events and changing heads of studios. A producer may make a deal for a television show in April only to see it cancelled in September by a new head of programming. The three editors planning to work on the show from August to March are suddenly scrambling for jobs when most commitments are already made. Most shows are given a commitment of six to thirteen episodes which can be cancelled at any time depending upon the ratings. If you're lucky, in December the network commits to six or thirteen more shows. If not, you're looking for work at Christmas.

In features, you contact your friends to see what projects are starting and what position might be available to you. There are always delays in starting and often cancellations. You may start a project and after two weeks, the director is fired and the editor goes with him. Some assistants work with only one editor and work steadily which is good except that no one else gets to know you. What happens if the editor retires or gets ill? On the other hand, working with different editors from job to job, you're never sure about your picture.

The minority program that got me into the industry ended after about five years. To achieve integration of the motion picture industry, those minorities admitted under special circumstances should have progressed to a level where they could make it easier for the next generation. But progress has not been made in most cases. The producers and department supervisors are still getting their friends and relatives in first.

My present job will end in a few weeks. I have no idea what I will be doing next. I want to stay in features. That may mean passing up television jobs until a feature comes along. The director I'm working with now is always negotiating for another movie. If he's successful, he will probably have the same editing crew. But, maybe he won't.

Curtis Choy

Hey! How's it going? Sorry I never write, but, honest to Kwan Kung, I been busy doing a billion things that ain't nothing to write home about. You know. Making a living, keeping the wheels running, cleaning house. All right, so I was in Asia half of last year. I was too BUSY, okay? Working long and hard and getting paid not so good. So you think I must be writing now to gripe about something, right? Like you're right about me marrying a girl from the old country.

What it is, is: The workers do the work, and those above-the-line[1] cop the credit, the awards, and the big bucks. This is annoyingly undemocratic, and it doesn't have to be this way. Now I ain't knocking nobody in particular (you fill in your own blanks), but check out the rags put out by different organizations. Who gets written up? Who gets left out? And what is success? Who defines it? Who needs it? Ain't it amazing how the answers all point in the direction of the mainstream money and honkie notions of success? Is public masturbation really good form?

I ain't no foreigner to work. Look at my father, who worked at the post office as a clerk. Spencer's father's a gardener.[2] Michael's father's a grocer.[3] Myron's father sells insurance.[4] These guys aren't recognized. They don't have academy awards—they're not successes in the celebrated sense. Nor are their sons.

Many of us below-the-line[5] film workers, who do all the schlepping and dirty work, do not seek the spotlight, but instead accumulate the experience that translates into production value in someone else's intellectual property. We are the ones that do not blow our own horns and whose labor makes possible the receipt of hoopla that's bestowed on those above-the-line. Us older farts, we aren't badly-off starving paupers, and we're not unnecessarily cabdrivers or busboys. But we aren't recognized much either.

This may sound corny, but there isn't much room out on the cutting edge. (My last time out near the edge, my film was called too radical, audaciously using poetry where no documentary had before. Oh, yeah, and I forgot to use a British narrator.) So those basking on that public edge should give a little credit to those pioneers who've boldly seized the means of production, lost their shirts, and who continue to support newcomers. They've put out to put us where we are. Like, we weren't always HERE, right? (It's further galling to feel shunned as competitors by other yellows in pro-

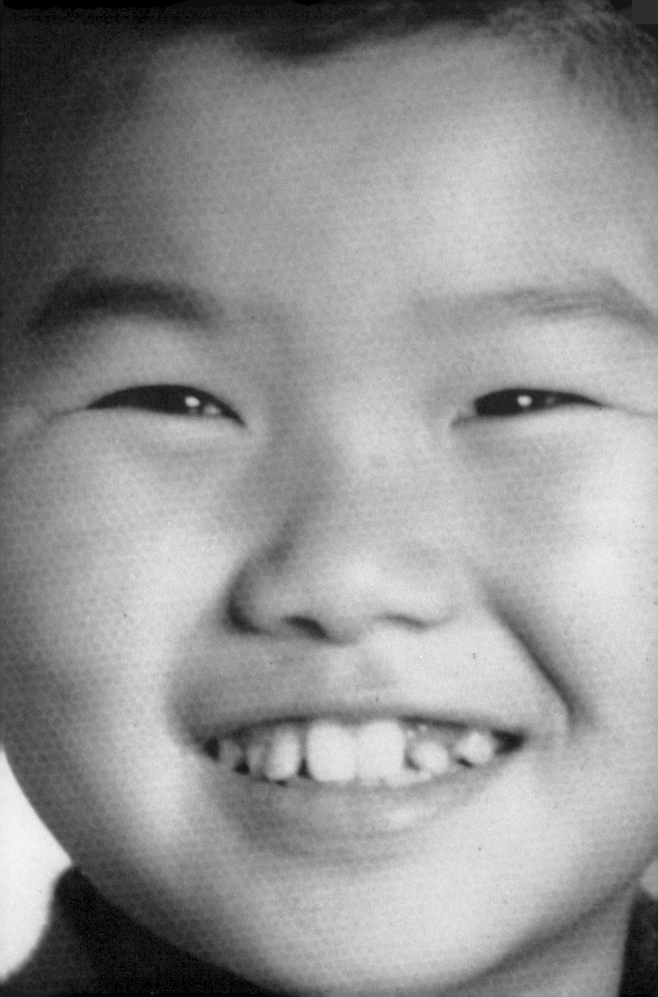

duction, given our early history of helping out. Too bad no one will reveal the mystery of why San Francisco Asian media people can't stand each other.)

A lot of naifs think we have the best job in the world: traveling, meeting strangers, the glamour of premieres and film festivals, sunglasses, big tits everywhere. What they don't understand is how complicated it really is. Those of us who have developed Asian Amerikan consciousness haven't subverted the "white" market. You can penetrate this market and never find any AA consciousness. (I do my bit by explaining the "Chonk Moonhunter" labels stuck to my gear.)[6]

Above or below the line, a yellow has three choices: do Asian/community subjects/productions exclusively, do only "professional" white gigs, or try to do both. In practice, those of us doing both simply get reamed from all directions. Above-the-line is perpetual underfunding and peer competition, or else a slimy dungheap of gladhanders and backstabbers scrambling for the biggest piece of cake. For work below-the-line, the "community" only calls when it needs a freebie (spending hard cash only for "outside" help) and we ain't white enough to be hired on the well-heeled white productions. When Michael is told he doesn't have enough feature experience or I'm told I don't have enough feature experience (often by people with little feature experience), what they mean is we don't have enough white feature experience—then they will casually hire a white person who has less experience than us.

Paradoxically, whites stigmatize us for working in the Asian media ghetto, but are jealous because they think we have first dibs on Asian jobs. Another contradiction for you yin/yang east/west duality splitheads: From a professional point of view, the Asian stuff is a drag because it never pays full rate. But, to tell you the truth, I like working on cheap features in Asia just because me and my craft are treated with some respect. I don't feel like a pawn in some occupation army telling locals to stay off their street and that they can't go home.

So I'd define success as making a living with a clean conscience—doing whatever it is we do without crossing that line that is selling out. The irony is that fifteen years ago I would have accused my present self of being a sellout. I do the work for money. A gun for hire. Legal prostitution. (Agents are really pimps, aren't they?) I unknowingly signed onto an ad with Exxon the week after the Alaska oil spill. When I found out, I could have walked off righteously, but I played "professional" and did my job. We're not stealing food out of the mouths of babies. How complicit am I? Is this any better than someone doing army training films? Where do you draw the line? (Well, I won't work for the War Department or the CIA.) The commercial is the ultimate propaganda of a capitalist society. The message is BUY BUY BUY trendy plastic eco-suicidal shit, and keep the fattest cats fat. The joke on me is that my 1969 intention was to be a Propagandist for The Revolution, and a creative artist on the Chonk frontier. Who knew that the yuppie/raygunnite scum would stop up the whole damn toilet?

But back to my gripe. Asians toasting themselves with awards are playing the yellowannabe Hollywood game of mirrors and appearances. Only the first few names on the credits get recognized, and the value of most workers simply goes unsung. (My personal regret is not having the equal opportunity to turn down an Academy Award on national television.)

In the end, I have only this two-bit advice to you would-be filmmakers:

get your MBA, and sell real estate. Then, you'll have the capital to make films, and the option to do something else when you see the folly of it.

P.S.: I'm NOT bitter. And don't forget to stay for all the credits.

NOTES

1. Above-the-line: the so-called "creative people"—writers, directors, actors, producers; on a budget form they are literally above the line (the vastest amount of money is assigned here).
2. Spencer Nakasako is a writer and director, and directly responsible for the birth of NAATA. He is below-the-line in spirit.
3. Michael Chin is a cinematographer and director of photography, producer of one of the earliest Asian American documentaries, *Inside Chinatown* (1973).
4. Myron Chan is a remote broadcast tech at a T.V. station, bass player, and godfather of Asian American audio. He taught the author basic microphonology and how to coil those pesky little wires.
5. Below-the-line: the technicians responsible for lights, camera, sound, truck-driving, first-aid . . . you know, the workers.
6. *Chonk* is a term describing that which is "Chinese American," coined during the rise of the Asian American movement by a poet in San Francisco. *Moonhunter* comes from the legend of the Iron Moonhunter, a train to China that Chinamen workers built by ripping off parts at night from the Transcontinental Railroad.

CHARACTERIZING COSTUME

Terence Tam Soon

Our family home was on a hill in Honolulu, overlooking Waikiki. At the bottom of that hill was the local neighborhood movie theater. My grandmother found that the best baby sitter was the movies. So every weekend, I went to the children's show for nine cents in the morning. I'd rush home for lunch in order to run back to the movie to catch the matinee for twenty-five cents. Sometimes I lived in the theater for twelve hours on weekends. I became a prisoner of fantasies and technicolor.

For my twelfth birthday, my mother got me a ticket to the local production of the musical, *Oklahoma*, my first live stage performance. I became hooked on the colors, lights, sets, and excitement of the theatre. At the age of five, I started to draw. The nuns at the parochial school encouraged me. Out of a class of about ninety students, I was the only one who wanted to be an artist. Others wanted to become doctors, lawyers, engineers, teachers, government officials. I told my parents I wanted to go to art school. My father said: "Become a commercial artist, not a fine artist!"

In Los Angeles, I attended Chouinard Art Institute (Cal/Arts). I was voted top three in Fashion Design in my graduating class. While my fellow classmates went right into the film industry—Bob Mackie and Judy Evans—I could not break into the studios as easily. So I went into the fashion industry, and sold my designs at Neiman Marcus, Bendel's, and other high fashion stores. But I still had the desire to do costumes for stage and film. So I left the garment trade.

Being the mid-sixties, my career got sidetracked. I tuned in and dropped out! With Frank Zappa's group, the GIO's, I became a dancer on Sunset Strip; I also opened an art gallery/boutique, "First National Nothing," with a friend from art school, Anthony DeRosa. He did the paintings and I did the fashions. Our customers were the rock groups of the sixties— the Byrds, Jimi Hendrix, Cher, John Sebastian, Cheech and Chong, etc.

My customers encouraged me to go back to costume designing, so in 1971, I joined the East West Players, not as a designer, but as an actor. When the costume designer left the company, I stepped in and did my first play, *The Inspector General* (Russia, 1850).

As a designer for East West Players, I was labeled an "ethnic designer." My first production away from them was at the Inner City Cultural Center.

The show was *One in a Crowd*, a black drama starring Beah Richards. This show, and *The Gold Watch* by Momoko Iko, led to my doing *Revolution* for the Mark Taper Forum. Because of the few minority designers at that time, I got jobs doing Asian, Black, and Latino plays. The Taper show that got me into television was *Me and Bessie*, a musical based on the life of Bessie Smith, with Linda Hopkins.

During this period, I went to several producers and complained about doing only ethnic shows. I told them, "Look, I was born and raised in Hawaii, which is part of the United States. I grew up on Cokes, french fries, and rock and roll. As a costume designer, I have studied all periods of costume history." One producer complimented me on a color scheme for the costumes: "You have that delicate Oriental palette," disregarding my four years at art school studying color and design.

In the industry, I am known for my color schemes and fabrication of costumes. Also, because of my high fashion background, I am known as a "woman's designer." Some of my ladies include Joan Chen, Lee Remick, Nancy Kwan, Lauren Hutton, Alfre Woodard, Nobu McCarthy, Karen Black, Shelley Duvall, Teri Garr, Kim Miyori, Beah Richards, Beulah Quo, Lisa Lu, and many more.

I prefer to work in theatre because I have more time to develop my designs. The pace of films or television is very fast—from five days to five weeks. But be it stage or film, I take the same basic approach. First, I read the script to do what is called a costume breakdown. This is a list of which characters appear in what scenes, including the number of costumes per person and the look of the costume itself. The script tells me the time of year, day, and location. I meet with the director, and touch base with the author to obtain their ideas. Taking a cue from the stage designer, I blend my costumes with the sets to create visual continuity—a painting. No polka-dot dresses against striped walls or chartreuse clothing on a purple couch!

Lighting is critical to costuming. Gels create a mood on the set. Direct or white lights are used in films, but on stage, the lighting designer may use a color gel that will change a fabric's coloring. Recently, I did the costumes for *The Chairman's Wife*, by Wakako Yamauchi. In the final dream segment between Madame Mao and Wang Guanmei, the script called for a green dress to be worn by Wang Guanmei, as based on historical notes. I chose a dark jade green fabric. But the dialogue went thus:

Madame Mao: "Is this the dress you wore to Jakarta?"

Wang Guanmei: "The black dress you suggested was too warm for Jakarta."

The lighting designer had gelled the scene with red, and the green dress turned black under the lights. So we quickly adjusted the lights. I also must measure the actors, and present them with my designs based on the characters they portray. I note their body types: my designs either accentuate their best points or cover their faults—all within the character. As the show or play proceeds, I attend rehearsals and watch the director and actors develop the roles; I observe how the actors move and note what colors they wear personally to know their likes and dislikes. Period shows especially allow me to do a rendition of an era, whereas modern plays pay less attention to the historical "fit" of clothes to the character.

Though I am now in the mainstream of costume designing, I still like to

TERENCE TAM SOON

work on Asian American plays and films. Of the five major Asian American plays that have been presented on PBS Television, I have had the honor of designing *And the Soul Shall Dance*, by Wakako Yamauchi; *The Gold Watch*, by Momoko Iko; and *Paper Angels*, by Genny Lim. As an Asian American, I can show by my work that we are contributing to the industry. And, when films and plays concerning Asians are produced, I as a designer can costume them creatively, drawing upon my historical research, experience, and Asian Pacific sensibility.

IT'S AMERICA

IT'S AMERICA

GEORGE LEONG

George Leong

A day in the life of a boom operator who happens to be Asian American. I'll keep it short and let it ramble. . . .

And so that alarm went off again. My right arm, the only part of me out of bed slithered pass a mostly full can of beer, its fingers trudging a gray across a filled ashtray. I smashed it silent. A foot fell out of the bed to land on Takaki's *Strangers from a Different Shore*. The next foot followed tripping over Jessica's *Dogeaters*.

Called home last night to tell her of an upcoming back-to-back job. Got as far as saying it was out of town when she hung up. Didn't have a chance to tell her that I love her. Maybe tonight if I wrap out early enough.

Forewent the breakfast line. The breakfast burritos at this point could have been made by Tupperware. Same texture. Ahead of me, young Asian woman, well dressed with a bit too much makeup. Some big shot's assistant, probably. I was going to say hello, but she didn't seem comfortable to be near me. No offense. I'm just a boom operator. She must have had her reasons.

Same crap over and over every day. Who thought of this Chinese, the dolly, the lights and all that crap. The Jap-a-lantern crap. It was bad enough when the black rap became Run-D.M.C. The other day, some guy thought he was making a joke when he saw one of these actors sneak up behind to yell into the microphone. Before I could fake a startled look, the gaffer shouted, "hey, you turned George American!" I suppose he meant that I turned white with fear. And for second meals, let us not forget the Chinese lunch (no longer considered a real meal in New York City). You know, that get hungry in . . . nonsense. Everyone ate with chopsticks off those Styrofoam plates, even that Asian woman. Everyone but me. I did what any sensible Chinese would do. Used a fork. Off the plate, the rule is short grain/hashi okay, long grain, especially fried rice/chopsticks, stupid. That's what bowls were made for. At any rate, I thought all this nonsense had passed, when lo and behold, the actress, the star of the film went off a spool of ching chong crap. The mixer looked over to me and shook his head. Only a week to go before we wrap. Okay, not every shoot has been like this. Some have been better, some have been worse. Attitudes are different in different towns as it were. It's America. We're all still addressed as foreigners, just as Native Americans are addressed as extinct. As my fiancee, Beverly Singer (Santa Clara

Pueblo) describes it, "It's a micro of a macro." The craftspeople in this industry are no different. As with the rest of America, these heads have been slow to turn, at least to what I had naively expected going into the 1990s, but they have turned. The term Asian American has even been used in sets recently. And movies by people of color depicting accurate images of people of color have been hitting the screen with success. Success equals jobs. And in this business, money talks very loudly. Perhaps in the 90s, people of color wouldn't have to be twice as good to get a foot into this chunk of industry door.

DEAR SPENCE

MICHAEL CHIN

Michael Chin

While Michael Chin was ripening into one of America's finest cinematographers in the fertile Salinas Valley of Central California, Spencer Nakasako was honing his own spiky, crustacean perceptions a few miles west in the brawling cannery town of Monterey. Mike and Spence, however, were not to encounter each other until much later when their paths fatefully crossed during work on the Asian American films and videos which blossomed forth in San Francisco during the early eighties.

As "below-the-line" craftsmen whose labors have given reality to the visions of many an Asian American "auteur," the two friends share an informed, pragmatic and often jocular view of their lives and work—an outgrowth of their years of involvement in the quirky Asian American media subculture of the Bay Area. Most recently, Spencer collaborated with Wayne Wang as writer and actor on Life is Cheap . . . but Toilet Paper is Expensive, while Michael has continued his incomparable camera work on such highly-acclaimed productions as Forbidden City, U.S.A., Eyes on the Prize and Roots of Resistance: The Story of the Underground Railroad.

The following is the latest in a series of ongoing philosophical exchanges frequently batted back and forth between the two irascible veterans. This one, appropriately, is a thoughtful meditation on longevity in Asian American filmmaking—and the virtues of a genuine paste wax car polish.

John Esaki

July 4, 1990

Hey, Spence!

How ya doin'? Haven't been over lately, but the ol' bus stopped running again. Think maybe it's about time to dump the ol' thing? Kind of looks like a camouflaged combat truck with a couple of patches of the original green showing through all the grey and red primer, but I keep thinking it's my only link to some pretty amazing times.

As a Tinseltown hack might pitch it, every dent's got a story. I remember once during *Chan Is Missing* back in '80, we had an Elemack Dolly in the back. Kept rolling around, banging into the sides—almost took a header through the side door. Never did get the door to close right after that, and every time I try to force the thing shut, I think about how we never even used the damned dolly.

Too bad you couldn't have seen it when it was new, back when I was working on "Bean Sprouts" with Sara [Chin] and Dean [Wong]. I guess we all looked better then, but loads of video gear, a producer you couldn't say "no" to, and herds of those hyper kids all took their toll. I still see all the little reminders: dings in the paint; rips in the upholstery where the video cart went out of control; and the handy little pieces of gaffer tape that have never come unstuck. It was a tough initiation, criss-crossing the city with kids and equipment for two and a half years. What a way to get into "the biz." But looking back, I guess it's hard to top the combination of production and community involvement.

Long hours and low budgets didn't faze us back then. *Monterey's Boat People* was a gas to work on (though I never did like that title). Hey, fresh squid after fourteen straight hours out on the Bay—who could beat that? And I think staying with your folks gave us all a sense of belonging to a larger struggle; seeing the similarities between those Vietnamese fishermen and the earlier generations of Japanese gave us more of a history lesson than we probably realized at the time.

Thinking back, all those drives back and forth to Moss Landing jammed in the van with all the gear weren't so bad after all. Maybe even brought the crew a little closer together. We learned from that and from each other, and I think it carried over to *Q It Up* (1985) and *Talking History* (1984). It wasn't just getting our technical stuff together. We had a dedicated group of individuals who had an unspoken, single-minded loyalty to the mission at hand.

You were always a pretty cocky guy, Spence, but back then we all had that certain youthful energy that carried us through anything. I mean, even though you ran down the van battery out there on the plains of South Dakota trying to pick up the 'Niners game while we were filming the sacred tribal lands, we managed to survive and get some pretty fair footage, don't ya think?

Well, through the years the odometer has turned over "0" too many times to count, and now I wonder if that spirit has grown along with our skills. I mean, I've enjoyed the "perks" of the business as much as the next guy—per diem, exotic locations, big budgets and bigger, better crews. You think anyone is still willing to cram themselves into the ol' van on a long haul to the Black Hills for fast food and fourteen hour days?

Somewhere between looking for Mr. Chan, "Go for Broke," semiconductor art, smoking prison peace pipes, the *Dim Summer* of '85, WGBH, WQRD, ABC, CBS, AWU, a Yosemite mule train, portraits of Hershey kisses, the Chinese Frank Sinatra, Haitian Hitmen, and a hundred other productions with their own special memories, it seems the ol' engine isn't quite hitting on all fours anymore. Know what I'm talking about?

You've always been a smart guy. Am I going soft, or what? You think the past is a done deal?

Just finished working on a doc about the S.F. Opera. For one scene we filmed a soprano finishing her number, then taking her curtain call. As I looked through the camera, watching her respond to her applause, she literally beamed, totally consumed in all the attention she was getting. I flashed on the fact that that's what anyone wants in this business: a chance to get some applause for a creative effort.

MONTEREY'S BOAT PEOPLE (1982)
Michael Chin

So, although I was leaning towards a sleek new American cruiser, like a Caravan or Jeep Cherokee, I started to think about the old van, and how it took years to build up that fine patina. You know, maybe I'll just refit the seatbelts, put in some new upholstery and add a few more touches of paint. I guess the wheels that got me this far could carry me a few more miles. . . .

I'll be over as soon as I've got it up and running.

Love to your folks,
Mike

194

I watched the Watts riot on television...

Appalled, inwardly cowering, I watched the burning and looting on the screen and heard the reports of the dead and wounded. But beneath all my distress, I felt something else, a tiny trickle of warmth which I finally recognized as an undercurrent of exultation. To me, the tumult in the city was the long-awaited, gratifying next chapter of an old movie that had flickered about in the back of my mind for years....

HISAYE YAMAMOTO DESOTO

"A Fire in Fontana" *Rafu Shimpo*, 1985

ROJAK

CHENG-SIM LIM

Cheng-Sim Lim

I. The most important thing in my grandmother's life is food. She speaks in gastronomic metaphors. Her being Chinese and all that, it's not surprising. The second most important thing in my grandmother's life are her grandchildren. She likes to combine both interests. Therefore, if someone—a polite relative, say—asks after her grandchildren, my grandmother is always quick with the answer. *"Rojak,"* she'll say, referring to a salad made from pineapple, mango, guava, jicama, cucumber, tofu, squid, hoisin sauce, chili peppers, ground peanuts, and shrimp paste.

My grandmother is clever, you see. By that one word, *rojak*, she saves a lot of breath. In one minimalist stroke she's made clear what she thinks of her grandchildren. They're like people possessed by spirits: capable of speaking in several (very vulgar) tongues and exhibiting several (very vulgar) personalities. But no one who's asked my grandmother about her grandchildren has ever bothered to ask how they came to be so. It's understood that they "came of age" in the 1970s, buffeted by the multiple influences of polyester, Southeast Asian monsoons, Chinese school teachers, the Royal Australian Air Force Weekly Top 40, the Partridge Family, Queen's English, kung fu movies, and bedtime ghost stories.

II. Of late there's been a chap with balding hair who's offered an English translation of my grandmother's *rojak*. But though these days my grandmother worries about little, except which virgin will fall prey to the villain's scheming in the next video installment of her favorite Hong Kong soap opera, the fellow in question wasn't so lucky. The Ayatollah Khomeini sentenced him to death. But I think Mr. Salman Rushdie remains quite the unrepentant infidel. He wrote not too long ago that he takes pride in the bastardization (the word is, indeed, a quote) of cultures, that he is a product of such an enterprise, and that he will continue to write accordingly.

III. I am neither as succinct nor as eloquently long-winded as my grandmother and Mr. Rushdie, respectively. And I have given no great cause to the Ayatollah, who may be dead but isn't gone, to sentence me to purgatory. (I can't say though that I've been spared that fate by low-budget producers.) Nonetheless, in my own very small way, in my filmmaking, I try to express what I see around me.

STEVE TATSUKAWA,
VIETNAM ANTI-WAR DEMONSTRATION
Visual Communications

I live in Los Angeles and my neighbors are Mexican, Cuban, Chinese, Italian, Kampuchean, Vietnamese, English, and Lebanese. During the last year, a golden-domed Ukranian church has sprouted in full view of my living-room window that faces east while the south window looks onto downtown and its skyline of highrise corporate ego. The Dodgers play ball on the hill at the end of the road. WASPs have found their way to the local Buddhist vegetarian restaurant. I heard Spanish rap in the laundromat the other day.

My auto insurance company says all of this adds up—reduces is more like it—to a high crime district then proceeds to extort me. But as there's always another weasel to out-slime the last one, there's Hollywood to upstage the insurance industry on this one. I can't remember the last time Hollywood made a movie about the kinds of people in my neighborhood without trivializing, pandering, painting a picture of only dire suffering or only false cheer. (One can make a good case that the abject few Hollywood films that haven't swept aside complex realities in the same breath they purport to be about those realities have more to do with the Spike Lees who do the right thing than Hollywood itself.)

Which is why no matter how much Hollywood tries to fool me with "seamless" cuts, continuity, character motivation, three-act structures where on the dot of the 120th minute the last loose end is tied up, it has never been able to disguise the fiction of its fictional narrative from me. That is not because I'm especially clever or worse, want to hold Hollywood to its promise of naturalism. (Who today will deny that movies are equally constructed whether they're 1990s Hollywood or 1920s German Expressionist?) No, it's simply that the Hollywood Script which I'm told plays everywhere may, in fact, play only in Peoria.

IV. My neighbor Hector was Mexican. He died last year. He'd almost bought a house in Texas and was planning to retire there. Five months later his wife is still living next door. Texas is up in the air. My neighbor Lillian is Italian, loves England, can't stop talking about England fifteen years after she moved away. But she doesn't think she'll go back. It's not that she's grown to love Los Angeles. She just prefers not to do anything about England. My neighbor Rick is gay, middle-aged, and single. I don't know his ancestry. He likes to mow his lawn. Some days he takes his dog for a walk and some days he doesn't.

Assuming that one day Hollywood decides to make an ethnic movie starring so-and-so name actors as Hector, Lillian and Rick, then Hector would retire to Texas before he dies, Lillian would learn that she actually hates London and really, really loves Los Angeles, and Rick would always mow his lawn and always take the dog out for walks. In the end, everybody would feel good.

V. These days I am trying to unlearn the language of Hollywood. I am doing it because I know it is not my language. I am trying to remake my image in myself. I am trying to construct narratives that speak to the fragmented, pluralistic, unpredictable, funny, sad, complex, simple, and even dull realities I see around me. I haven't been successful. Not in all ways. Not altogether at one time. But I am trying.

CHENG-SIM LIM'S GRANDMA
AND GRANDPA (circa 1930)
Lim Family collection

"WHAT IS IT ABOUT THIS WORLD?"

SUPACHAI SURONGSAIN

What is it about this world which makes it impossible for a man to choose where he wants to live?

from *Pak Bueng on Fire* (1987)

I am a Thai filmmaker, a newcomer to America. The stories I want to tell are different than those of Asian Americans who were born and raised here. While recent Asian immigrants are struggling to settle themselves and their families in this country, those already here are fighting for justice and an equal place in American society. There are many issues which face newcomers—whether immigrant, student, or worker—yet little media attention is given to our experiences from our point of view. As an immigrant who is also a filmmaker, it is up to me and others to tell our stories, anew.

Pak Bueng on Fire is the memory of my collective experiences here: those of a close friend during our years in school, and the lives of other Thai friends who have lived in Los Angeles for many years before me. In the early 1960s when middle-class Thai parents started to send their children to study in the United States, there were three to four hundred students in Los Angeles. Now, in L.A. alone there are over a hundred thousand Thai; the other two large Thai communities are in San Francisco and New York. Most Thai in the United States are first generation. We are still transitional in this country. Our young community has not yet fully developed a system of community support or organizations that can help an individual in need. Ron and Charlie, the main characters in my film, are newcomers struggling to survive. Because they live in a small social sphere, they are forced to develop a bond of trust between themselves. Against this background of the Thai community I scripted my story. But after I finished, I needed actors. There are no Thai actors available in Los Angeles; those who were actors in Thailand pursue other occupations here and no longer act. So I ran an ad in the local Thai newspaper. From the responses I received, I selected two non-actors to fill the main roles. Next, I scouted for locations. I was lucky that a lot of people let me use their places: a Thai restaurant, the Thai *wat* or temple, etc.

As a filmmaker, I chose every image consciously. And I think we ought to be honest to our audience. In *Pak Bueng on Fire*, the film presents both the

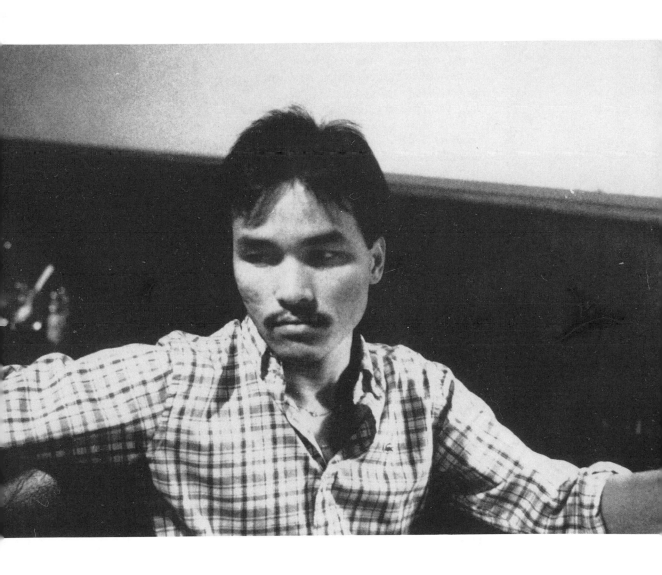

PAK BUENG ON FIRE (1987)
Supachai Surongsain

positive and negative sides of living in America: a struggling Thai student, illegal Thai immigrants, white high school shoplifters, a group of Thai gambling addicts, and a confrontation between Charlie and a shoplifter. As a filmmaker, I must take risks, yet make careful choices.

The opening scene of the immigration raid on the Thai restaurant is a true story passed on to me by friends. The manager of the restaurant where we shot the film told me that a similar incident had occurred there. Stories like these have great emotional impact on newcomers to this country who come seeking the "American dream." The film allowed me to share these stories common to newcomers, stories which most Americans may find peculiar and hard to believe.

The over-scene dialogues, which are delivered by the characters in an established space and continue to play over into another space, were originally scripted to play this way. My approach to making *Pak Bueng on Fire* is to substantiate contradictions through cinematic devices—to reveal the gap between human beliefs and desires and harsh realities. A key example is the intercut between the establishing shot of Ron and Charlie in the restaurant and the shot of the elderly cook in the kitchen. The dialogue between Ron and Charlie, played over the montage of the cook as she smashes, cuts Thai greens "*pak bueng*" and tosses them on the steaming wok, symbolizes the vulnerable environment of Thai workers and immigrants. In this scene, Charlie works to convince Ron that education alone will ensure him a good job in the United States. Ron resists the argument, explaining that he does not want to remain a draftsman for all of his life. Here, bringing in the shot of the elderly cook as the dialogue continues to play, is an example of someone with a job sufficient to provide a minimal salary, but difficult work for an elderly person to endure daily. Immediately after, the immigration authorities enter the restaurant causing havoc and fear. The parallel editing of sound and images over two spaces was done not for the purpose of showing two events happening at the same time, but serves to further counter Charlie's argument. Such common incidents present life in a society where labor exploitation is a real issue for new immigrants, quickly eradicating their dreams.

In the film, I also experiment with sound tracks, i.e., ambient tracks which not only add spacial depth to scenes but link screen space to the characters' mind levels. In the apartment scene, the close-up of Ron's hand as he reaches to dial the telephone, and as he hesitates making a call to set up another job interview after receiving rejections, reveals his difficulty with bureaucracy.

The sets were designed for the specific characters involved: Ron and Charlie. Ron comes from an educated background; Charlie, from a working class family. Each has different goals in life. As a design student, Ron fills his apartment with makeshift furniture, arranged with aesthetic appeal. Charlie's room is a little messy, with a poster of a basketball player; he owns a sports car. Such relationships between persons of different class backgrounds would rarely occur in Thailand. Here, however, these unique relationships are often developed among Thai immigrants. While both work at the liquor store, one attends school and the other is somewhat of a hustler. Yet both work seven days a week and spend many hours together.

When ethnic characters are on the screen, we tend to analyze the way they are portrayed. We have been sensitized to look for stereotypic portrayals.

But what I hope I am doing is giving depth to my characters and their situations. In my film, I paint the gray tones of the Asian immigrants as opposed to black and white. By portraying a Thai student and a worker, we get to know who these persons are, why they are here, and their goals in various scenes. In the pool scene, for instance, after-hours entertainment for late shift workers, Charlie tells his friends about the INS pursuit of the illegal workers at the restaurant where he and Ron had gone for dinner. One of Charlie's friends reveals that one of the waiters is a student who risks his student visa status because he needed to work more hours to support his schooling. The dialogue plays over the intercut between the pool hall and Ron's apartment to make the connection between past and present, and to hint the future in the pattern of obstacles that Charlie and his friends have encountered, and which may also happen to Ron. Charlie and his friends have dropped out from their schools, becoming illegal immigrants and thereby limiting their chances for better jobs and confining them to their own small community. Ron and the waiter are both in similar circumstances as students who must work illegally to support their schooling. Charlie realizes that Ron may be ensnared in the same pattern. The scene leads to a question raised innocently by one of Charlie's friends, a question of human rights: "What is it about this world which makes it impossible for a man to choose where he wants to live?"

Class issues always occur in film; *Pak Bueng on Fire* is no exception. Under a capitalistic system and in a society made up of various ethnic groups, we cannot separate the issues of class, racism, and art in filmmaking. However, my execution of each scene was not based on a need to merely reproduce or reflect reality. My filmmaking approach is to use cinema to reveal the underlying contradictions between human ideals and social reality, as I see it.

RITUALS
REVISITED
CINDY HING-YUK
WONG

RITUALS REVISITED

Cindy Hing-yuk Wong

Born and raised in Hong Kong, I was not aware of stereotypes of Asian Americans until I came to the United States. While faced with different questions about colonial mentalities and orientalism, I did not feel that I belonged to a group characterized as inscrutable, mysterious, exotic, and at times "weird." After spending eight years here, I have learned to appropriate the stereotypes and even to use them to my advantage by revealing their fallacies. While it may be easy for me to discard the stereotypes of myself, making a video on Asian Americans poses a different dilemma.

When I embarked on my video documentary, I did not consider at length the problem of representation. My subject is a Chinese-Vietnamese couple who, late in life, became a Buddhist monk and nun in Los Angeles. When I was little, I saw Buddhist monks and nuns all the time. They neither fascinated nor repulsed me; they formed part of my everyday existence. However among my various white American crew persons, one of them found it hard to tell the men from the women, because monks and nuns all have shaved heads. Only then did it strike me that the monk and nun would probably look quite different to the average American.

During my research, I spent a great deal of time with Rev. Tue Quan Chich and Rev. Tue Wai Xiu. They devoted time to ceremonial pursuits which constitute the more public side of their lives. However, they also eat, drink, cook, and lead lives which do not differ from anyone else. At the early stage of production, I knew that the video would encompass the monk's and nun's life stories; however, I remained unsure of the focus. I could talk about rites and rituals, and try to explain Buddhism from that perspective. I could talk about their own experiences, their relationship toward one another and to their children, and their migration from China, to Vietnam, and finally the United States.

Working within a visual medium, rituals appear tempting. They are colorful, attractive, and aesthetically pleasing. Rituals provide excellent tools to create the desired mood for movies. I could have more control choreographing my shots, since many rituals are rigid and repetitive. Lastly, enthnographic films have long concentrated their effort on recording rituals, recognizing that many rituals are self-contained events which give an illusion of completeness; and believing that rituals epitomize certain values of a given society. Thus, rituals become a shorthand guide to that culture.

However, had I concentrated on the ceremonial aspects alone, the audience would think that the monk's and nun's lives are totally ritualized. They would fulfill stereotypes of exotic Asians who live their lives by these wonderfully elaborate and bizarre ceremonies, thus perpetuating orientalist attitudes to the viewer. If I had chosen to emphasize ritual, I would not be lying, but retelling actual happenings in real life. However, what truth am I telling?

Given the limited depiction of Asian American life in the media as well as in ethnographic films, most audiences do not get an in-depth, balanced and yet diverse picture of the Asian American experience. As a film/video maker, I do not live in a vacuum. I work in an age where many discuss ethnic diversity, but this does not always translate to the visual representation of ethnic difference. As an Asian American film/video maker working with Asian American subjects, it becomes my responsibility to present alternative perspectives to dominant stereotypes.

So I decided to downplay the ritual aspect of Rev. Tue Quan Chich's and Rev. Tue Wai Xiu's lives. To exclude any ritual scene in the work would be erroneous, because rites and rituals are important to their lives as ordained Buddhists. Moreover, the problem does not lie so much in rituals themselves, but in how a film/video maker uses these images. Do the rituals in the work carry a level of meaning that is beyond their visual appeal? Do the rituals help to accurately represent the characters? Finally, are they meaningful events within the videotext?

There are six different ritual events in the video; they take up about one-third of the tape. All ritual scenes are contextualized, so that they are not mysterious, but become meaningful subtexts for the video. For example, the tonsure scene comes after the audience has gained an understanding of the event by seeing both the nun's and monk's tonsures in stills and words. When the more immediate form of representation—live action—presents itself, the audience has been well coached. Also at the Buddha Bathing Festival scene, the audience witnesses the monk and the nun pouring water onto a small Buddha statue. The action is introduced first, then Rev. Tue Wai Xiu gives me a description of the festival. She concludes by telling me how the festival has deepened her relationship with the Buddha. These rituals thus provide meanings that are immediate, yet personalized.

Downplaying, normalizing, and contextualizing the ritual aspects of the monk's and nun's lives combat stereotyping; however, I also needed to introduce other aspects of their lives such as their relationship to one another and their past experiences. These facets of everyday experience in turn provide them with a sense of history unique yet comprehensible. Their life experiences became active responses to histories which they endure.

In making this documentary, my subjects and I cemented a strong relationship. In our everyday dealings, I have never viewed them through the filter of ethnic stereotypes; in turn, the stereotypes failed to create a barrier between us. The monk and the nun are at ease in front of the camera. They interact directly with me on camera; in turn, the subjects and I are equals. Most important of all, the absence of preconceived stereotypes has allowed me to view my subjects afresh, and in turn, produce a work that provides alternative faces and voices to Asian Americans.

ELECTRONS &
REFLECTIVE
SHADOWS

Directing Memory

206

ELECTRONS & REFLECTIVE SHADOWS

JANICE TANAKA

ELECTRONS & REFLECTIVE SHADOWS

Janice Tanaka

Memories are not always an understood compilation of linear ideas. They seem instead to be fragments of stored, synthesized, edited sensory stimuli; bits of personalized perceptions. Film and television oftentimes play a major role in the process of subliminal inculturation by creating a criteria for self-evaluation. Consequently, our self-image, our role models, what we know and expect of our society and the world, are greatly influenced by the media. Somewhere caught between the crevices of concept and production lay the elements or perhaps the reflective shadows of who and what we are. This exquisitely complex structure of electrons prophetically examines nature.

I once saw a sign that read, "Life is a test, only a test. If it weren't, we would have been given instructions on what to do." I guess my work, through electronic reflections, is about trying to discover what to do.

I describe my tapes as follows:

Memories from the Department of Amnesia (1989) is about the death of my mother and the process of grieving. Section one: chaos, evasion, impotence, fear and denial. Section two: an attempt to escape the inescapable, the transitional void where images from the past resurface from the abyss of forgetfulness. Section three: surreal absurdity, the aftermath of grieving. Section four: following a catastrophic event old defense mechanisms are relinquished and memories once locked and translated in childish language are relived and redefined in the present.

The Heisenberg Uncertainty Principle (1988) is a video opera occurring in five acts and four interludes. The score is original and vocal performers are members of the Chicago Lyric Opera. The visuals incorporate both "real" and computer-generated images. The five acts are titled "The Gloria," "Pursuit for Plastic," "Greetings and Salutations," "He Who Dies with the Most Toys Wins," and "Hope Extraordinaire."

In quantum physics, the Heisenberg uncertainty principle states that when using a subatomic particle to measure the position and velocity of another subatomic particle the action of one affects the other. Consequently, a precise measurement of either the velocity or the position of a particle is possible, or a rough estimate of both quantities, but never a precise measurement of both.

The philosophical implications of this principle are profound when applying its basic tenets to the way in which we perceive and interact with each other and the world. We are not neutral entities that are insensitive to or nonreactive with the environment or others. Who and what we are cannot be accurately predicted. On the one hand, we have the creators of Auschwitz and Buchenwald and on the other, the Mother Teresas of the world.

This video opera reflects upon those factors that affect the human condition.

New Untitled Project: After the death of my mother, I began looking for my father, a second-generation Japanese American whom I hadn't seen since I was ten. I located him in a halfway house in East L.A. for the chronically mentally ill. This tape is about my father and the cultural values that shaped him. His good looks, intelligence, and charismatic personality allowed him to survive in the mayhem in which his life seemed to be directed. He was declared insane when he rebelled against internment; he continued a life of rebellion by escaping several mental institutions; by delivering unordered donuts to various police stations and then billing them at the end of the month; by writing fraudulent checks to the government thereby collecting redress long before it became a political issue. He survived internment in Manzanar, confinement in mental institutions, shock therapy, drug therapy, and legal incarceration. His life exemplifies what is possible in this country of contradictions.

This project will not be a visual documentary of his life. Rather, the narrative will hang behind images of contemporary society bridging the parameters between one man's personal insanity and the institutionalized insanity of a society.

mate (Lily

***MEMORIES FROM THE DEPARTMENT
OF AMNESIA*** (1989)
Janice Tanaka

AN(OTHER)

REFLECTION

ON RACE?

Directing Memory

208

AN(OTHER) REFLECTION ON RACE?

AN(OTHER) REFLECTION ON RACE?

Roddy Bogawa

RODDY BOGAWA

...We all speak from a particular place, out of a particular history, out of a particular experience, a particular culture, without being contained by that position as 'ethnic artists' or filmmakers. We are all in that sense ethnically located and our ethnic identities are crucial to our subjective sense of who we are. But this is also a recognition that this is not an ethnicity which is doomed to survive, as Englishness was, only by marginalizing, dispossessing, displacing and forgetting other ethnicities.

Stuart Hall, *New Ethnicities*

Making pictures is to clean, like a window you clean to be able to see.

Jean-Luc Godard

Last year I was asked to be on a panel discussing "Asian-American aesthetics" at a film festival which happened to be in my hometown, so I invited my parents. My presentation revolved around a new film I was scripting that examines conflicts of assimilation and ethnicity within the main character. The film isn't a straightforward narrative and as in my previous work, elements of autobiography, fiction, and documentary material weave in and out of its structure. While I was in the middle of talking about the formal strategies of the film, my mother (probably recognizing the autobiographical details in the story) stood up and said she had a question. I wavered between fainting or going into shock, though of course no one but me knew the woman was my mother. In her opinion, she said, I wasn't one bit "Japanese," nor "Asian-American." Moreover she claimed I was clearly "American," and thus why was I doing this film or attempting to define an "Asian-American aesthetics." The bluntness of her questions startled everyone until my father next to her jokingly yelled out, "Answer your mother!" With his humorous aside everyone broke into laughter, the tension was relieved, and I got out of addressing the question by protesting back, "I can't take you guys anywhere."

Parameters of an Identity Crisis

For artists of color, expectations of what their work should investigate simultaneously dictate what the work should not explore. In most contexts, for instance, I am introduced as an "Asian-American filmmaker" or a variation of that description. These are not arbitrary or neutral labels. They construct Asian-American filmmaking as a uniform practice, ignoring the diverse complexities of each film and each filmmaker. Their function is to stereotype, control, and marginalize. To preface a work racially is to inherently reduce in many ways the discussions to one—is the film Asian-American or not?

Here is an appropriate place to ask what a short black and white 16mm documentary film about a four-year-old boy (white) who grows up in the projection booth of an art house movie theater has to do with Asian-American aesthetics? Or how does an experimental narrative about a delivery driver for a pharmacy and a few characters he meets (an elderly Irish woman who runs a bed-and-breakfast, a receptionist for a doctor's office) speak of race or ethnicity? These questions come up at almost every screening of my work, regardless if the program is a selection of documentary and experimental films or "Asian-American films." In both situations, the same expectations exist—that my ethnicity should be apparent within the work by the choice of subject matter or form. Some questions arise:

- Why should the work be discussed in terms of my racial identity?
- Why isn't the same criteria applied to issues of "whiteness"?
  Other more difficult questions are foregrounded:
- What happens when we only think of ourselves in relation to immigrant stories? What other representations are left out?
- Can an ongoing dialogue be established that is supportive of the multiplicity of perspectives, image-making, and practices?

Fragments of a Resolution

The hardest artistic/critical decision I have made is to write, direct, and edit a film about an "Asian-American topic." The answers "probably nothing" and "who knows" won't suffice this time around. The project developed similarly to my other films through storytelling, note-taking, and collaging fiction and documentary material. Though concerned with many of the same formal issues, it would be dishonest to claim that choosing this subject is unrelated to engaging and theorizing issues of identity which have emerged at screenings of my work and in writing and discussions with friends and peers.

Some Divine Wind is a film about the paradox of assimilating into a so-called melting pot. By focusing on moments of contradiction within one's identity, I hope to resolve these issues by talking about the questions rather than answering them. In this respect the film is a non-traditional narrative, unconcerned with plot closure and immersed in layering strategies of disparate images. The film doesn't attempt to reconstitute World War II but examines the effects on the generations once or twice removed from its horror, juxtaposing "popular" history versus a subjective experiential one.

To be an "Asian-American filmmaker," a "Japanese-American independent filmmaker," etc., and so on, means in some way to belong to all of these categories as well as simultaneously define yourself between each. I remember moments when friends would say how they never thought me Japanese because I was so "Californian" and other times when people would assume I was a tourist and begin to speak in long passages of Japanese, of which I only understood "hello."

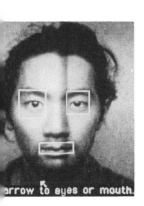

arrow to eyes or mouth.

SOME DIVINE WIND (1991)
Roddy Bogawa

Perhaps two friends of mine describe my current thinking best. One, a Japanese/Chinese friend confiding that she has always felt herself on an "invisible edge" between ethnic labels (often you are either inside or out), says it is a daily struggle to identify and articulate her uneasiness. Another says the time has come to explore the significance of the hyphen in what it means to be "Asian-American," an identity neither "Asian" nor "American," as well as both.

One's practice is linked to one's identity and one's identity is often one that is put upon you. I never really questioned whether I was "American" except for the times I've been called "Jap" or, mistakenly, "Chink." Now, two years into a project about race and identity, there are still no clear-cut solutions but I have realized that there aren't any.

Identity is not as transparent or unproblematic as we think. Perhaps instead of thinking of identity as an already accomplished fact, which the new cultural practices then represent, we should think, instead, of identity as a "production," which is never complete, always in process, and always constituted within, not outside, representation. This view problematises the very authority and authenticity to which the term, "cultural identity," lays claim.

Stuart Hall

LABTALK

MAR ELEPAÑO

Mar Elepaño

One day when I was rummaging through the old aluminum film cans in the vault of the motion picture lab of the then USC Film Department (now it's called a school), I came across a can of old rubber stamps. Each stamp was no bigger than 16mm in width and several inches in length. They were used at one time to identify rolls of film. They carried technical information like "Ektachrome," "Answer Print," "Head Start," "A Roll," and were stamped on film leader.

I was fascinated by these little rubber stamps. I knew that I had to do something with them. At that time, I was running the film lab. I had been working there for the past six years. I would make short graphic films when I had the time in between those endless hours of processing and printing millions of feet of black and white 16mm film. The little stamps encapsulated my life for the past twelve years. They reminded me that film permeated and continues to permeate my adult life. It was not just film as a technical reality but also film as an aesthetic experience. It was hypo and gamma mixed in with kinestasis and intuitive motion. It didn't occur to me till much later that in spite of the sometimes difficult working conditions I encountered, I was very lucky and privileged to have access to film technology and was able to experience its aesthetic possibilities. But above and beyond all that are the people I met and befriended. They made the experience total.

That became the answer to how I would deal with the rubber stamps. I decided to get my friends, who also worked with me at the lab at that time, to talk about those little stamps. Of course we drank several bottles of burgundy and bordeaux. That loosened things up. I recorded the revelry. The result was quite pleasing. I edited it down to a manageable length (three minutes, anything more I consider madness) and proceeded to use simple metamorphic animation using the stamps as my "lines" and "dots" to create the images.

I was pleased with the result. It became my very own personal souvenir of my friends like an old faded photograph. They have all gone their separate ways but I still keep in touch with them. We once joked that we would cut the film print into four pieces. We would each keep a piece and splice them back at random each time we would have a reunion and screen it amidst obligatory drunkenness. We were never able to do that. I don't think we will ever come back together as a group. Thankfully, the film is still in one piece.

212

You see farther. Farther and farther. Beyond what you are made to see and made to see only. You pass the mark, even though you say nothing. Everyone who has seen, sees farther. Even farther than allowed....

THERESA HAK KYUNG CHA

Dictee (1982)

BITTER SOUP

BITTER SOUP

ARNE WONG

Arne Wong

My life as an artist/filmmaker has been, and still is, a difficult but satisfying one. Difficult in the sense of being true to myself and expressing ideas that are important to me. Satisfying in that I am still able to make a living at drawing, which is what I love to do.

When I was eighteen, I had a vision of making mind-blowing art that would change the world. I imagined myself a mutant revolutionary within an old and dying society, awakening the walking dead souls with lightning bolts of truth. I was ready to enlist in a lifetime-underground resistance dedicated to suffering and pain for the salvation of our minds. Everything was going great until I came off the acid, and found myself face down in a bowl of bitter melon soup, at the family dinner table, with my parents staring at me in disbelief.

In my first year of college, I discovered animation. I made several short animated films inspired by a love for the ocean and surfing. They were well received, and I was offered commercial work soon after.

My parents never understood what I was doing. Self expression was not valued in my parent's home; it was feared and suppressed. Being an artist was not a valid profession in my father's eyes; he wished that I had chosen a profession whose value they understood, like medicine or law. Every time I came to visit them, I would get a lecture on "fitting in with society," or "don't make any waves." I wanted so much for my father's approval and support of me as an artist. I felt I had to prove to him and myself that I could be as successful in my work as any doctor or lawyer. I compromised my inner vision to be a good son.

I've spent a lot of my time in the past twenty-two years creating films for someone else, for money, and also to learn the craft. I figured I would become a successful commercial animator, make lots of money, then after that, I could really get into my creative stuff and make my own films.

Whenever I felt a passionate vision come into being, I would find myself face down in bitter soup. I would deliberately sabotage myself into that soup each time, not surfing into the Mystery, but retreating back to shore where it is safe. And each time, my parents were there wiping my face whispering "Please stop dreaming, wake up and face reality."

It has been rare moments when I have taken the chance of creating my own visions, and I am just beginning to see through my own bullshit of

DEPOT DUET (1983)
Art Nomura, Mary Daval

SKETCH OF ARNIE WONG
Moebius (1990)

"pleasing someone else so they will like and buy my films, so I'll become rich and famous, and live happily ever after."

A mentality fearful and at times antagonistic towards freedom of expression is not just something "out there" in American society. It is also present within my own Asian "tribe," my family, and more important, myself.

The patriarchal mentality is also a heritage of China, a mentality that does not welcome anyone whose words or visions challenge the status quo. The acquisition and misuse of power, control, and "respectability," did not just pop up in America and Europe alone. In my family, and in the Chinese and American communities I grew up in, women and artists who pursue the areas society has cast off as feminine—surrendering into the unknown—are a threat in every way to the household. A man was not a man unless there was someone beneath him. That is what is meant to be a man. People with more power—especially men—were respected. The despair and devastation this brought to the souls of the women in my household, to the crushed feminine part of my father, myself, to other Asian men I know. The lack of joy, and the rigid control we demanded of ourselves, the terror of feelings, the terror of JOY, the terror of all that was out of their control. Art included.

When I hear about racism in America toward Asian artists, it makes me face my own shadow. In this society, the Chinese and other minorities are often the victims of racism. But in China, the same kind of harmful attitudes have existed for thousands of years, dominating the minority cultures— such as the Tibetans; enjoying the privileges of hierarchy, "the right of the stronger to take over the weaker." Is it really a shock to find the same attitudes present in American culture, or is it the shock of being on the receiving end.

As a Chinese American, I grew up with a lot of racist voices. It seems to go hand-in-hand with cultures that have become identified with the need for power and domination.

The enemy is not outside of Chinatown, nor is it within our own culture. The enemy dwells deep inside our psyche, disowned voices echoed in the closed dungeons of our ancestral memory banks. It's not going to go away by ignoring it, seeing it in others, or feeling guilty about it.

Racism is now a scourge on this earth. The place I must attend to first is within myself and those close to me.

In my family they say, "We are old-fashioned Chinese and you must respect our ways, and keep the bloodline pure." I heard these words when my brother married a Japanese, my sister married a "white ghost," and worse yet, when I introduced to my parents my Cherokee/Russian/ Caribbean/everything-but-Chinese girlfriend. We must all get to the point where we can see beyond race.

My work now is to return to being an artist, to bring these things to light. To be a harbinger of the future. The future that has been stubbornly resisted in China for a long time. Eros has been feared and hated.

My work as an artist or explorer, as I see it, is to explore honestly and share what I find. A different attitude than fighting, rebelling, or blaming others. To seek, to discover, to uncover, to be an explorer. To bring back my dreams to the "tribe," to help the greater "human being" tribe.

Kuan Yin, the goddess of beauty and compassion, has been in the shadows too long.

MOVING THE IMAGE, REMOVING THE ARTIST, KILLING THE MESSENGER

DARYL CHIN

If the Asian American International Film Festival is any indication, 1989 was one of the best years for Asian American media. The range of work from that festival was astonishing; in addition, the fact that there were so many new filmmakers was encouraging. 1990, of course, has proven to be a less notable year. Not that there haven't been any revelations (every year for the past few years, there has been some fresh new talent) but there hasn't been the same excitement. How can there be? The Asian American Film Festival is still founded on independent filmmaking, and independent filmmaking is dependent on forms of funding, patronage, and support which are not standardized into commercial formulae. Quite frankly: for any independent filmmaker, after the completion of one film, there is the period of distribution, exhibition, and promotion. After that, there is the period of gestation for the next project, which usually entails fundraising as part of the preparation for the new film. Unless you find a way of generating a constant cash flow, the problem of fundraising will be one always with us.

Is there any way out of this dilemma? I honestly don't know. I couldn't even begin to suggest ways and means of continual financing for independent filmmaking, but if anyone has suggestions, especially as pertains to Asian American media, please feel free to share the suggestions with the rest of us. Right now, I know of several projects in various stages of development by a wide range of filmmakers. Some are still in script stage, others in the purgatory of post-production, where a few thousand dollars are needed for the final sound mix or for negative cutting, but all are doing that hide-and-seek of trying to find the needed cash. Trying to be theoretical is all well and good, but that's not going to answer the practical questions that are coming up about Asian American media. The practical questions relate to access: to funds and equipment, to distribution and exhibition, even access to publicity. Before we can talk about Asian American filmmaking, there must be Asian American films. It's as simple as that.

But any simple proposition is always fraught with paradox. If we are to encourage the production of Asian American films, then we arrive at the question, what are Asian American films? When the first Asian American Film Festival was being organized in New York City, the decision was made to define an Asian American film as a film whose principal creator was an Asian American. Even that definition is subject to ambiguity: an Asian American

WOK LIKE A MAN (1987)
Art Nomura

could be an American of Asian ancestry, it could be an Asian living in the United States, or any variant thereof. And this definition still finds debate. This year, for example, the question arose as to what were we to consider nonwhite natives of the Pacific Islands, in particular, aborigines from Australia? Australia is a country in the Pacific Rim; aborigines are nonwhite natives of Australia; are aborigines to be considered "Asian?"

These questions may seem unimportant, even absurd, yet these questions do have bearing on what gets shown and what gets considered in terms of screening, exhibition, distribution within the network of Asian American media. At this time, for example, the countries of the Near East (what used to be called Asia Minor) have been annexed to Asia, and so films from Iran, Turkey, Morocco have been included in showcases of Asian films. If this is true (and it is), then why not show films by aborigines? That this should be controversial is a symptom of the difficulties in identifying the definition of Asian. Another point: identification of Asian becomes important within the American context, signifying the status of minority in contradistinction to a majority culture. But what defines majority and minority in terms of a multicultural, polyglot, multiethnic society? Or is there an admission that this is a multicultural, polyglot, multiethnic society?

These questions have played a part in the formation of the ethnic arts movement: workshops, festivals, exhibitions showcasing the work of artists united because of ethnic heritage. Moving beyond the established boundaries of the ethnic arts movement, is there a way for fundamental changes to be made so that there will be continuity within the ethnic arts movement?

I'd like to get down to several specifics. In 1988, I was asked by John Hanhardt to begin a project for the Whitney Museum regarding Asian American independent filmmaking. For this project (which remains unrealized), I got in touch with those filmmakers and video artists who were working in the 1960s and 1970s. Most of these artists had been working in ways which could be described as "experimental," and I tried to get as many filmographies as possible. From these filmographies, and from discussions with many of these filmmakers, certain issues emerged.

I do not believe that the system of nonprofit media centers is overtly or inherently racist; it is more like an oversight which is perpetuated. If a number of avant garde filmmakers emerged during the 1960s (examples: Ernie Gehr, Barry Gerson, Larry Gottheim), their reputations and their credentials were established within the network of alternative cinema which had been fought for by such people as Amos Vogel and, of course, Jonas Mekas. In New York City, by the mid-1970s, there were several organizations dedicated to independent, specifically experimental, film. These included the Filmmakers Cinematheque (which evolved into Anthology Film Archives), The Millennium Film Workshop, The Collective for Living Cinema, The New American Filmmakers series at the Whitney Museum, Cineprobe at the Museum of Modern Art. At that time, the demarcation of specific practices founded on ethnicity, sexual orientation, gender had not occurred, so that a single season of screening at any one of these places would include films which (at this time) we would designate as "Asian American," "gay," or "feminist." In short, the audience for "experimental" film was assumed to be in itself a "minority" audience, a specialized audience, and therefore did not need to be further divided.

By the mid-1970s that started to change. Anthology Film Archives had

THE LONG WEEKEND (O' DESPAIR) (1989)
Gregg Araki

established a hierarchy of filmmakers, and this hierarchy began to dominate the critical discourse attending experimental filmmaking practice. With this domination came the extension into exhibition, distribution, and funding. Thus, once it was established that Stan Brakhage was central to one definition of the avant garde aesthetic, and that definition became the dominant definition of the "the avant garde" (which is not homogenous, by the way), Stan Brakhage's work became dominant within the network of nonprofit media centers. I am not arguing that there is no reason for this ascendancy during that time; certainly, given the alternative nature of experimental cinema, Stan Brakhage has defined one of the most impressive non-narrative aesthetics in the cinema. However, that dominance meant the de-emphasis of further alternatives. Just as an example: Carolee Schneemann took the "Abstract Expressionist" ethos of Brakhage's work and reworked that ethos into an expression of feminine sensibility. Brakhage's manipulated imaging of direct vision was redefined in terms of female experience, specifically sexual experience, in Schneemann's *Fuses* (1967) and *Plumb Line* (1971). When *Fuses* was first released, there was a general critical acknowledgment of Schneemann's achievement, and *Fuses* received a substantial record of exhibition. By the time of *Plumb Line*, that critical acknowledgement was no longer available, and Schneemann's films became more difficult to place within a hierarchy being defined.

Critical biases had been unacknowledged: in the bluntest terms, there was the belief that work by white men was inherently more important. Although the work of the few women was included when these women were unavoidable (example: Maya Deren), many more women found their work excluded (examples: Storm De Hirsch, Shirley Clarke, Schneemann). For this reason, a number of collectives which arose during the mid-1970s arranged screenings of experimental films by women.

This was obviously the state of affairs for those filmmakers who were marginalized even within the alternative media network. I mentioned the development of women's collectives to create a counter-cinema to the nonprofit media network. This was obviously the case for those artists of color working in experimental modes.

The reason I bring this up is that many of the showcases and festivals which developed to serve the Asian American community were begun in this way, i.e., the Asian American International Film Festival, now administered through Asian CineVision. The person responsible for the Asian American Film Festival was Tom Tam, an experimental filmmaker who previously had shown work in group screenings at the Millennium Film Workshop. One of the motivating factors in starting the festival was to find out if there were other Asian Americans who were making movies. Certainly, there were collectives which dealt with community-activist documentaries; one such collective was Third World Newsreel. But the question was: were there other filmmakers? What kinds of films were they making? During the 1960s, a number of artists (painters, sculptors, even composers) decided to work in film, bringing aesthetic, theoretical, and conceptual concerns which revitalized experimental filmmaking. Among these artists were, of course, Andy Warhol, Michael Snow, and Tony Conrad. During this period, Asian American artists also worked in film, most notably Arakawa and Yoko Ono. By the 1970s, a number of Asian Americans were working in film in experimental ways, among them: Tam, Al Wong, Fu-Ding Cheng, Bruce and Norman Yonemoto,

Lambert Yam, Ruby Yang, and Wayne Wang.

I should mention that when I have brought up this fact of the neglect of many of these artists within the Asian American media community, I have been taken to task for bringing up "obscure" filmmakers. But isn't it disturbing that some in the Asian American media community would say such a thing about Asian American artists? Within the larger context of the American media industry, which Asian American isn't "obscure?" If the answer is Wayne Wang, then that is highly parochial, even patronizing. It presupposes that acceptance within the commercial mainstream is the only aim of Asian American media. As a corollary, I would like to bring up the example of African American media. During the past year, at screenings of work by a number of different African American artists (including Philip Mallory Jones, Marlon Riggs, and Charles Lane), someone in the audience (inevitably, a young African American) will bring up Spike Lee. What do you think of Spike Lee? What relation does your work have to Spike Lee's work? Have you discussed your work with Spike Lee? This was absolutely amazing. Even when Spike Lee had nothing whatsoever to do with the work being shown, his name would come up. Don't the people asking such questions realize how insulting the questions are? When I mention that Lee had nothing whatsoever to do with the work, I mean that, not just literally, but metaphorically: in most cases, these artists had been working prior to Spike Lee, and in forms and genres (documentary, media installation, experimental) which have nothing to do with Spike Lee. Why should Lee's work, which is traditional movie narrative now being produced within the commercial system, be central to a discussion of African American documentary? Or African American video experimentalism? Or an African American who has made silent comedies since the mid-1970s (years before Spike Lee ever made a movie)? Spike Lee did not influence these artists (since they'd been working for years before there was a Spike Lee), but to suggest his example, his importance, his influence as so all-embracing is insulting, because it shows that you are ignorant of the achievement of other African American artists (that's why I stressed that the people who asked questions were always African American).

Although there were many reasons for such ignorance, the situation points to the fact that, even within the margins of an alternative practice, there is further marginalization, especially from the alternative media community. And the person who is always at a disadvantage in this situation, as in most situations involving the cultural industry, is the artist. I don't think anyone who is not a "minority" artist can understand the situation. It's a vicious circle. If a media art center shows a renowned white male experimental filmmaker every two years (and most media arts centers do not have unlimited screening possibilities; usually, screenings are held two or three times a week, and only during certain months), those who are not as renowned (and that usually means artists of color and/or women) will find themselves programmed after those who are more famous. And that means being programmed every four or five years. A similar situation exists in terms of grants. Although funding panels do look at the work, they're also dependent on reputation, since panelists are more inclined to look more closely at work by artists they're heard of, and who will hear about you if you're not exhibited and written about?

By the mid-1980s, with the consolidation of Asian American media organizations, there was another curve thrown into this circle: Asian Ameri-

(Top) *FILM STRIPS II* (1966-70)
(Middle) *FILM STRIPS I* (1966-70)
(Bottom) *I SAW THE SHADOW* (1966)
Taka Iimura

WHITE IN BAD LIGHT (1979, 1989)
Fu-Ding Cheng

can artists were referred to Asian American media organizations. Since most of those organizations were not designed to present experimental work, they could not be expected to be responsive to those artists not doing work which was either documentary or narrative work overtly about Asian American issues. However, the mainstream media arts centers presumed that Asian American artists would find exhibition within Asian American media organizations (which then let them off the hook from showing Asian American artists). And those Asian American artists found themselves holding the bag (which was empty). Tom Tam's example is pertinent, because here was the person who had started the Asian American Film Festival, and he was disenfranchised when the festival's administration was taken over by a community arts organization, Asian CineVision. Tam has gone on to a distinguished teaching career, and he remains an Asian American activist: just this year, he organized the Asian American Heritage Day at the City University of New York. But the fact that he was disenfranchised from his own festival is a fact which has disturbed me.

For artists working in nontraditional ways, there is no idea of commercial reward. Experimental filmmakers and video artists know that their work will remain within a small circuit. But when that circuit gets even smaller, when that circuit shuts you out, the effects are devastating. Sometimes, just the encouragement of having your work exhibited within the context of a festival will be enough to motivate you to continue. But when you aren't even encouraged but actively discouraged, shunted from one excuse to another as to why your work can't be shown, there is confusion, frustration, anger.

If my response to my research, to my reestablishment of contact with many of these artists, has seemed shrill to many, it may be because my sense of outrage is intense. These artists did not deserve to be given such a runaround. Although inequity in this society is ever present, it has been my hope to even out some of the inequities within the cultural realm. Perhaps this can never happen. But if the inequities had been allowed to stand, there would have been no possibility of discovery. During the last few years, there have been a number of exceptionally talented young filmmakers. Most of them are under thirty years old, and most of them are working in ways which are not traditionally Asian American, that is, few of them are working in documentary forms regarding specifically Asian American issues. Many of these artists are beginning to receive recognition outside Asian American media movement. My hope is that their work will continue, and they will not be disenfranchised as had been previous generations of Asian American media artists. Furthermore, my hope is that ways will be found to help fund, or even to provide in-kind services, to Asian American media artists, so their work can be continued. In addition, we should find ways to establish networks working in the media, both in the industry and outside the industry. I have always been taken to task for this suggestion, yet it is important. Governmental funding for the arts is coming under attack, and other forms of finance may be needed. Why sneer at those Asian Americans working within the industry, just because many of them do not work on Asian American projects?

My aim is to see the continuance of our media art, not to prescribe what Asian American art should not be. Asian American artists have created many works of great merit, and we would be impoverished if we did not recognize and celebrate this fact. When I list the names of many of these artists, I am not doing this to be obscure, I am doing this to suggest that such work should be more widely known, even within the Asian American media community, because, when that work is known, it will reveal its beauty, humor and richness. During the past years, there has seemed to be a revitalization. Against all odds, Asian American artists are creating new works, and we should be celebrating that fact, and celebrating them, instead of trying to circumvent them for not living up to the media image of the model minority. Though the mid-1980s seemed a rich period for Asian American media organizations, it has proved a desperate time for many Asian American artists. That was the period of frustration for most of the Asian American experimental media artists who had been working since the 1970s (at the least). I would not like to see the same situation develop again. Funding remains a problem, but experimental media artists have been incredibly resourceful. They should not be marginalized or penalized further. Perhaps ways can be found to facilitate access, to funding, distribution, exhibition. That is the discussion that needs to be started at this time, not denunciations for daring to bring up "obscure" names. There's no reason why Asian American film and video can't be one of the most vital and resourceful and vigorous areas of independent media: with the artists that we have, and the variety of work, and the multiplicity of options, our media art could be a harbinger of the possibilities of the multicultural society which would fulfill the American dream.

TEN THINGS I HATE ABOUT AMERICA:
NOTES FROM A FRUSTRATED YOUNG FILMMAKER

Jon Moritsugu

1.
I hate it that no one knows who Jean-Luc Goddard is.

2. I hate MTV.

3. I hate the fact that filmmaking here is seldom an act of desperation but almost always an outgrowth of complacency.

4. I hate sequels.

5. I hate people who believe that being a production assistant (coffee server, floor sweeper, etc.) for a major Hollywood feature is more "credible" that struggling on your own independent film project.

6. I hate television adaptations of insipid paperback novels.

7. I hate MTV clones (see 2).

8. I hate the socio-economic forces that compel film school students to spend $50,000 of their parents' money on thesis projects.

9. I hate it that Tom Hanks' new video is now readily available at all supermarkets.

10. I hate waking up in the sunny California morning feeling marginalized, disenfranchised, and bankrupt, while under my pillow, my clock radio blasts some dopey soft-rock hit song from the seventies.

RASHOMON BLUES

ANTHONY B. CHAN

Anthony B. Chan

She's a New Yorker. Mother's an Italian and father's first generation Toy San. Looking like the placid, but gorgeous woman in *Rashomon* (1951), she knows that nurses popping cokes (the soft drink!) on 4 A.M. shifts means they've done triage in Vietnam. She's been there too.

And since no one's done this story about Asian American nurses before . . . maybe because it's just too painful for the right folks who could, convinced me to tell it. It's a mission. That's what I'm doing right now. Just calling it *Super Angels,* but after all the frames are shot, there'll probably be another title.

Asian American nurses, soldiers . . . in Vietnam. Chinese cafes in small towns. Chinese expatriates returning to Hong Kong. East Indians looking for a way out of Hong Kong and 1997. A trio of Japanese American artists/musicians showing all of us that what they paint or play is just part of being here . . . in America. These are some of the thirty or so documentary stories that I'm telling or have told on television, in festivals and community gatherings.

They need to be told because any time a story about the life of an Asian American is told, it means we're alive, we're here and we're staying. We have a history. And with a history, "We damn well know where we've been, so we damn well know where we're going."

Life sure isn't cute when you're an Asian living in America. It's worse when you're doing docs about the Asian experience in America. Part of the problem is that there are too many stories to explore. So you go with your gut instinct that this story and the people in it can connect, can make your life a little better because you, with your "technical competence," can make it all happen. But if you're doing docs to win awards, fame and fortune, sure sounds like a losing proposition to me. You'd make a better living selling real estate in Monterey Park 'cause making documentaries isn't money heaven.

Asian English

Once you get that "right" story with those wonderful sound bites, it's a feeling you just can't explain. But what if the "right" story gives you a lot of footage of patchy English with perfectly useable opinions and ideas.

Solving this problem used to be a big headache for me when I did street reporting for the Canadian Broadcasting Corporation in Saskatoon and Calgary. "Asian people, Chinee English, lousy interviews, no story." That's what news directors used to say. Then they'd insult me and the interview subjects by demanding subtitles.

Later, a seasoned Asian American reporter told me, "If you ain't got those pics, you ain't got that swing."

Pictures, visuals, B-rolls and cutaways—it all amounts to getting generic shots to cover those hesitant sound bites. In *Another Day in America* (1989), I had just that kind of interview. The Japan-born painter was shy, hesitant and wasn't all that fluent in English. But what she said made great copy for the story. Since my Filipino American shooter gave me plenty of painting footage, I solved this problem by cutting her sound bites—without the hesitations, without the ums and ahs—over visuals of the artist at work. That gave the story a great feel for the art and for her.

Themes Versus Individual Segments

This is always a big problem for me. The story's great . . . meaning the interviews are dynamite. In *Chinese Cafes* (1985), I worked with four Chinese cafe owners. The men and women talked about coming over, why they became cafe owners, racism, children, their futures: all provocative. In *Indian Struggle* (1986), complex issues like racism, being Indian in Hong Kong, and working as merchants were potential segments.

Once the story begins to take a shape of its own with each interview, the themes start to appear. But working in a thematic way loses the sensitive human feeling and personal touch that a documentary must have, or else it becomes either turgidly academic or mere propaganda.

I used the thematic approach in several documentaries that I produced for the English division of Television Broadcasts Ltd. in Hong Kong. Most of these dealt with economic issues like *Textiles: Tough Time . . . Again!* (1987) and political stories like *The Philippines: Buying Time* (1987). In the latter, two interview subjects (left/right views) gave their opinions on the ceasefire, Marcos, the military, the communist insurgents and Aquino's future. These were all thematic segments. Documentaries like these deal with ideas impacting on people rather than with people impacting on the shaping of ideas.

Since I've been through all the phases of more than thirty television documentaries and have narrated about seventy more, experience has shown me that idea stories lend themselves to thematic segments. People stories have their own individual segments. While the people stories give rise to specific themes like racism or sexism, the themes ought to be incorporated only within the segments dealing with specific individuals, families or people. It's an approach that suits me.

As a former television journalist, I also had a tendency to grab the best-paced natural sound or sound bite for an opener or teaser even in documentaries. This is what I called "deadline syndrome." This was resolved, especially in longer pieces by the story and interview subjects themselves.

Some people might think that a documentary producer of non-fiction television has total control. But you're only as good as your people. They're the ones who are the real storytellers. A producer/reporter is just the catalyst. That's because producing documentaries is a craft, a trade, nothing more and there is always more than just one approach.

VIDEO ART:
HOW MANY VOICES?

ART NOMURA

The terms "minority" and "mainstream" may seem antiquated in a field like video art which prides itself on its universal membership. Indeed, the reigning superstar and "father" of the artform, Nam June Paik, hails from Korea. But Paik, despite his Asian heritage, works with broad creative strokes often using the entire world as his canvas. He epitomizes the "universal" artist, that is, an artist who exploits life in the world at-large rather than confining himself to a single geographic area, ethnic background, or culture. Paik's unique way of working renders for the most part meaningless the label of "minority" artist.

For other artists from minority backgrounds, however, ethnicity and cultural values have a more obvious and fundamental effect on the artwork produced. The minority video artist is socially, psychologically, and artistically susceptible to his background and environment.

For example, let us consider a group with which I am intimately familiar: Asian American video artists. Asian American video artists are members of a "triple" minority. First, our ethnicity places us in a minority status within mainstream America. Second, the role of artist is clearly on the fringe of mainstream occupations and vocational pursuits (a status that all artists must endure). And finally, video art itself is a subset within the world of art and art-making.

On the face of it, Asian American works have little in common besides the fact that they are created by artists from similar backgrounds. Indeed, the work of Asian American video artists is diverse. It includes the soap opera influenced work of Bruce and Norman Yonemoto, the stylized explorations in light, color, and form of Norie Sato, and my own dance video collaborations and unorthodox documentaries.

But despite this diversity, we cannot escape our triple minority status. My video art illustrates this status.

For the past ten years, my passion has been to produce video art. Although I am a third-generation Japanese American (Sansei), I have never felt the need or desire to produce video art that is consciously "Asian American." And although I enjoy, respect, and am often enlightened by the efforts of the Asian American documentaries and conventional narrative producers working with minority themes, I am actually disinclined to make a practice of overtly presenting ethnic issues, problems, and experiences in my own work. I

WOK LIKE A MAN (1987)
Art Nomura

choose instead to remain open to a broader range of influences which naturally (and often, unpredictably) includes my inherent and learned ethnic and cultural sensibilities.

I think this inclusive attitude toward subject matter is common among contemporary artists of all backgrounds. My own work draws strongly from my experience and formal training as a sculptor and painter. So I therefore consider formal issues of composition, color, form, scale, and contrast in tandem with questions about narrative content, information presentation, and dramatic structure in my work.

Only two of my videos thus far, *Refugees From Laos* (1981), a documentary on the U.S. settlement of Southeast Asian refugees, and *Wok Like a Man* (1987), an experimental hybrid of music video and documentary about Asian American males, have explicitly addressed Asian American themes and issues. Nonetheless, I have been told that my "non-Asian" work, on occasion, appears to have connections to my mother culture, three generations removed.

For instance, a viewer once told me that my experimental dance video *Haute Flash* (1982), which I co-produced with choreographer Mary Daval, is visually evocative of the staging of classical Japanese *Noh* drama. Whether or not that assessment was primarily a projection of his personal racial stereotypes, or a subconscious choice on my part, is difficult to figure. I just know that I've never been a student of that traditional artform, but that I was probably exposed to such presentations as a child.

Of course every minority artist is free to make reference to his/her roots. But it seems that the more artists are concerned about and affected by their differences from the mainstream, the more an artist is apt to consciously bring minority issues into the work. Popular topics of concern for such artists include authentic depictions of minorities vs. stereotypes, cultural backgrounds and concerns, and speaking out about one's problems as an immigrant. These issues are reverently and frequently explored by traditional minority media makers in the documentary and narrative media arts.

These intimate and positive depictions of the Asian American experience, however valuable they may be, are in manner and content too conventional and obvious for the video artist. As an artistic minority even within the art world, video artists instead relish the opportunity to produce the innovative and unique *regardless* of subject matter. Nonetheless, ethnic and cultural values can often emerge in our work, in sometimes surprising ways.

For example, even though I work earnestly to be straightforward in my personal interactions and writings, I choose, in my video work, to offer a multi-layered, indirect path towards communicating with my audience. My rationale for doing so is because I believe that the most effective communication of new information and aesthetic concerns is possible when the receiver is relaxed, comfortable, and therefore, receptive. Upon examination however, it is also possible that the alleged Japanese tendency toward nonconfrontation has filtered its way into my art-making philosophy.

Accordingly, much of my work seems to be "soft," rather than "hard" hitting. This doesn't, in my opinion, detract from the work, but unfortunately runs *against* the western values of aggressiveness and self-promotion and *with* the eastern values of non-confrontation and cooperation. This conflict in values can be problematic, especially in regards to the exhibition of my work.

My belief that my video artwork is best served and communicated by a "soft" approach becomes a problem, ironically, not with the viewing public (who seem willing to accept different approaches), but with the learned members of the media community. Works that lack the "hard edge" of traditional western media are routinely passed over by programmers, curators, funding panels and critics for exhibition, sponsorship and thoughtful reviews.

My Asian background and Asian American upbringing has probably influenced my tendency to go "soft" with my work. And although I steadfastly believe that this mode of delivery is a superior one for introducing ideas, inducing communication, and fostering understanding, it is not an approach endorsed or supported by the arbiters of mainstream video art.

My dilemma then becomes that of every minority artist: "How do I create work that honestly incorporates my unique background, experiences and values, on both a conscious and unconscious level, and still receive acceptance, support and exposure from the mainstream art world?"

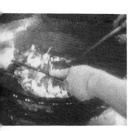

Regrettably, many minority artists choose to sidestep the issue by staying out of the mainstream art world, with its predilection toward narrowly focused western sensibilities and values. But that choice, although practical and less confrontational, is both exclusive and more than a little short-sighted. It is, of course, possible to exhibit in "side show" exhibitions (and publications) such as "Contemporary Black Women Artists," or "Asian American Videomakers," but those venues, although helpful, should not and cannot be considered the end-all of artistic presentation by minority artists.

The aesthetic concerns and expressions of minority artists are, in every way, as valid as those in the mainstream. In a more perfect world this reminder would be unnecessary. We would all approach art-making with the confidence of Nam June Paik. Each would be free to draw from the past, interpret the present, visualize a future, and convey a mood in their own unique manner and have an equal opportunity to present that expression.

But such is not the case. Few minority artists will ever be able to match the combination of talent, energy, luck and opportunity that has propelled Paik to his enviable position. Therefore, every minority artist in my view must pursue an inclusive attitude in the presentation of his/her work.

Finally, those that exhibit and critique art must realize that the face of America has changed. To retain their relevance in the new America and indeed the world, those that see, judge, and write must critically examine time-worn, culturally specific standards. Then, and only then, will "triple minority" video artists and the innumerable other "outsiders" in our society receive the attention, support, and forum for creativity they need and deserve.

WOK LIKE A MAN (1987)
Art Nomura

Fu-Ding Cheng

The source and inspiration for my art, films and videos comes from my long-term involvement with the spiritual quest, the world of dreams, meditation, psychic studies and Kung-fu. The artistic challenge is to express these powerful experiences that often involve strange, surrealistic events without diluting them with normal logic and storytelling formulas *and* still making them accessible to the viewer. My experiments include:

Ethero (1968)
Inspired by the Tibetan Book of the Dead and its view of the life-death cycles, I structured the film as a tone-poem and allowed the flow of images—a three-eyed fetus, a first nightmare, etc.—to unfold as in a stream of consciousness.

White in Bad Light (1974, re-edited 1989)
The germinating impulse was a sequence of dream and meditation images that seemed powerful in how they revealed deep psychological events and yearnings: a man in a traffic accident flies away like a bird; a toilet crumbles in the middle of the desert; a hole in the desert emits a rainbow, etc. At first the film was edited as a tone-poem but in 1989 (fifteen years later!), I finally found the structure for the film: edited it in the form of a *myth* (dreams and myths come from the same place—an individual has a dream, a society has a myth).

Flight of Ideas (1978)
The reconstruction of a meditation session using the attitude of a newsreel documentary filmmaker—as if the camera is in the brain. All conscious experiences whether "real" or imaginary are documented objectively for the film following the thought patterns of the mind as it hops, steps and jumps toward increasing stillness and awareness. (This prize-winning film although filled with "fantasy" sequences was invited to the Bilbao International Documentary Film Festival.)

Spirit of the Dream House (1982).
The hero of the story is a *house*, who tells how he got built, the families that

THE WINGED CAGE (1989)
Fu-Ding Cheng

lived inside him, loved him and abused him. The material, again from a powerful meditation centered on a house that continually changes its appearances, and three years later a dream of the same house, was this time put in the form of a fable, or a fairy tale. (In Jungian thought, the best repository for the suppressed psychological events of a culture are their fairy tales.)

How to Become a Fascinating Speaker (1987)

A surrealistic comedy about a shy man at a party who hears a strange voice and learns to become a fascinating speaker. One of the first of the series of my "Zen-Tales for the Urban Explorer." These allegorical stories are in the great tradition of mystical literature—Aesop fables, Sufi stories, Taoist tales, Biblical parables and Zen tales. On the surface, they are very simple stories accessible to the most casual viewer, and at the same time they reverberate with the profound insights on metaphoric level. In this case, the instructions given by the "voice" are based on the ancient wisdom of the "Vedas."

The Winged Cage (1989)

Another in the series of "Zen-Tales for the Urban Explorer." Continuing with my explorations with allegorical levels, this film interweaves experiences of super-normal consciousness with the normal reality of everyday human interaction. Actors, dramaturgy, humor and irony flesh out this film allowing super-ordinary dream and meditation experience to be accessible to a general audience.

Full Contact (in pre-production).

This feature-length, martial arts film follows the adventures of a kick-boxer who after a vision during a serious injury, gradually transforms himself from a macho street-fighter to an impeccable warrior. Throughout the film the character experiences different realities, which help him expand his vision of life and adds to his self-mastery.

ON EXPERIMENTAL
VIDEO

ON EXPERIMENTAL VIDEO

Valerie Soe

VALERIE SOE

Part of establishing a voice and perspective for the Asian Pacific community has been demanding recognition for our point of view. This aesthetic acknowledges the legitimacy of experiences outside of the dominant culture. Experimental film and video work likewise expands the boundaries of conventional forms, using unusual structures or visual languages, or approaching unlikely topics or themes.

As a case in point, my experimental video work often uses unconventional devices to carry its message. *All Orientals Look the Same* (1985) is a non-linear, non-narrative piece using slide dissolves of the faces of several Asian Pacific Americans to contradict the title phrase. *Scratch Video* (1986) and *Eggs* (1987) consist mainly of static shots of mundane activities with a voiceover describing personal experiences and concerns. *New, Parts I & II* (1987), respectively makes use of storybook drawings and re-edited film and television images. None of these approaches follow the broadcast television narrative or documentary format, thus presenting me with the challenge of reaching the viewer and effectively conveying my concerns.

I've found that despite the unorthodoxy of my methodology, I can communicate my message by maintaining a distinctive perspective, which can be as simple as speaking in the first person relating an individual experience, or as broad as examining an issue of concern to the Asian Pacific American community. By balancing an unusual formal structure with more immediate conceptual concerns I've been able to create accessible yet challenging work.

My next avenue of investigation is expanding my conceptual base, trying to broaden the scope of the Asian Pacific American perspective. The definition of what constitutes community concerns as the community changes. Similarly, my concerns as a Chinese American woman have grown and changed throughout my life. I hope that the community will remain as supportive and receptive to my newer work, as it has been in the past, as the issues I deal with change.

Two of my upcoming videotapes will deal respectively with interracial marriage and my response to the October 17th earthquake. Although one piece can be more directly perceived as "Asian Pacific American," since it deals with an immediate concern of the community, I believe that my second tape just as legitimately comes from an Asian Pacific perspective.

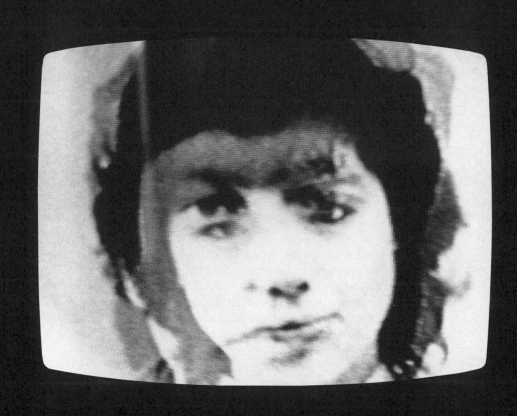

As Guillermo Gomez-Pena has stated, within each community there is a multiplicity of communities, and within each artist a range of concerns that speak to that community's needs. It's more important not to pigeonhole Asian Pacific artists into only dealing with culture specific topics and themes.

The Asian Pacific American perspective by definition recognizes the validity and importance of visions outside of the mainstream. In turn, I hope that such a tolerant world view will allow for the evolution of my particular point of view, in which I seek to further expand the definition of the Asian Pacific creative voice.

ALL ORIENTALS LOOK THE SAME (1986)
Valerie Soe

EARRADIATION: "GOLD MOUNTAIN" RADIO

Theo-dric Feng

The "Gold Mountain" radio program in Washington, D.C., which I produce and host (as a volunteer) presents material on Asian/Pacific Americans. "Gold Mountain" includes interviews, speeches, panel discussions, and music. I am both an advocate and conduit of Asian/Pacific American views and sensibilities.

Interviews

I prefer to conduct and air in-depth interviews. They are more enjoyable and intellectually stimulating. Sometimes problems arise when the interviewee manipulates the interview or responds with vague answers or statements. For example, an interviewee may say, "You should ask about this rather than that." If the suggestion is given in a commanding tone, I feel like a publicity flack receiving an order.

Equally bothersome is when an interviewee answers a question with something innocuous or oblique. I feel like grabbing them by the lapels and saying, "Look, you better answer the question or I'll stuff this microphone down your throat!" It is not decreed anywhere that the interviewee must answer all questions to the questioner's satisfaction. For that matter, where it is written you have to like the person that you're interviewing?

It's annoying when the interviewee launches into a rehearsed phrase or discourse. (You realize they're just trying to cover their ass.) I recall asking an official for a major movie studio about his company's affirmative action and EEO, knowing this was his area of expertise. "We stand by our record," was his response. In subsequent questions, I couldn't get much more detail. Needless to say, it was a short interview. I found out later that one reason the fellow was so tight-lipped was because a representative was in the room from the movie company that had just bought a controlling interest in the movie studio. The interviewee didn't want to say anything that could be used against him in any possible personnel reshuffling.

Sometimes the response appears to have little to do with the question and ends up dissipating in a vapor of platitudes. One time, I tried to ask a visiting Asian political candidate from the West Coast about issues he was covering in his campaign. He replied that as a first-timer in running for office, he learned a candidate should not debate the issues. He then launched into some fuzzy rhetoric. (He seemed to be inferring that a candidate shouldn't try to alienate any voters. I was a little frustrated, especially since my listeners were obviously not potential voters in that election.)

Ultimately, I tend not to air material that doesn't say much or isn't particularly educational or illuminating. Neither will I give much airtime to dirty laundry.

One example of controversy within the Asian/Pacific American community occurred in the Jim Loo case. Several months after Jim Loo died from an assault by a white racist, I wondered whether or not I should try to explore the differences of opinion between two groups organized to bring the white assailants to justice. I happened to be personally acquainted with the leader of the smaller of the two groups. His words and actions had become a focus of controversy in the advocacy efforts.

Ultimately, I decided that it wouldn't be terribly interesting to the listeners to understand the controversy, the disagreement over tactics and strategy as well as personal animosities. Moreover it would have probably used up lots of time and effort in getting the interviews and writing and editing the script.

Music

Being mindful of one's audience is key in any communicative endeavor. This is especially true when choosing music for broadcast. By and large, I have great respect for musicians for their skills, talent, and the difficulties they face in performing and disseminating their music. I feel it is vitally important to support Asian/Pacific musicians. Unfortunately, some of their music that I acquire I deem unsuitable for broadcast on "Gold Mountain." Certain pieces sound too raw, dissonant, abstract, or uncoordinated. Some music may be fine for 2 A.M., but not right for 2 P.M. (Mondays, which is when the show airs).

Another problem I've run across is slow tempo. I can think of two releases that were recorded at a slow tempo to ensure all the notes were played accurately. The problem with that is the recordings sound dead. I can't speed up the music very much before the pieces start sounding like they were recorded by Alvin and the Chipmunks.

The question conscientious APA music programmers might ask themselves is whether to play certain music because of a felt obligation to support APA creative endeavors or not play it because it's difficult to listen to or there's something technically wrong with it. It used to be more of a problem when few recordings by APAs existed. Nowadays, there are quite a few releases. And since I play contemporary and traditional music from Asia and the Pacific Islands as well, the problem recedes into the background. I'm also averse to airing music that sounds too derivative or fairly commonplace. This especially applies to music that draws heavily on fusion, rock, pop, disco, rap, New Age, or muzak.

The fulcrum of this whole discussion is the tradeoff between objectivity and advocacy. How do you balance the desire to be supportive and the need to be objective or critical? Most solutions wind up being a function of lack of time to prepare a program and the abundancy of material to choose from.

Everywhere I roam I listen for
my native language with a
crying heart because it means
my roots in this faraway soil; it
means my only communication
with the living and those who
died without a gift of
expression.

CARLOS BULOSAN

June 2, 1953

SURVIVING IN THIS PLACE CALLED THE UNITED STATES

ESTHER G. BELIN

if i was japanese
i would be a nisei
i am second generation
off-reservation

my mother comes from
the land of enchantment
now also
the land of poverty
drugs
illiteracy
and confusion

my mother
like many japanese during WWII
was relocated
off the rez
to a federally-run
boarding school
in riverside, california, USA

there she experienced
a five-year program
of assimilation
of humiliation
goal:
annihilation
of the savage race

now
many years later (yes, we are still around)
i honor
my mother

NATIONAL ASIAN AMERICAN TELECOMMUNICATIONS
ASSOCIATION SCREENING
Bob Hsiang (1989)

who like most indian people
is a survivor

she continues to struggle
to make my path
—even if it's the same path as hers—
a little easier
survival—by any means necessary

she endured what was called "civilization"
in 1956
to see me graduate
from high school in 1986
with honors
then on to u.c. hyprocrisy

her dreams
her amazing strength
survive
through me
and what i create

though my path is easier
i still struggle
with ills she faced in '56
racism
sexism
classism
homophobiaism

i cringe at
how this place
called the united states
sees me and my people:
indian princesses
     & rotund squaws
     & blood-thirsty braves
     & ungrateful drunks
     & specimens (dead or alive)
     for projects in the name of science
     & progress
     & non-existent after the 1800s
     & some of the richest people in the u.s.
via
     hollywood's image
     anthropological data
     & reagan's quote to the russians

survival tactics for me have always been my mother
whose faith in our creator and in me
keeps me moving and shaking

on the aside:
facts they don't tell you in history books
about this place called the united states:
there are no tepees in northern arizona or new mexico
leonard peltier is a political prisoner
native people occupy less than 2% of their original land base
there are over 300 separate indian nations
migration is a theory, not fact

facts you might already know:
i am urban, but definitely indian
i am a survivor and definitely moving the image

PUBLIC MEDIA: SERVING THE PUBLIC INTEREST?

JAMES YEE

"Thirtysomething" of Public Television

In 1990, as public broadcasting (PBS) enters its twenty-third year, it finds itself in the grip of a severe bout of "thirtysomething," a grappling for purpose, for redefinition, for new directions. Created in 1987 during Lyndon Johnson's great society initiative, the Corporation for Public Broadcasting (CPB) is the primary national organization charged with the development of public television and radio in the U.S. Its purported mission is to provide high-quality, educational, informational and cultural programming for all Americans.

To fulfill this charge, CPB provides funding for national programs, distributes grants for operations and programming to stations and producing organizations and provides regulatory assistance, research, and broadcast training. Public television and radio were intended to be non-commercial, producing and broadcasting programs which are both alternatives to commercial programs, and representative of the cultural diversity of American peoples.

In its twenty-two years, public television has created programming that has served as standards of excellence such as "Sesame Street," "NOVA," "The MacNeil/Lehrer News Hour," "Great Performances," "Frontline," etc. But in the process, public television has also become complacent. In recent years, it has found itself unable to respond creatively and programmatically to the nation's trends and problems, e.g. drug epidemics, AIDS, the reformation of the global economic order, and the impact of changing population patterns in America. Equally disturbing is the lack of programming on minority issues and works by minority producers on public television.

Compounding public broadcasting's problems were the technological advances in satellite communication. Vigorous marketing strategies in the last decade have led to the rapid emergence of cable television from HBO, Disney, CNN and Discovery channels which has eroded public (and commercial) television viewership.

At this juncture lies an opportunity for the minority communities to assert their presence in shaping future public television policy, in decision making, and in pushing for multicultural programming and production.

Why the Asian Community Must Involve Itself in Public Television

The entry of minorities has always been an uphill struggle. The 1960s Civil Rights movement led to a few openings in film, television, and radio for people of color, but overall not many minorities advanced to decision-making roles as producers, programmers, and managers.

In the 1990s, the U.S. census projects that we will become a nation in which no single group will assume a racially-based majority. This demographic change requires that Asian Pacific American communities must involve ourselves in the creation and dissemination of our own images and voices within public television and radio.

Since the mid-70s, the Asian Pacific American media community has made modest gains in producing documentary and narrative films and videos on public television. Audiences who supported Asian American artists, writers and directors grew within, and without our immediate ethnic communities. Nonetheless, the productions which have explicit ethnic/racial points of view are few and far between. Access, control and distribution of Asian Pacific works in film, video, television and radio must remain central to our political strategy.

A quick glance at the numbers of minorities employed within public broadcasting confirms the limited participation of minorities. For example, the overall number of minorities employed in public broadcasting in 1989 is 16.3% or about 2,400 out of 14,713 employees. In the category of 'professional,' the figures are 14.9% or 790 out of 5,288. As to being in major decision-making positions, CPB's survey of 29% of television stations showed that only 11% are minorities with any key decision-making roles. Parity of numbers of minorities in decision-making roles is a high priority.

Asian Pacific American Independents

The figures above do not include the independent minority filmmaker or media organizations who work outside the station environment. This community of independents produces some of the finest programming on public television and radio. (See Norman Jayo's "The Last Game Show," in this book.) Without the contribution of these independent producers, public broadcasting would lack the uniqueness and diverse fare that it should provide.

At the same time, the independent makers need to have their works broadcast to the widest audience possible through these several hundred television stations across the nation. For the better part of the 80s minorities have struggled to be included in national public programming.

The creation of the National Asian American Telecommunications Association (NAATA) came about at the behest of minority producers and community groups who saw the need for an ongoing vehicle and advocate for having their works seen on public television. Created out of the first Asian American media conference in 1980, and active since 1982, NAATA became a national presenter of Asian American films and video programs for public television. In its eight years, the organization quickly evolved to becoming a clearinghouse that provides makers and communities with services including public broadcast programming, exhibition, non-broadcast distribution, research, information, publication, and advocacy. With core funding from CPB, it immersed itself initially in acquiring, packaging and presenting works

'The 1960s Civil Rights movement led to a few openings... but overall, not many minorities advanced to decision-making roles as producers, programmers, and managers."

(From left) JAMES YEE, LONI DING, AND WAYNE WANG,
NAATA CONFERENCE (UCLA, 1985)

by Asian producers on PBS. Given the marginal funding from CPB, NAATA expanded its activities and its funding base to assume a media arts center role.

Within the Asian American community, we can take pride in seeing works truly about the Asian American experience in this nation made by our own makers. These filmmakers and writers include Wayne Wang, *Eat A Bowl of Tea* (1989); Christine Choy and Renee Tajima, *Who Killed Vincent Chin?* (1988); Loni Ding, *Color of Honor* (1987); Spencer Nakasako, *Monterey's Boat People* (1982); Steven Okazaki, *Unfinished Business* (1984); Lise Yasui, *Family Gathering* (1988); Philip Gotanda, *The Wash* (1988); Genny Lim, *Paper Angel*; Felicia Lowe, *China: Land of My Father* (1979); Arthur Dong, *Forbidden City, U.S.A.* (1989); Lisa Hsia, *Made in China* (1985); Karen Ishizuka and Robert Nakamura, *Fool's Dance* (1983); and others who can't be named due to space limitations.

New Initiatives

Every three years, the Congress (with the White House) must reauthorize the Public Broadcasting Act as part of its legislation responsibilities. During this review process federal laws can be amended and changed in light of debate raised by either legislative bodies. The past several years, NAATA has participated in a national coalition of independent media groups, civic organizations and minority producers to seek improved access and greater funding for minority/independent works. Our efforts to cooperate with the Corporation for Public Broadcasting, the Public Broadcasting Service and public stations in insuring a successful reauthorization of the 1988 Public Broadcasting Act to benefit all parties were refused. We were perceived as a threat (and correctly so) to the "old boys" approach of conducting business as usual.

Despite these obstacles, sympathetic and knowledgeable legislators heard our collective pleas. This resulted in the 1988 public broadcast legislation which designated nine million dollars a year for independent and minority production and programming. Congressional leaders were critical of the paucity of programming that failed to encompass the breadth of America's ethnic and racial minorities. The lack of quality multicultural children's programming further propelled the Congress to provide legislative language to address these concerns, regardless of CPB assurances. In short, both the Senate and House insisted that CPB and the public broadcasting community of stations be held accountable for future efforts which recognize multicultural/minority communities as part of the overall public and not simply as "special" groups separated from the rest of the American audience.

The impact of this new legislative language was a sharp rebuke to the public broadcast community's management of this public stewardship. The Congress perceived that this public mandate was being undermined by stations which broadcast old Hollywood movies, blurring the distinction between non-commercial and commercial television.

What's Ahead

It takes somewhere an average of three to five years to make a documentary film or video. Much of the time is devoted to fundraising before a frame of film is even shot. If Asian American media is to attain a regular, ongoing presence on public television, we must reduce the turnaround time between conception and completion and increase the number of production efforts by the Asian American and other minority communities.

This is the immediate task before those of us in production or programming support. The solution is partly having more funds designated for research and development. Later this year, NAATA will provide modest grants for new startup projects.

Secondly, members of the public station system must be persuaded to accept and broadcast new programming produced by a non-white producer. Station and program managers are still hesitant about including minority produced programs given their thinking that minority programs are for minority viewers only. In light of the fact that minority audiences are proportionately small compared to the larger viewership, there is great reluctance to broadcast those works during those "prime times" when there are larger audiences watching public television. A fundamental error made by many of these program and scheduling managers is their failure to see that minority programming is as relevant to non-minority viewers.

The response to the PBS special, "Eyes on the Prize" (1990) series certainly speaks to the universality of these issues. Unfortunately, "Eyes on the Prize" is an exception rather than the rule, as its producer, Henry Hampton, would testify. The road to acceptance of minority production remains far from equitable both from a funding and programming perspective. To affect greater minority production, we must collaborate with national PBS programming entities such as "American Playhouse," "American Experience," and "Wonderworks."

There is underway a daring, long-overdue effort for a new national program model where all decision-making and funding will be housed under a single office and director at PBS, the nation's public television station network. At this writing, it is unclear what plans this new vice president to national programming has for bringing in greater minority participation to national programming. Recent PBS proposals and discussions have been receptive to the concerns of its minority advisory board members as well as to those raised by the minority and independent producing community. It is too soon to tell what will actually take place other than a verbal acknowledgement of multicultural programming. "Multicultural," in my view, should be applied to those ethnic and racial minority groups who have been historically disenfranchised and excluded from being part of the mainstream. At a later time, "multicultural" should embrace all cultures and races but it is premature until there is, indeed, inclusion and equitable integration of the present ethnic and racial minority communities into public media.

A recent experience by this writer perhaps illustrates the difficulty we face in order to gain acceptance of minority programming within the public media. National producers and station programmers met this spring at Hilton Head Island to discuss the state (and plight) of primetime programming on PBS. Outside of the few minority producers in attendance there was little interest in how to address assuming a multicultural and racially diverse makeup. "Minority programming," "multicultural programming" were rarely uttered by this national group of producers.

The attendees were predominantly white males whose energies were focused around their own programming turf issues. For the few women and minorities in attendance, seeing their dynamics gave us a much needed reality check of what public television is all about . . . and it isn't about us!

In all those discussions, Bill Moyers brought home most eloquently what public broadcasting is supposed to be all about.

. . . public broadcasting must always be an alternative to commercialism; not just to commercial television which is now the dominant strain in American life. The economic animal is devouring America. . . . There has to be an alternative to that mentality (commercial television) in the production of art, journalism and public service. . . . We are still the only broadcasting community charged with the dynamics of the U.S. Constitution, which is being the Public Broadcasting Act of 1967, to produce our art, our journalism, our theatre without regard to those little lies and fantasies that are incorporated into the merchandising process of America today . . . we can save public broadcasting if we keep in mind that our purpose is to serve the public. The audience will always leave you, but if you serve the public, they will be there when you need them most.

I hold Bill Moyers' remarks to mean that the future of public television will have to integrate a multicultural public.

Public Television In a Self-Censoring Role

We can sympathize with the fact that public broadcasting is an inherently poorly funded system. In the past two decades, stations have proven adroit in raising funds from their viewing audiences and from a host of other public and private dollars. Their ability to raise funds has led to the impression that the public television station community is assuming characteristics not that different from its commercial cousins.

Ratings, serving the donors and the subscriber paying members, are becoming priorities; programming is treated as an afterthought. While all this may have been necessary to insure the well-being of the station, one cannot but sense the hesitancy of the stations to air programming that may challenge the sensibilities of their viewers. This cautionary and self-censoring behavior inhibits any kind of innovative or minority programming except on holidays and anniversary events. This safeguarding of viewers' donations versus carrying out the mission of providing all kinds of images, opinions and information to the American public creates a contradictory situation. Viewer subscribership ideally should support invigorating, non-commercial alternative programming.

Change or Perish

Innovation and risk-taking will come elsewhere, predictably from the independent and minority producing communities. Our minority communities must see themselves as part of the new American public, insisting on seeing a diversity of images, stories, aesthetics that are theirs, created to be shared with others.

If the new national program leadership is willing to make a fundamental change and take risks in creating new primetime programs in partnership with independent/minority communities, then the nation shall benefit immensely in the years and decades to come. But if these steps are not taken, the effectiveness and purpose of a public broadcast mandate may come to an end, leaving our families, communities and public without any true alternative to the commercial barrage of mediocre programming. The Asian Pacific community will continue to suffer under the new stereotypes that are being created by the same industry that has ill served us for so long, and our minority producers will, indeed, become an endangered species.

"'Multicultural' should embrace all cultures and races but it is premature until there is... inclusion and integration of the present ethnic and racial minority communities into public media."

Norman Jayo

Ed. Note: "The Last Game Show," a two-hour, four-part futuristic radio drama by Norman Jayo, features a multicultural cast with Brock Peters, Abbey Lincoln, George Takei, Robert Ito, Danny Valdez, and Mako. Set in the year 2045, the hundredth anniversary of the atomic bomb destruction of Hiroshima, the production portrays an Orwellian, cyper-punk society, where passive citizens are hooked up to computer workstations and spend their leisure time plugged into an electronic entertainment system that transports them into a variety of "virtual reality" diversions, from travelogues to game shows. "Virtual reality" is an existing technology, a marriage of artificial intelligence and robotics developed by NASA and others.

Not many people realize upon hearing "The Last Game Show" for the first time that it was written, produced, directed and engineered by Asian Americans. Most people just get right into the story, into the characters, and the theme of the game show, played out against the backdrop of our dying planet. They want to know what's going to happen in the end because they have a vested interest in the outcome. They don't think to themselves: Wow, this was done by Asian Americans! That information comes only by way of the titles and credits. They don't really care who's telling the story. The fact that "The Last Game Show" is an Asian American product represents an expanded strategy for minority production.

This strategy began in June of 1983, when Jim Yee, of the National Asian American Telecommunications Association, asked me to write something on the state of people of color in the media as a precursor to developing the long range goals of the organization. In the library, I read up on the history of civil rights, the Kerner Commission, Vietnam and the women's movement. During these sessions, something began nagging at me from deep within. I kept finding the word "minority." Each time I read it, I felt resentment. It was with this word in mind that I began to write "Minority Production in the Twenty-First Century—Leaving the Revolving Door

THE LAST GAME SHOW (1989)
Linda Mabalot

Behind." In short, the paper goes, as follows:

In the sixties and early seventies the stability of law and order was threatened much the way law and order is threatened in South Africa. Sparked by the struggles from Selma to Watts, from Alcatraz to Wounded Knee, from the great marches and demonstrations in Washington, D.C., to the Chicano Moratorium, people of color began to raise their voices with the same common demands for equal rights. In reaction, the word "minority" was pulled from the Constitution, and used in a pretext to define us by the smallest possible numbers. This was a division by race of the "have-nots." Out of that violent period came the "cooling-off" language and legislation, designed to chill the anger and send promising breezes through the streets of the neighborhoods and ghettos of America. Word was out; opportunity was on the streets and willing to talk.

When we made our entrance into the world of media, we stepped through the revolving door of "equal opportunity" and found ourselves in the front lobby. That's where we received our first minority application. With great anticipation, we began checking the boxes, and at that very moment, the psychology began to have its way with us. A certain mindset kicked in, and consciously or unconsciously, we began doing business as minorities. The first matter of business we learned was that all the doors leading from the lobby are entered by appointment only; appointment to interviews, leading to little training, and even fewer jobs; appointments to meetings, where we heard the same replies, on countless occasions—That's a great idea, however, it's not quite up to technical quality!—That's absolutely the best 'stuff' I've seen on your people!—It's not mainstream subject material!—There's no audience!—It's not a good investment.—It won't make money!—We'll run it on Sunday morning, 3 a.m. public affairs slot!"—If you stack these replies on top of one another, you can measure just how far we are from the top.

To say we are a minority, under the influence of this pretext, is to begin the process of separating ourselves from the whole by the absurd criteria of simply not being white. The word, used in this way, is a constitutional disgrace; a fantasy in denial of all equitable reason. It has the same underlying intent as the words chief, chink, nigger and spic, which it has diplomatically replaced. You can also see the same fundamental logic at play when examining the case of women who themselves make up more than half the population. The constitutional needs of women are the same as people of color. Together, as the "have-nots" of equal rights, men of color, white women, and women of color—who stand alone on a bridge of double jeopardy—we constitute a majority. Yet, as people, we continue to act with the mindset of a minority.

In the original constitutional context, the word "minority" was used to guide and protect us against tyranny by any single faction while at the same time protecting the rights of each individual citizen. In our case, it is the latter that we need, the former that we endure. According to Madison and the Federalist Papers; "A faction is any group of citizens who are united around some common interest, which is antagonistic to the rights of other citizens. A power to control the democratic process." Certainly we have a minority faction in control. We see them! We recognize them! We deal with them every day. We know them to be a faction dominated by white men. This faction is bound together by a desire to remain in power. They are not part of a single conspiracy but rather a far-reaching alliance which has its own potential for splintering. It is not beyond this faction to make great compromises in order to maintain the status quo, even if it means including limited numbers of women and people of color, some more mindful of personal wealth and power, and who have little regard for the struggle for equal rights.

In order to deny the needs of the majority, the Constitution must be denied. Attitudes of superiority and arrogance are fundamental to this end. Likewise, attitudes of inferiority and passivity are equally necessary if the pretext is to be carried out. Our productions reflect this. Our programming range is based on this denial. When we end the denial, our perspectives will broaden, and reveal that we represent a substantial current of the mainstream.

For the "gatekeepers" of media, the "mainstream" is big business. The bottom line is cash at the box office, increased subscriptions in the public venues, and the going rate for a thirty second commercial spot on the networks. From their perspective, the minority product has very little value. The whole social obligation towards women and people of color is painfully endured by most media executives as a necessary burden, like taxes. Their hearts are not in it.

For us to continue doing business from this minority mindset means economic failure in the market place. In accepting the terminology, as defined, we have accepted the rules and regulations which restrict the fulfillment of real affirmative action. Our product has become ghettoized. As long as we continue to think of ourselves as a minority, it will remain so. We will be bound by negative limitations with few viable options. We have the power to broaden the range of our perspectives, to expand our view of the whole, to see ourselves in a universal context leading to our own empowerment. No longer should we regard any subject material as the private exclusive reserve of white producers. We should be making mainstream movies, reporting prime time news, covering major events, from local street fairs, to flights of the space shuttle. All subject material, currently considered to be mainstream, should now be considered as viable production options for women and people of color. However, the ground which we have managed to gain thus far as producers should remain the bedrock from which we build. We must continue to produce projects reflecting our personal experiences as women and people of color. But we must also expand our production diet to include a range of choices not yet on our programming menu. We alone hold the key to expand our perspectives as producers and audiences. There is no end to what we think of as people, and certainly no end to what we see happening in the world around us. The only difference we should be concerned with is that what we see and feel about the world as a whole is fully represented.

In summary, the paper on "Minority Production in the Twenty-First Century—Leaving the Revolving Door Behind," concludes with the presentation of a programming menu, consisting of over forty project concepts, each a paragraph in length. The menu reflects dozens of ideas in news, drama and public affairs. Every possible selection is treated from a universal point of view presenting Asian Americans in context as part of the whole. After reading the paper, Jim Yee and Janice Sakamoto of NAATA selected "The Last Game Show" from the programming menu as our first target production using this strategy.

> *"To say we are a minority… is to begin the process of separating ourselves from the whole by the absurd criteria of simply not being white."*

Now, after seven years of struggle to see both the story told and this production strategy applied, we have delivered our product to the marketplace. Response has been representative of a broad multicultural base. Acceptance by the listeners has been all that we as independent producers could ask for. Inquiries about the two-hour drama continued well after the national broadcast on Earth Day, April 22, 1990. Acknowledgement from the industry has also been broad and diverse, with requests for carriage coming from local community stations here in the States, to the British and Australian Broadcasting Corporations overseas.

"The Last Game Show" received two awards. Mentioning these honors is not intended as a boast for they are signs validating our production strategy. The first award was the Golden Reel for Best National Radio Drama, from the National Federation of Community Broadcasters (NFCB). The NFCB is the community wing of broadcast radio in the U.S. and represents the main media venue where women and people of color have gained the greatest ground since the sixties. On the other side of the spectrum, the production received the Gold Medal for Best Audio Art/Experimental by the International Radio Festival of New York, a commercial wing of radio, involving twenty-five programming and advertisements. This is one of the media venues where women and people of color have gained the least ground. Recognition from such a diverse range of the industry tells us that each market has placed some common value on our product. We suggest that this common value can only be fully appreciated from the viewpoint of a production approach which hinges on the rejection of the traditional minority posture, and the acceptance of ourselves as part of a whole.

By portraying ourselves in a broad "multicultural" perspective, we have defined, in a more honest and real context, our view of the world, rather than being defined by the limitations of the current standards and perceptions about people of color. Again, the fact that Asian Americans wrote, produced, directed, scored, performed in and distributed "The Last Game Show" was not the first aspect to be realized about the project. As that becomes clear, heads have turned with a constitutional jerk.

A TALK STORY POEM
FOR OPEN DIALOGUE III
PETER NIEN-CHU KIANG

The following poem was written and read by Peter Kiang for the plenary session on Leadership and Empowerment at the Open Dialogue III national conference of The Association of American Cultures (TAAC) in Washington, D.C., June 9-12, 1988.

We as artists, as advocates, as activists.

    We gather together in Washington—
Making history, opening dialogue for a third time
To celebrate our soul, to share our struggle.

For it is the Year of the Dragon,
    The dawn of a new day
    As eight long years come finally to an end.

We look to the future—the signs are clear:
    Nuevo Latino;
    The Pacific Rim Era;
    and What Does Jesse Want.

America is changing—We are changing America.
    Our colors are primary; Our cultures are precious;

But our presence is threatening.

Talk Story 1
Memorial Day Weekend in Boston, 1985.

White kids out from school, killing time by the hours.
Rambo opens at the movies, killing gooks by the thousands
    As the audience cheers him on.

One day later, kids attack a family of Vietnamese refugees,
    Breaking into their home, screaming "Go back to China!"

Two days later, Cambodians are harassed and beaten.
    They're told, "Go back to Vietnam!"

Racist violence runs rampant, like Rambo and Reagan,
    Making way for immigration control and English-only

To weaken our presence, to limit our numbers,
    To stop our influence.

A good lesson to learn—

We speak of leadership and empowerment in a social context
and struggle to understand our role,

We as artists, as advocates, as activists.

Talk Story 2
Boston, 1982.

Riding the Green Line subway to the edit studio
    To finish a videotape on Boston Chinatown's History.

As three Vietnamese get off at their stop,
    The big ugly white guy next to me mutters, "Chink"
    under his breath.

Full of pride and passion, I seize the moment,
    "What did you say!"

With no response, I repeat, "What did you say!"

He answers, "Chink," and, not thinking,
    I slap him in the face.

We rumble in the aisle . . . and he kicks my ass.

When he exits at the next stop,
    I look at the African American brother next to me,

A witness.

He tells me, "That was really stupid,"

And then adds, "Next time, use your fist!"

A good lesson to learn—

Pick your fights wisely.

One person alone, no matter how proud,
One person alone is not enough.

We must have organization.

Talk Story 3

Almost fifty years ago.

The Chinese Consulate in Los Angeles
    Grows weary of Fu Manchu, tired of Charlie Chan.

My grandfather, at once distinguished and indignant,
    Goes to Hollywood on behalf of the Chinese government
    To discuss multicultural awareness with Louis B. Mayer.

"Mr. Mayer," he demands,
    "This chinky chink Chinaman shit has got to stop!"

The next morning, all eight of the Chinese American actors
    in Hollywood come to see my grandfather.

"How could you do that," they ask.

"After you left, he told us we'd lose our jobs
    if you complain any more."

My grandfather, still distinguished, yet indignant,
    snaps back:

    "Your jobs, what jobs?
    You play houseboys and number one sons.

    Instead of caring only about yourself,
    you should have been there with me.

    Maybe we could win something for everyone."

A good lesson to learn—

Unity is our greatest resource.

We must be united.

Talk Story 4

New York City, 1983.

A National Third World Media Conference.

The Master is there, Steve Tatsukawa,
    producer of Asian America's first feature film, *Hito Hata*.

The last time I would ever see him.

Steve reminds us of the time
     Visual Communications was videotaping
     a Little Tokyo rally against redevelopment.

But they are not outside observers,
     Merely documenting the day's demonstration.

As the rally builds; the crew drops their cameras,
     Or at least puts them down gently,

To raise the banner and join the rally themselves.

Because the fight is for empowerment,
     And empowerment means everybody.

A good lesson to learn—

We are accountable to our communities.

Their struggle for empowerment must also be ours.

Talk Story 5

And this is true in my experience, too.

Developing Asian American art and culture
     Over the years in Boston Chinatown.

From festivals and folksinging
     to coffeehouses and cable television,
     Our work was strong and significant.

But the greatest contribution we ever made
     Was organizing a community coalition
     After Long Guang Huang, an elderly Chinese immigrant,
     Was assaulted by the police in Chinatown.

Out in the streets, fighting for our rights;
     We set a standard for progress and movement.

People still talk about that case, remembering with pride
     that the Asian community stood up and testified.

A good lesson to learn—

Long after Heritage Week is over
     and the Dragon Boat Festival has ended,

The impact of the Huang case continues.

So our role become clear—
    We as artists, as advocates, as activists.

To tell the truth, offer new visions and dreams,
    Inspire pride, build respect.

But who has touched our people,
    more broadly and deeply, perhaps,
    than any of us can imagine?

Who else but Jesse Jackson?

Telling the truth, offering new visions and dreams,
    Inspiring pride, building respect.

A good lesson to learn—

The best example we have seen—

From Jesse Jackson we understand
    The meaning of leadership and empowerment.

In this, the Year of the Dragon,
    As eight long years come finally to an end.

For it is 1988, and we are here in Washington;
    Crossing borders, extending boundaries.

You see, Open Dialogues are naturally multilingual.
    We code-switch across dialects and disciplines.

Hito Hata Ageru!—We raise the banner!

¡Si, Se Puede!—Yes, it can be done!

We can win!—Yes, We can win!

We as artists, we as advocates, we as activists.

Gregg Araki

After earning his B.A. in film history/criticism from UC Santa Barbara and his MFA in film production from USC, Gregg Araki turned to filmmaking, creating award-winning independent pieces such as *Three Bewildered People in the Night* (1987) and *The Long Weekend (o' Despair)* (1989). Araki acknowledges that changing the world is not possible, but that he is willing "to die trying."

Esther G. Belin

Esther G. Belin, a self-described "U.R.I." (Urban-Raised Indian) from Los Angeles, has made three videos with the support of the UC Berkeley Native American Studies Dept., including *Beyond The Squaw and The Princess*, which was part of the L.A. Festival film and video series. She currently attends UC Berkeley.

Roddy Bogawa

After studying filmmaking at UC San Diego and the Whitney Independent Study Program in New York, Roddy Bogawa wrote and directed two 16mm films, *A Small Room in the Big House* and *Four or Five Accidents, One June*. He is doing post-production work on a feature-length 16mm film, *Some Divine Wind*.

Anthony B. Chan

Anthony B. Chan has done extensive work in television in Canada and Hong Kong. He produced the documentary, *Reorganizing the Shop* (1987), on the downfall of Hu Yaobang and is currently an instructor at Cal State Hayward and an independent producer. His latest work is about Asian American nurses and soldiers in Vietnam.

Fu-Ding Cheng

Artist/video filmmaker Fu-Ding Cheng started as an architect, but used his income to finance his films in 1968. In his series of works, "Zen Tales for the Urban Explorer," Cheng delves into myths, dreams and the meditative experience. His *Winged Cage* (1989) won the Gold Prize at the Houston International Film Festival, but feels his upcoming piece, *Full Contact*, might be his best.

Daryl Chin

New Yorker Daryl Chin is currently preparing a program of recent Asian American films for a tour of Japan in the winter of 1990-91. A playwright and a director, Chin co-founded the Asian American International Film Festival in 1978 and the Asian American International Video Festival in 1983.

Frank Chin

Los Angeles-based playwright Frank Chin was born in Berkeley in 1940. He broke new ground with his play, *Chicken Coop Chinaman*. A well-known writer, editor, and critic, Chin's latest novel, entitled *Donald Duk*, was released in Spring 1991.

Michael Chin

Born in Salinas, California, Michael Chin is one of Asian America's leading cinematographers. His work on major independent Asian American motion picture and television productions includes Loni Ding's *Bean Sprouts, Nisei Soldier*, and *Color of Honor*, and Wayne Wang's *Chan is Missing*, and *Dim Sum*. Recently, Michael was one of the four cinematographers on *Eyes on the Prize*, parts one and two.

Christine Choy

A professor of film at New York University, Christine Choy is also executive director of the Film News Foundation in New York City. Along with Renee Tajima, Choy produced the Academy Award nominated documentary, *Who Killed Vincent Chin?* (1988) and thirty other films in her career.

Curtis Choy

Production sound mixer Curtis Choy has won numerous awards, including the James D. Phelan Art Award in Filmmaking in 1988 and a first prize in the Atlanta Film Festival in 1986. Besides having worked on almost every Wayne Wang film, Choy has done extensive work in the Far East. He is working on a screenplay entitled *Banana Splitz*.

Loni Ding

A twenty-year independent film and TV producer, Loni Ding was a founding member of NAATA and ITVS (Independent TV Service). A media activist, Ding is also a lecturer at UC Berkeley in ethnic studies and the media. Ding, a writer and a director, who produced *The Color of Honor*, credits her family for their support.

Mar Elepaño

Mar Elepaño runs the motion picture lab at USC. The Philippine native is working on a graphic film based on photos of Filipino immigrants. His favorite work was a piece created under his guidance by Vietnamese and Cambodia high school students on their journey to the U.S. KCET-TV will air the documentary.

John Esaki

The director of *Yuki Shimoda: Asian American Actor*, John's prolific credits include: sound recordist, *Nisei Soldier*; cinematographer, *Conversations*; and co-writer, *Hita Hata*. Born in Monterey and educated at U.C. Berkeley, he taught at Carmel Middle School for five years before earning his MFA in film at UCLA. John is a staff member of Visual Communications.

Theo-dric Feng

Theo-dric Feng has worked on the Asian American radio show, "Gold Mountain," in Washington, D.C. for the last decade. A graduate of UCLA, Feng, who earned his master's from San Francisco State, is a behavior analyst for the Army Research Institute. He is currently developing radio pieces on the *Miss Saigon* controversy.

Luis H. Francia

Poet, journalist, critic and film curator, New York-based Luis H. Francia has written extensively on Asian and Asian American film. He has programmed films for different organizations such as the Whitney Museum of American

Art and the Anthology Film Archives. An anthology of Filipino stories and a book of his poems are set for publication next year.

Richard Fung

Writer and independent video producer Richard Fung has produced such tapes as Fighting Chance: Gay Asian Men and HIV (1980) and My Mother's Place (1990) while contributing articles to FUSE magazine. Born in Port-of-Spain, Trinidad, Fung has lived in Toronto since 1973. A graduate of the Photo-electric Arts Dept. at the Ontario College of Art and the University of Toronto Cinema Studies program, Fung will publish a book, "How Do I Look."

Stephen Gong

Currently the general manager of the Pacific Film Archive in Berkeley, Stephen Gong is a writer and media art administrator. Long associated with the Asian American media, Gong serves as a NAATA board member and on the advisory board for the Asian CineVision. Gong formerly was a program officer for the National Endowment for the Arts.

Karen Ishizuka

Karen Ishizuka is a writer/producer with a diverse background in Asian American Studies and the social sciences. In addition to her own films, she works in project management and media consultation and is currently producing a series of films on the Japanese American experience for the Japanese American National Museum. She heads up JANM's Photographic and Moving Image Archive.

Norman Jayo

L.A.-born Norman Jayo has lived in the Bay Area for twenty years. In that time, he has many credits, including directing the live stage radio drama, "Juke Box—Music To Live By." He wrote "The Last Game Show," which won the Golden Reel and a gold medal as Best Audio Art in an Experimental Series in 1990 from the N.Y. International Radio Festival.

Peter Nien-chu Kiang

Educator and Boston Asian American community activist Peter Nien-chu Kiang is a lecturer for the University of Massachusetts, Boston. One-time program director of the Asian American Resource Workshop in Boston, Kiang has written numerous articles and has director, produced and written video documentaries on many Asian American issues.

Yoshio Kishi

In his lengthy career in film, Yoshio Kishi has worked as editor on *Dim Sum* (1984), *Raging Bull* (1980), *Fame* (1980) and *Finnegan's Wake* (1965) and was the writer/director/editor of *Lombardi*. Besides working on over 100 documentaries, Kishi has been active in the Asian American community in New York for many years.

Geraldine Kudaka

Artist, poet and filmmaker Geraldine Kudaka noted that she has been making films "most of her life." Now finishing up a videotape on massage that she plans to market herself, Kudaka resides in Los Angeles.

Kyung-Ja Lee

After immigrating from Korea in 1971, Kyung-Ja Lee earned a master's degree in psychology from Columbia University in 1980 and worked as a psychiatric social worker until 1985. Kyung-Ja then entered the American Film Institute and was graduated in 1989.

Charles L. Leong

Charles L. Leong (1911-1984) was a pioneer Asian American journalist and editor. In the 1930s, he described himself as "a working man, from working people, who has stepped into the sphere of higher education." A graduate of San Jose State College and Stanford University, Leong was the founder of the California Chinese Press (1940), an English language paper for Chinese Americans. His autobiography, *The Eagle and the Dragon* (San Francisco, 1976), was written for the Chinese Bilingual Program.

George Leong

Besides his extensive credits as a boom operator in *The Abyss, Teenage Mutant Ninja Turtles, The Night of the Living Dead , Dim Sum* and *Pee Wee's Playhouse,* George Leong has been active as a founding member of the Asian American Jazz Festival and a writer. He now resides in New York.

Russell C. Leong

Of Cantonese blood and spirit, Leong has written for *Aiiieeeee! An Anthology of Asian American Writers, The Seattle Review,* and the *Far Eastern Economic Review.* Two video documentaries are *Morning Begins Here,* and *Why is Preparing Fish a Political Act? Poetry of Janice Mirikitani.* A member of San Francisco's Kearny Street Writers' Workshop, he is editor of UCLA's *Amerasia Journal* and of *Moving the Image.*

Cheng-Sim Lim

Cheng-Sim Lim was born and raised in Malaysia. In the days when she knew better, she was a journalist, a development agency researcher and a painter. Now mostly an unpaid filmmaker who metamorphizes into a lighting electrician to pay her bills, she recently made a video, "My American Friends," which aired on KCET-TV in May.

Linda Mabalot

Linda Mabalot, executive director of Visual Communications, has been a long time community activist in the Asian and Pacific American communities. She serves on the boards of the National Alliance of Media Arts Centers, the CPB-created Multicultural Programming Board, and was an originating member of the National Coalition of Multicultural Media Arts and the National Coalition of Independent Public Broadcasting Producers. A former photo journalist for *Philippine American News,* she has produced *Planting Roots: History of Filipinos in California,* and is currently co-producing *You Still Can Hear Me Singing.*

Diane Mei Lin Mark

Writer Diane Mei Lin Mark, born in Arizona and raised in Hawaii, has been a reporter in Hawaii and a developmental director in Washington, D.C. and New York. Author of *A Place Called Chinese America, Chinese in Kula* and

Seasons of Light, Mark works as a program specialist for the University of Hawaii, putting together film, literature and arts workshops.

Trinh T. Minh-Ha

Filmmaker, writer and composer Trinh T. Minh-ha has produced several books, including *Woman, Native, Other*, and *En minuscules* (poetry) and films such as *Reassemblage, Naked Spaces - Living Is Round* and *Surname Viet Given Name Nam*. An associate professor of cinema at San Francisco State, she hopes to film in China one day.

Jon Moritsugu

Originally from Hawaii, Jon first came to acclaim through his work at the Brown University School of Semiotics, from which he graduated in 1988. His films include the shorts *Sleazy Rider, Mommy, Mommy, Where's My Brain?* and the apocalytic *Der Elvis*, as well as his first feature effort, *My Degeneration*.

Carlton Moss

Carlton Moss is a lecturer in the comparative culture program, social science division, at the University of California, Irvine. He wrote and acted in the classic *Negro Soldier* (1943) from the Frank Capra unit Signal Corps, U.S. Army, World War II, which has garnered many national and international awards.

Robert Nakamura

Robert Nakamura, one of the founders of Visual Communications, made pioneering films in the early 1970s that presented the Japanese experience to U.S. audiences throughout the country. A graduate of the Art Center School of Design and the UCLA Department of Film and Television, Bob is currently an associate professor of motion picture production at UCLA AND director of the Heritage Film Series at the Japanese American National Museum.

Joyce Nako

is a staff member of Visual Communications. She is a founding member of Pacific Asian American Women Writers-West, a Los Angeles-based writing group. She is the assistant editor of *Moving the Image*.

Art Nomura

Art Nomura is a video artist and an assistant professor of television production in the Communications Arts Department of Loyola Marymount University in Los Angeles.

Maricel Pagulayan

Media activist Maricel Pagulayan has worked extensively in radio and theater. She has been involved with Great Leap and the Pacifica Radio Foundation and has done several documentaries for radio. Maricel was one of the founders of Laikha, an organization that spotlights Filipino arts and culture based in San Francisco. Pamela Burton, another media activist, contributed to Pagulayan's article.

Irvin Paik

Irvin Paik has worked in the motion picture and television industry for over twenty years as a film editor, cameraman, actor, props and sound, and production manager with Warner Brothers, Universal, and Paramount. A second generation Korean American, he also has written television scripts and articles on the Asian American experience.

Van Troi Pang

When Van Troi Pang was 13, he took an animation class. His final project was a two-minute piece entitled, *Mochi Monster*, which has been called a "cult classic." Now 19, Pang lives in New York and attends community college. He is an active member of the East Coast Asian Student Union.

Hye Jung Park

Hye Jung Park, the director of community affairs at the Downtown Community TV Center in New York, is working on "The Revolution Will Be Televised: Social Movements in Asia" with producer Shu Lea Cheng. In conjunction with J.T. Takagi, Park has launched Third World News Reel.

Janice Sakamoto

Janice Sakamoto is the programming director for the National Asian American Telecommunications Association (NAATA), a media arts organization based in San Francisco.

Valerie Soe

Artist Valerie Soe, a fourth-generation Chinese American, has concentrated on making videos that are a personal expression of her own experiences. Her "All Orientals Look The Same" (1985) won the Best Foreign Video at the 1987 Festival Internazionale Cinema Giovani in Italy. A published critic, Soe is on the faculty at San Francisco State.

Terence Tam Soon

Having designed costumes for over one hundred films, stage, dance and TV productions, Terence Tam Soon earned an Emmy as a researcher for the documentary, "James Wong Howe—The Man and His Movies." A founding member of the Asian Fashion Designers of Los Angeles, he is director of the L.A. Center of Asian American Film Studies and Research.

Supachai Surongsain

A native of Bangkok, Thailand, Supachai Surongsian earned his MFA degree from the UCLA Film/Television Department in 1987. His film, *Pak Bueng on Fire*, examined the social and cultural adjustments that confront the latest Asian Pacific immigrants in California, the Thai community. The film won the Best Dramatic Film award at the 12th Atlanta Film & Video Festival.

Renee Tajima

Independent filmmaker Renee Tajima has made an impact with her documentaries, *Who Killed Vincent Chin?*, *The Best Hotel on Skid Row* and *Fortune Cookies*. A writer and film critic for both the *Village Voice* and National Public Radio, Tajima is executive producer for the Film News Now Foundation and was once director for Asian CineVision.

Nicky Tamrong

Born in Bangkok, Thailand, Nicky Tamrong has written two plays in 1990: *Mothballs* and *Two Feet Away*. Tamrong has done documentary videos, including *Thailand - Not Taiwan* and *Nok Lare*. The assistant director on the film, *God at Bran Bang Poon*, Tamrong has directed many stage productions.

Janice Tanaka

Japanese-American media artist Janice Tanaka says her dual heritage has given her work a socio-political bent painted with tongue-in-cheek humor. Her videos have earned awards from the American Film Institute, the National Endowment for the Arts and several regional fellowship programs.

John Kuo Wei Tchen

Associate director of the Asian/American Center at Queens College (CUNY), John Kuo Wei Tchen is a historian and cultural activist who co-founded the New York Chinatown History Project in 1980. He authored *Genthe's Photographs of San Francisco's Old Chinatown* in 1980 which won an American Book Award.

Peter Wang

Filmmaker Peter Wang was born in Beijing, but moved to Taiwan when he was nine. After earning his Ph.D. in electrical engineering from the University of Pennsylvania, Wang changed careers and produced such works as *A Great Wall*, *Laserman*, and his latest, *First Date*.

Arne Wong

Arne Wong, who has worked and traveled to Taiwan, Hong Kong, Hawaii and France, was the animation supervisor on the animated feature, *Pico & Columbus* and layout supervisor on 13 half-hour animated shows for the TV series, "Wizard of Oz." Wong won an International Clio Award for "Best Animated Commercial" in 1986.

Cindy Hing-Yuk Wong

Cindy Wong is an independent film/videomaker residing in Sarasota, Florida. Wong, who earned her master of arts degree in visual anthropology from the University of Southern California, recently produced the piece, *Leaving Home*.

James Yee

James Yee has been the executive director of the National Asian American Telecommunications Association (NAATA) since 1981. He is responsible for the group's TV and radio programs while maintaining communication with the Asian American media community and organizations. Yee was a producer and consultant for WGBH in Boston.

Bruce Yonemoto

At home in the City of Angels, video artist Bruce Yonemoto, along with his brother and frequent collaborator Norman, has represented the cutting edge of the field of video art. Among the Yonemoto brothers' groundbreaking works are *Green Card*, *Framed*, *Blinky*, and their most recent work, the cinematically-inspired *Made in Hollywood*.

Amerasia Bookstore
129 Japanese Village Plaza
Los Angeles, California 90012
213 680.2888
Resource materials on Asian American and Pacific Islanders communities.

Asian American Arts and Media Program (AAMP)
1851 Columbia Road NW #501
Washington, D.C. 20009
Exhibitor.

Asian American Resource Workshop
27 Beach Street
Boston, Massachusetts 02111
617 426.5313
Develops Asian American curriculum programs in the schools; production
and exhibition.

Asian CineVision
32 E. Broadway
New York, New York 10012
212 925.8685
Asian American International Film Festival, Asian American International
Video Festival, Children's Film Series, and produces quarterly publication,
CineVue, and an Asian American media reference guide available for pur-
chase at $19.95.

Film News Now
625 Broadway, #904
New York, New York 10012
212 979.5671
Fiscal agent, consultations and workshops.

International Center for 8MM Film and Video (IC8FV)
Toni Treadway/Bob Brodsky
10-R Oxford Street
Somerville, Massachusetts 02143
617 666.3372
Provides technical assistance and broadcast quality transfers (1″ or 3/4″) of
small format productions.

Japanese American Curriculum Project
414 E. Third Avenue
San Mateo, California 94401
415 343.9408
Distributor of productions and publications of Asian America for educational
market.

National Alliance of Media Arts Centers (NAMAC)
Robin Reidy, Chair, Membership Development
c/o 911 Contemporary Arts Center
8540 18th Ave., NW
Seattle, Washington 98117
206 682.6552
Media Arts, quarterly publication; Member Director; annual conference; Media Information Network; and mailing lists of media arts centers.

National Asian American Telecommunications Association (NAATA)
346 Ninth Street, 2nd Floor
San Francisco, California 94103
415 863.0814
Cross Current distribution.

Third World Newsreel
335 W. 38th Street
New York, New York 10018
213 947.9277
Distributor.

UCLA Asian American Studies Center
3232 Campbell Hall
University of California
Los Angeles, California 90024-1546
213 825.2968
Book Publisher, *Amerasia Journal*, and other media materials.

Visual Communications
263 South Los Angeles Street, #307
Los Angeles, CA 90012

Voice: 213 660.4462
Facsimile: 213 687.4848
email: viscom@vc.apnet.org.
WWW: http/vc.apnet.org/-viscom/

Since its founding in 1970, Visual Communications (VC), the nation's old-est Asian Pacific American media arts center, has been dedicated to the creation and presentation of works by and about Asian and Pacific Ameri-cans. VC, through its productions, educational projects, books, photo ar-chives, and workshops, develops audiovisual and electronic images and texts which illuminate the path to a more just, humane, and culturally diverse American society.

Linda Mabalot, Executive Director of Visual Communications

UCLA Asian American Studies Center
3230 Campbell Hall
University of California, Los Angeles
CA 90095-1546

Voice: 310 825.2974
Facsimile: 310 206.9844
Publications email: dmar@ucla.edu
WWW: sscnet.ucla.edu/aasc

The Center, as one of UCLA's four ethnic studies centers, has pioneered new research, publications, curriculum, and campus and community classes since its founding in 1969. Its research and publication programs, the *Amerasia Journal,* its library and archival collection, graduate MA and BA degree programs, and student community projects are known inter-nationally for their excellence and innovation in Asian American Studies.

Don T. Nakanishi, Director of the UCLA
Asian American Studies Center

Permissions and Acknowledgements XIII

We are grateful to the authors and/or publishers for giving us permission to reprint selections which originally appeared in the following publications:

Al Robles, "Hanging on the Carabao's Tail," _Amerasia Journal_ 15:1(1989), 195-218.

Him Mark Lai, Genny Lim, and Judy Yung, editors and translators, _Island: Poetry and History of Chinese Immigrants on Angel Island 1910-1940_ (San Francisco: Hoc Doi Project, 1980), 122.

Emilya Cachapero, "miss philippines at the miss universe contest," _Liwanag_ (San Francisco: 1975), 33.

Marlon K. Hom, editor and translator, _Songs of Gold Mountain: Cantonese Rhymes from San Francisco Chinatown 1911-1915_ (Berkeley: University of California Press, 1987). Copyright by the Regents of the University of California.

Hisaye Yamamoto DeSoto, "A Fire in Fontana," _Rafu Shimpo_, December 23, 1985.

Carlos Bulosan, _Sound of Falling Light, Letters in Exile_, edited by Dolores S. Feria (Philippines), 1960, reprinted in "Selected Letters of Carlos Bulosan 1937-1955," selected by E. San Juan Jr., _Amerasia Journal_ 6:1 (1979), 153-154.

Diane Mei Lin Mark, "The Reel Hawaii," _CineVue_ 4:1 (1990), 4-7.

Janice Sakamoto, "Wayne Wang Interview," _Gidra_ (Los Angeles: _Gidra_, 1990).

Frank Chin, "James Wong Howe," in _Yardbird Reader_ 3 (1974), xvi–38.

We also express thanks to, and acknowledge:

Bernadette Cha, for sharing out-of-print materials with us, including, Theresa Hak Kyung Cha, _Dictee_ (New York: Tanam Press, 1982), 47.

Yen Le Espiritu, for sharing _Vat Nang_ (Boulder, Colorado: Vietnamese Students Association, 1990), and Quach Quynh Hoa, "Spring Night on the Island," 33-35.

Photos:

All photo stills are used with permission of the film/videomakers, unless otherwise noted.

Hollywood silent film stills are from the Yoshio Kishi collection, the Terence Tam Soon collection; historical photos are from the Visual Communications Photo Archives.